The social history of Canada

MICHAEL BLISS, EDITOR

INTRODUCTION BY MARILYN BARBER

Strangers within our gates

OR COMING CANADIANS

JAMES S. WOODSWORTH

UNIVERSITY OF TORONTO PRESS

© University of Toronto Press 1972

Toronto and Buffalo

ISBN (casebound) 0-8020-1891-2

ISBN (paperback) 0-8020-6149-4

Microfiche ISBN 0-8020-0231-5

LC 76-163836

Printed in the United States of America

The original edition of this work appeared in 1909

An introduction

BY MARILYN BARBER

Strangers within Our Gates was first published in 1909 by the Young People's Forward Movement Department of the Methodist Church. The book was intended to draw attention to the challenges facing Canada and the Methodist Church in Canada as a result of rapid and increasing immigration. It was written by J. S. Woodsworth, superintendent of All Peoples' Mission, Winnipeg, at the suggestion of Dr F. C. Stephenson, secretary of the Young People's Forward Movement, and with the aid of A. R. Ford of the Winnipeg *Telegram* who contributed several chapters. As Woodsworth himself stated, the book was written at odd moments during a busy winter and had no literary pretensions. Indeed, *Strangers within Our Gates* is largely a compilation of government statistics and publications, selections from United States immigration literature, and quotations from Winnipeg sources, pasted together with comments, suggestions, and interpretations by the author. However, with all its literary deficiencies, and with all the complications which such a hasty mingling of sources has created for later interpreters, the book has become a valuable source of information. It both provides evidence of the evolving social thought of J. S. Woodsworth, first leader of the CCF, and illustrates the sort of ideas and assumptions which influenced the social attitudes of many Canadians and helped to determine the response of the Protestant churches to one of the most important social problems confronting Canadians in the early twentieth century.

James Shaver Woodsworth inherited from his parents the traditions and values of Ontario Methodism. He was born near Toronto in 1874, the eldest of six children of Esther Shaver and James Woodsworth, an ordained Methodist minister, and his earliest years were spent in Ontario where his father travelled the Methodist circuit. In 1882 James Woodsworth moved his family west to Manitoba where, in 1886, he became the first superintendent of Methodist missions in the northwest. As a result, J. S. Woodsworth grew up in a western environment, attending high school in Brandon and graduating from Wesley College – the Methodist College in Winnipeg – in 1896.[1] His entry into the Methodist ministry was, according to his biographer, almost automatic, and he spent the next two years as a probationer or circuit rider in the mission field of southwestern Manitoba. However, in spite of the formative influences of a closely knit Methodist family and a Methodist higher education, Woodsworth did not

accept his role in the Methodist ministry easily or without serious
doubts. From his first work as a probationer until his final reluctant
resignation from the ministry in 1918, he continually questioned his
own position and principles and those of the church itself, its
dogmas and its role in society.

Woodsworth's questioning was the product of an inquiring mind
with a deep interest in people and their welfare. During 1898-9,
while studying theology at Victoria College in Toronto, Woodsworth
observed the steadily worsening living conditions in the poorer areas
of Toronto and became acquainted with the work of the Fred Victor
Mission among the Italians. The next year he spent at Oxford in
order to gain direct knowledge of another society and absorb the
ideas of another culture. Mansfield House, the university settlement
house in East London, particularly interested him, and he spent two
weeks at Christmas attempting to assess the settlement work being
conducted in the slums of London. As a result of his observations in
Britain, Woodsworth came back to Canada with a knowledge of the
serious social problems which could result from extensive industrialization and urbanization.

Upon returning to Manitoba in the summer of 1900, Woodsworth
was ordained into the Methodist ministry, but he did not find the
next years of service, first in rural areas and then at Grace Church in
Winnipeg, very satisfying. Twice he attempted to resign from the
ministry and twice the Manitoba Conference dissuaded him, the
second time in 1907 by offering him the position of superintendent
of All Peoples' Mission. Woodsworth cited his rejection of important
tenets of Methodist doctrine and his lack of personal conversion as
reasons for resignation, but there were other reasons as well. Grace
Church, wealthy and respectable, did not provide Woodsworth with
an opportunity for the kind of service which he so desired to give.
His daughter understood when she later wrote: 'James . . . simply
didn't want to be a preacher. He wanted to get out of the pulpit and
among the people. He wanted to minister to them practically without having to bother with the screen of dogma between him and
them.'[2] The opportunities for such direct social service were almost
overwhelming at All Peoples'.

Winnipeg, 'the Gateway to the West,' was not only the main
distributing point for immigrants to western Canada but also the
centre where many remained temporarily or permanently. Its

population grew rapidly as immigrants who lacked money or agricultural ambitions settled in the crowded tenements in the North End, on the wrong side of the tracks, safely removed from the stately homes of South Winnipeg. In the early twentieth century the immigrant community of North Winnipeg thus became a demanding mission field. All Peoples' Mission, the first and major Methodist mission working among foreign immigrants in western Canada, was initiated by individual endeavour and concern, not as a result of church policy or philosophy. In 1889 Miss Dolly Maguire, a young Methodist sunday school teacher, founded classes for children of German and other nationalities whom she collected from the streets. From this beginning, the work expanded and became more diversified until a separate building was acquired to provide more adequate facilities. The mission became known as All Peoples' from the scriptural passage, 'My house shall be called a house of prayer for all people' (*Isaiah* 5:7). With Woodsworth as superintendent, emphasis was placed on work among non-English-speaking immigrants, and particularly on work with immigrant children through a kindergarten department conducted by certificated workers at a time when the city provided no kindergarten classes at all. The children were the hope of the future and they also provided a means of entrance into immigrant homes for workers who wished to encourage mothers to attend classes in sewing or kitchen-garden work or to stress the value of all adult immigrants coming to the night schools to learn English. In addition to the educational work, All Peoples' made provision for nursing and for fresh-air camps and hospital treatment for sick children.

Woodsworth wrote *Strangers within Our Gates* during his second year as superintendent and the book reflected his concern and sympathy for the plight of the immigrants, some of whose problems he had come to know well. He wanted to introduce the immigrants to other Canadians who were not so well acquainted with them, and he emphasized that the immigrants should not be regarded as members of an anonymous group without faces or personalities but as individuals with individual hopes and fears — that the owners of names ending in 'stein,' 'nski,' 'owitz,' 'zak,' were after all men, women, and little children, not merely immigrants (p. 39). However, Woodsworth defeated much of his own purpose when he presented the immigrants by nationality divisions — British, Scandinavians, Germans, French, Southeastern Europeans, Austro-Hungarians, Italians,

Orientals. Although the divisions were not too carefully defined, nevertheless in such a categorization the individual is almost inevitably subsumed into a group and given a set of group characteristics.

Since the most obvious way of identifying immigrants was by nationality, the set of characteristics assigned to each group is significant. Woodsworth seemed to be trying to present as favourable a picture as possible of the various groups. Nevertheless, the degree of his enthusiasm varied considerably. Americans, apart from the Mormons, were welcome, as were the Scandinavians and Germans; but the acceptance of immigrants from Austria-Hungary and from southeastern Europe, in which category Russia was placed, was much more qualified. Thus *'the most intelligent and progressive of the Slavic races* are the Czechs, or Bohemians' (p. 108) and 'the Hungarians, or Magyars, are, on the whole, *probably more progressive than the majority of the Slavs*' (p. 116).[3] To be best among the Slavs or even to be better than the Slavs was a questionable honour, and serious doubts were raised about the majority of Slavic immigrants. An exact interpretation of Woodsworth's views is difficult since Arthur Ford wrote the sections on the Scandinavians, Doukhobors, Ruthenians, Poles, and people from the Balkan states and it is he who was most enthusiastic (about the Scandinavians) and also most pessimistic (about the Ruthenians and Poles). According to Ford, 'taken all in all there is no class of immigrants that are as certain of making their way in the Canadian West as the people of the peninsula of Scandinavia. Accustomed to the rigors of a northern climate, clean-blooded, thrifty, ambitious and hard-working, they will be certain of success in this pioneer country, where the strong, not the weak, are wanted' (p. 77). By contrast, his comments on the Ruthenians or Galicians acquired even greater force. 'The Galician figures, disproportionately to his numbers, in the police court and penitentiary. Centuries of poverty and oppression have, to some extent, animalized him. Drunk, he is quarrelsome and dangerous. The flowers of courtesy and refinement are not abundant in the first generation of immigrants' (p. 112). Such a condemnation was much more direct and harsh than any provided by Woodsworth in either *Strangers within Our Gates* or his other contemporary writings, but nevertheless Woodsworth was willing to acknowledge general authorship of the book in which it appeared.

Woodsworth has been described as an 'untypical Canadian,'[4] but he could not escape the context of his times. Concern for others and

an inquiring mind do not necessarily lead to a rejection of the
dominant ideas of a society. Woodsworth's view of the immigrants
was that of an actively involved and well-read English-speaking
Protestant Canadian of 1909. Woodsworth had read much of the
current American literature on immigration, and at the beginning of
Strangers within Our Gates he placed a list of American books and
magazine articles to which he directed the reader for further information. Throughout the book, he relied extensively on these
sources; many of the chapters are prefaced with direct quotations
from one or more of the suggested books and concealed within the
chapters are other lengthy quotations from the same sources. The
American material is thus responsible for establishing much of the
tone of the book. In turning to the United States as an important
source of information and ideas, Woodsworth was a very typical
Canadian. The United States was well in advance of Canada in
material expansion – in the settlement of the west and in industrial
and urban growth. Therefore, Canadians were very aware of the
United States as an example, both of successes to be emulated and
of problems and failures to be avoided.

Immigration seemed to be a particularly pertinent subject for
comparison. By the twentieth century a reaction had developed in
the United States against large-scale immigration and particularly
against the immigrants from southern and eastern Europe who began
arriving in increasing numbers in the 1880s and settled mainly in
large cities along the eastern seaboard and the Great Lakes.
American writing, setting forth the problems posed by immigration,
the difficulties of assimilation, and the need for a more restrictive
immigration policy, greatly influenced those Canadians who, for
economic, social, or political reasons, were concerned about the
effects of immigration. Woodsworth compared the Canadian situation with that of the United States: 'Just when restriction leagues
are being formed in the United States and rigid immigration laws are
being enacted, Canada adopts a "progressive immigration policy,"
and puts forth every effort to secure immigrants ... When the United
States contained our population they received one settler – and
found it difficult enough to Americanize him. We receive thirty-six.
What about our task?' (pp. 165-6). If the United States was taking
greater care in the selection of immigrants, would Canada become a
dumping ground for all the undesirables rejected by the United
States? If the United States was having difficulties assimilating the

new immigrants, would not the difficulties be considerably greater
for Canada with her much smaller population?

In his emphasis on the necessity for assimilation to a uniform
standard and in his assumptions concerning the proper values and
ideals for the Canadian nation, Woodsworth reflected the dominant
ethos of his society: Canada was and should remain an Anglo-Saxon
nation, and as such Canada could embody the highest principles of
Christianity and civilization. Woodsworth accepted the common
view that northern races and northern civilizations were superior. He
quoted without contradiction or qualification a very explicit statement of the division between European civilizations:

A line drawn across the Continent of Europe from northeast to
southwest, separating the Scandinavian Peninsula, the British Isles,
Germany and France from Russia, Austria-Hungary, Italy and
Turkey, separates countries not only of distinct races but also of
distinct civilizations. It separates Protestant Europe from Catholic
Europe; it separates countries of representative institutions and
popular government from absolute monarchies. It separates lands
where education is universal from lands where illiteracy predomi-
nates; it separates manufacturing countries, progressive agriculture
and skilled labor from primitive hand industries, backward agriculture and unskilled labor; it separates an educated, thrifty
peasantry from a peasantry scarcely a single generation removed
from serfdom; it separates Teutonic races from Latin, Slav, Semitic
and Mongolian races (p. 164).

The quotation is from an American source, but Woodsworth did not
need to turn to American sources for an expression of the conviction
that immigrants who did not come from northwestern Europe were
inferior in religion, government, education, and all other characteristics of a progressive civilization.

Favourable economic conditions and a vigorous government
immigration policy brought more and more immigrants to Canada
during the period from 1897 to 1914. In the decade between 1901
and 1911 immigration for the first time exceeded emigration, and
the number of immigrant arrivals grew from 21,000 in 1897 to reach
a peak in the fiscal year 1912-13 with a recorded total of over
400,000. Much of the increase was accounted for by the rising

numbers from both the British Isles and the United States, many of the Americans being of German or Scandinavian origin; together these two groups always constituted the majority of immigrants entering Canada. But there was also a new element which entered the immigration pattern: for the first time immigrants from southern and eastern Europe began to constitute a recognizably large proportion of the total immigration. Those who received the greatest publicity were the Doukhobors, approximately 7,400 of whom arrived in 1899, and the Ukrainians, called Ruthenians or Galicians since the majority came from the Austro-Hungarian provinces of Galicia and Bukovina, whose large-scale migration to Canada began in 1896.

As the influx of immigrants attracted wide attention, statistics, although not accurately kept, were frequently quoted to show by cold mathematics not only the impressive numbers but also the range of nationalities and the stark truth concerning the percentage who were 'foreigners' to whom Canadian institutions and customs were totally alien. Woodsworth followed the statistic tradition when he placed numerous tables at the beginning of *Strangers within Our Gates.*

The statistics showed that there were significant groups of Orientals in British Columbia, a fact which the Vancouver riots of September 1907 had publicized. For Woodsworth, the Orientals were isolated by a colour difference which formed an obvious and permanent racial barrier to assimilation. His assertion that essentially non-assimilable elements such as the Orientals should be vigorously excluded from Canada (p. 232) would have been emphatically supported by most citizens of British Columbia and actively opposed by few in Canada. The problem for the federal government was to devise a means of excluding Asiatics without appearing discriminatory and adversely affecting Empire relations or the possibility of increased Canadian trade with Japan.

The Oriental question, however, was of immediate concern primarily to British Columbia and the federal government. In the statistics of growth and development, the issue which appeared of greater significance to most Canadians was the revealed strength of the new immigration from southern and eastern Europe. The 'new immigrants' who often established group settlements on the western prairies or congregated in immigrant communities in cities and towns

were frequently labelled 'undesirable.' Southern Italians were defi-
nitely inferior to northern Italians, but it was particularly the Slavic
immigrants who were characterized as an inferior group, ignorant,
illiterate, dirty, lacking initiative, and involved in drunken brawls
and crime of all sorts. As Arthur Ford pointed out, 'Galician' had
become a term of reproach, applied indiscriminately to all immigrants from eastern Europe. The condition of many of these
immigrants during their first years in Canada gave rise to many of
the objections. There was no doubt that illiteracy was high, that
many arrived practically destitute after the long journey, and that in
general their standard of living was low; surveys of both rural and
urban areas revealed overcrowding and unsanitary conditions. The
hostile response, however, was also a result of racial prejudice: the
Slavic immigrants by dress, language, and custom were set apart as
obviously strange and different, not willing or able to conform
immediately to the standards of the majority – although, unlike the
Orientals, they might eventually be assimilated.

The majority were assured of the superiority of their standards by
a conviction deeply rooted in the Canadian experience. North was
superior to south; the northern races were inherently superior to
southern races. Race was a vaguely defined but commonly used
term. To the northern races were assigned the virtues of self-reliance,
initiative, individualism, and strength, whereas the southern races
were seen as degenerate and lacking in energy and initiative. Canada
was a northern country, and the myth of the northern race, a hardy
race created by a stern and demanding climate, had been used to
express Canadian nationalism and pride in country since Confedera-
tion. In the Canadian context the idea of the northern race also had
strong agrarian or rural connotations and it was perhaps partly
for this reason that Canada actively sought only agricultural
immigrants.

The myth of the northern race was reinforced by concepts which
Canada inherited as part of the North Atlantic cultural community.
From Britain, and particularly from the British imperialists of the
1880s and 1890s, came the sense of mission, Kipling's 'white man's
burden' which portrayed the Anglo-Saxon race as carrying the
highest principles of Christianity and civilization. Social Darwinism
was used to give scientific credibility to the theory of Anglo-Saxon
superiority – the Anglo-Saxon race had achieved its dominant
position through a process of natural selection of the fittest. Such

views reflected pride, confidence, and an optimistic belief in progress. There was no cause for alarm concerning the effects of immigration as long as it was believed that the superior Anglo-Saxon race would dominate and that immigrants could be assimilated by environmental forces.

However, other, less optimistic, conclusions could be drawn from the emphasis upon race and the idea of biological competition. In the United States immigration restrictionists watched the declining birth-rate of the native-born population and the rapid multiplication of the immigrant population and feared that in the conflict for survival there was no guarantee that the superior race would win. They argued that when forced to compete with immigrants who had a low standard of living, Americans reduced the size of their families in an effort to maintain their higher standards. The competition thus caused the superior race to commit 'race suicide.' The fear of 'race suicide' was reinforced by developments in genetic theory. After 1900 eugenicists refuted the idea that characteristics acquired through education and acculturation could be inherited and instead warned that heredity was fixed and that characteristics acquired during the life of an individual would not be passed on to the next generation. In a less scientific application of the theory, racial characteristics became fixed and immutable. Thus, from the United States came the fear that immigrants would not be assimilated and that immigration could destroy the traditions and standards of Anglo-Saxon civilization.

For most English Canadians in the early twentieth century, the ideas of nationalism and imperialism, pride in country and pride in tradition, combined to support the view that Canada should develop as an Anglo-Saxon nation. English Canadians, however, did not reach the same agreement upon the seriousness of the immigration problem. Woodsworth was a true representative of English-Canadian nationalism when he assumed that Canada would achieve her highest destiny as an Anglo-Saxon nation, but he was less representative in his conclusions about the effects of immigration.

In the optimistic boom years of 'Canada's Century,' pessimistic warnings of future problems were not widely heeded. There were a few writers in university magazines and other Canadian periodicals who did accept the arguments of the American racial nativists. According to J. R. Conn, writing on 'Immigration' in *Queen's Quarterly* (July 1900):

In departing from the traditions of half a century ago, our friends to
the South are perfectly justifiable ... The higher civilization has a
moral right to displace the lower. This alone can justify European
occupation of China, American conquest in Cuba and the Philip-
pines, and the assertion of Britain's sovereignty in South Africa. This
same right of the higher as against the lower types of life justifies the
people of this continent in shutting out such alien elements of
population as seem likely to lower rather than raise the general type
of life (p. 119).

The implication that the higher civilization would not necessarily
prevail over the lower was made more explicit in an article in the
Canadian Magazine (February 1908) by W. S. Wallace. Writing on
'The Canadian Immigration Policy,' Wallace looked at the American
experience and concluded:

... it is possible that what applies to the United States may not apply
wholly to Canada; but it appears to be shown here clearly that there
are grounds for believing that the tendency of inferior immigration
(and nearly all immigration is, in the nature of things, inferior), is to
lower the birth-rate of the native-born population. The native-born
population, in the struggle to keep up appearances in the face of the
increasing competition, fails to propagate itself, commits race
suicide, in short; whereas the immigrant population, being inferior,
and having no appearances to keep up, propagates itself like the fish
of the sea (p. 360).

Immigrants of an inferior racial type could not be assimilated and
therefore should be restricted from entering Canada since to admit
them would lower the standard of Canadian life and perhaps destroy
the higher civilization altogether. This was an extreme argument and
not likely to win many converts in a period of general prosperity and
expansion.
    The predominant mood of English Canadians seems to have been
one of confidence that the immigrants would be assimilated and
would contribute to the growth and development of the country.
The assimilative powers of the Anglo-Saxon race were stressed.
'Canada is Anglo-Saxon and will remain Anglo-Saxon. Foreigners
may come in their thousands, and they, too, if not in the first, then

in the second generation, will also be Anglo-Saxon.'[5] The emphasis here is on assimilation to an Anglo-Saxon norm, but in some cases it was suggested that a new and better race would be created by the mingling of elements. Ralph Connor in the preface to his novel, *The Foreigner*, wrote: 'Out of breeds diverse in traditions, in ideals, in speech, and in manner of life, Saxon and Slav, Teuton, Celt and Gaul, one people is being made. The blood strains of great races will mingle in the blood of a race greater than the greatest of them all.'[6] It is questionable, however, whether the distinction is significant since the new and better race envisaged seemed to retain the obviously superior Anglo-Saxon characteristics and the contribution contemplated from other sources was minimal.

Woodsworth accepted neither the pessimistic belief that Canadian standards would be destroyed by immigration nor the optimistic assurance that assimilation was inevitable. His was the middle position of concerned Canadians who feared that there would be serious problems unless care was taken to ensure that the new immigrants were assimilated. For these Canadians, assimilation was not a natural and inevitable process, but one which required assistance and direction. Among those most concerned with the problems of immigration and assimilation were a considerable number of educators and Protestant clergymen, since the schools and the churches could perform an important role as agencies of assimilation. Woodsworth was in the vanguard of those Methodists actively involved with assisting the process of assimilation.

The Methodist Church saw itself as a national church and viewed its responsibilities in national terms. Its mission was to Christianize, that is, Protestantize, and Canadianize the immigrants – the two purposes were inextricably related. Methodists saw Canada as not only an Anglo-Saxon nation but as an Anglo-Saxon and Protestant nation. In Methodist literature Protestantism was equated with the Anglo-Saxon virtues of initiative, industry, freedom, and democracy, whereas Catholicism was equated with superstition, ignorance, and autocracy. Naturally, Methodists were concerned that Protestant values should be maintained in Canada and that the Roman Catholic Church, with its base of power among French Canadians, should not be permitted to extend its sphere of influence. The immigrants from southern and eastern Europe therefore posed a serious problem and challenge for the Methodist Church. Not only could these immigrants be regarded as members of an inferior race but the majority were also non-Protestant, being Roman Catholic, Greek Catholic, Greek Orthodox, or Jewish.

In response to the challenge of immigration, the Methodist Church supported missions designed both to proselytize the immigrants and to improve the social conditions of the immigrant communities. Missions and homes in urban areas, All Peoples' Mission in Winnipeg, the Fred Victor Mission in Toronto, and others in Edmonton and Vancouver attempted to deal with the new problems created by industrialization and urbanization. The Methodist Church also carried on more traditional evangelical missionary work in the west under the Home Department of the Missionary Society and the Women's Missionary Society. In 1901 Rev. C. H. Lawford, MD, was sent to Pakan, Alberta, to do both evangelical and medical work in the large Ukrainian colony northeast of Edmonton. The work was greatly assisted by the construction of the George McDougall Memorial Hospital which was opened at Pakan in 1907 and became the core of the mission. The medical mission was augmented by educational work sponsored by the Women's Missionary Society in the same area. The school homes of Wahstao ('A Light on a Hill') and Kolokreeka ('The House by the Creek') were conducted by dedicated women who lived among the new settlers, learned their language, and not only taught the immigrant children but also tried to interpret Canadian customs to the settlers and thus facilitate their integration into Canadian society. The medical and educational aspects of the work were considered important in themselves, but were also highly regarded as a means of attracting the immigrants and winning them for Christ and the true Christian religion. As Dr Lawford reported in 1903: 'The medical work has proven a most successful agency in overcoming the prejudices of the people and establishing a strong feeling of friendship between us, thus leading to permission to hold services on Sundays in many homes.'[7] Indeed, the medical work seemed 'the one thing used of God to prevent us being defeated in our efforts to gain an entrance to the people.'[8]

Methodist ideals for Canada and Methodist responsibilities for achieving those ideals were well summed up in an article in the *Missionary Outlook* in June 1908:

If from this North American continent is to come a superior race, a
race to be specially used of God in the carrying on of His work, what
is our duty toward those who are now our fellow-citizens? Many of
them come to us nominal Christians, that is, they owe allegiance to
the Greek or Roman Catholic Churches, but their moral standards
and ideals are far below those of the Christian citizens of the
Dominion. These people have come to this young, free country to
make homes for themselves and their children. It is our duty to meet
them with the open Bible, and to instil into their minds the principles and ideals of Anglo-Saxon civilization.

Strangers within Our Gates emphasized these principles, responsibilities, and ideals. Woodsworth stressed the need for assimilating the
immigrants into an Anglo-Saxon civilization through the work of
such agencies as national schools, labour unions, the press, and the
churches. Much importance was attached to the preservation of
Protestant ideals and values which were seen as an integral part of
Anglo-Saxon civilization. Numerous references were made to the
threat of the Church of Rome, and the Mormons too were presented
as a serious menace to Western civilization as their system was antagonistic to freedom, morality, and true religion. The octopus of
Mormonism with its black tentacles stretching across the map is one
of the more vivid images in the book. The religious threat became
particularly acute when combined with difference of race: thus
German Catholics appeared more acceptable than Polish Catholics.
    The values which Mormonism and the Church of Rome threat-
ened, the values which immigrants had to accept in order to be
assimilated, were Protestant rather than particularly Methodist
values. Methodists co-operated with Presbyterians and Baptists in
dividing the mission work of western Canada, and from the need to
co-operate in the vast areas of the west came the movement for
union which led ultimately to the formation of the United Church
of Canada. In conformity with such an ecumenical spirit, Woodsworth's solution to the problem of non-Protestant immigration was
not to convert the immigrants into Methodists but to help them
work out their own salvation by means of 'Independent' churches.
'Independence means that the people are taught to think for themselves; it means that the Bible is placed in their hands; it means that

their children attend the Public Schools instead of the parochial schools; it means that the people ally themselves with Protestants rather than with Catholics. *Independence affords the opportunity for reformation'* (p. 256). Direct proselytizing among the members of another faith was neither completely acceptable nor practical. Independence in 1909 seemed to offer a hopeful compromise for worried Protestants, but its prospects for success soon became less bright as Roman Catholic bishops and the Catholic Church Extension Society responded to the challenge of western immigration and waged a campaign against proselytizing Protestants.

The response of the Methodist Church to the challenge of immigration resulted not only from the national ideals of the church but also from the conviction of some influential Methodists that the church should work with the community and not solely with the individual, that the Kingdom of God should be sought in this world and not solely in the next. Grace Church in Winnipeg was witness to the fact that the Methodist Church was becoming a church of the respectable and established and was losing its position and influence as a church of the people. The Methodist interest in social welfare developed from a concern for the historical traditions of the church in Canada, as well as a recognition that the rapid and undirected growth of cities together with rapid immigration were creating new problems which demanded new kinds of solutions on the part of the church. What has been called the Social Gospel, the gospel of love, co-operation, and brotherhood, directed the development of city missions and settlement houses. Society's emphasis on excessive materialism and advancement at the expense of others was decried; instead, it was urged that 'the stranger that sojourneth with you shall be unto you as the homeborn among you, and thou shalt love him as thyself.'

In *Strangers within Our Gates* the stress on Protestant values was incorporated into a general concern for the development of Canadian society. Although Canada should develop as a British country, not all immigrants from the British Isles were welcome. The remittance men, the assisted immigrants from the slums sent out by the charity societies, the diseased or mentally incompetent, these were not acceptable because they lacked initiative or self-reliance and became a burden on the Canadian communities. Woodsworth's interests were those of a social worker rather than an evangelist, and

Strangers within Our Gates was well received by reviewers as a pioneer sociological study.[9] The problems of the city attracted considerable attention in the reviews, for Woodsworth had painted a dark picture of urban conditions. 'Ignorance of the language, high rents, low standards of living, incompetency, drunkenness and other evils are already producing conditions as bad as are to be found in the slums of the great cities. Unless certain tendencies are checked at once, it is appalling to think what will result with the growth of the city' (p. 217). The photographs of overcrowding and unsanitary conditions in Winnipeg tenements provided visual proof of appalling conditions, particularly in contrast to the other photographs of picturesque but progressive immigrants adapting to the country and aiding in economic development. Woodsworth was particularly concerned with the need to find solutions to the problems which accompanied the development of cities, and his concern led to the publication in 1911 of *My Neighbor* as a companion volume to *Strangers within Our Gates.* By 1913 Woodsworth found that the Methodist Church no longer offered sufficient scope for his developing commitment to secular social service and he resigned as superintendent of All Peoples' Mission to become secretary of the Canadian Welfare League. During his years at All Peoples', Woodsworth's observations and study thus led him from questioning the role of the church to the belief that social problems demanded more fundamental solutions than those which could be supplied by the church.

In 1909, however, Woodsworth was still emphasizing the importance of the church, especially as the champion and protector of essential Protestant and national values. In *Strangers within Our Gates* the focus was not on the city and city problems or even on the west and western problems but on the nation and national problems. The assimilation of immigrants was a vital national problem which should concern all Canadians. Canada had 'certain more or less clearly defined ideals of national well-being' (p. 232) and these ideals must be maintained. Immigrants were welcome only if they conformed to Canadian standards and could be assimilated into Canadian society. Woodsworth had travelled widely and warned against 'a certain arrogant superiority and exclusiveness, perhaps characteristic of the English race' (p. 240). Nevertheless, he accepted the need for a common standard for all and assumed that this

standard should be based on Anglo-Saxon Protestant values. Thus
the immigrants from southern and eastern Europe were a questionable acquisition, as were certain classes from Britain. Canada was not
to be a dumping ground for undesirable British immigrants, or
continental European or Asiatic immigrants. There was active concern for the immigrants in Canada, but the gospel of love was
subordinate to the gospel of nationalism.

NOTES

1 Kenneth McNaught, *A Prophet in Politics* (Toronto, 1959), provides the most complete biography of Woodsworth.
2 Grace MacInnis, *J. S. Woodsworth: A Man to Remember*
  (Toronto, 1953), pp. 56-7.
3 My emphasis.
4 F. H. Underhill, *James Shaver Woodsworth: Untypical Canadian*
  (Toronto, 1944), and quoted in McNaught, p. 37.
5 *Manitoba Free Press,* 8 July 1898.
6 *The Foreigner: A Tale of Saskatchewan* (New York, 1909).
7 *Missionary Outlook,* Sept. 1903.
8 *Ibid.,* Aug. 1904.
9 *Globe*, Toronto, 6 March 1909; *Manitoba Free Press,* 22 April 1909.

SUGGESTED READINGS

Allen, Richard. *The Social Passion: Religion and Social Reform in
Canada.* Toronto, 1971

Berger, Carl. *The Sense of Power: Studies in the Ideas of Canadian
Imperialism, 1867-1914.* Toronto, 1970

Berger, Carl. 'The True North Strong and Free,' in Peter Russell, ed.,
Nationalism in Canada. Toronto, 1966

Emery, George. 'Methodism on the Canadian Prairies, 1896 to
1914.' PH D thesis, University of British Columbia, 1970

Higham, John. *Strangers in the Land: Patterns of American Nativism, 1860-1925.* New York, 1966

MacInnis, Grace. *J. S. Woodsworth: A Man to Remember.* Toronto, 1953

McNaught, Kenneth. *A Prophet in Politics.* Toronto, 1959

Underhill, Frank H. *James Shaver Woodsworth: Untypical Canadian.* Toronto, 1944

Ziegler, Olive. *Woodsworth: Social Pioneer.* Toronto, 1934

Strangers within our gates

JAMES S. WOODSWORTH

The stranger that sojourneth with you shall be unto you as the homeborn among you, and thou shalt love him as thyself.
LEV. 19. 34

Assemble the people, the men and the women and the little ones, and thy stranger that is within thy gates, that they may hear, and that they may learn, and fear the Lord your God, and observe to do all the words of this law; and that their children, which have not known, may hear, and learn to fear the Lord your God, as long as ye live in the land.
DEUT. 31. 12. 13

STRANGERS WITHIN OUR GATES

COMING CANADIANS

Contents

Introduction

Perhaps the largest and most important problem that the North American continent has before it to-day for solution is to show how the incoming tides of immigrants of various nationalities and different degrees of civilization may be assimilated and made worthy citizens of the great Commonwealths. The United States have been grappling with this question for decades, but have not yet found a solution. Canada is now facing the same problem, but in an aggravated form. A much larger percentage of foreigners, in proportion to our population, is coming to us just now, than came at any one period to the United States. The larger the percentage the more difficult is the problem of solution. Western Canada has this problem in an even more perplexing form and to an even greater degree than has the East. And the city of Winnipeg might, without any misuse of words, be called the *storm centre* of this problem for Canada. Mr. J. H. Ashdown, who has been Mayor of Winnipeg for the past two years, and resident in the West for over forty years, and who has perhaps given more time, attention, and money to the working out of a solution of this question than any other layman in the West, regards the problem as vital and fundamental.

I have been permitted to read the manuscript of the Rev. J. S. Woodsworth's book, entitled 'Strangers within Our Gates.' It should be stated that Mr. Woodsworth is Superintendent of 'All Peoples' Mission,' and of our foreign work generally in the city of Winnipeg, and has had special opportunity to meet and study these various peoples and divers nationalities. I can with confidence commend this pioneer Canadian work on this subject to the careful consideration of those who are desirous of understanding and grappling with this great national danger. For *there is a danger and it is national!* Either we must educate and elevate the incoming multitudes or they will drag us and our children down to a lower level. We must see to it that the civilization and ideals of Southeastern Europe are not transplanted to and perpetuated on our virgin soil. I would have all our young people between the oceans read and ponder the subject-matter of this book. 'Dry!' you say? No! vastly interesting and illuminating if you read and study it sympathetically. Here you will find tragedy and comedy combined in the actual lives of men and women, none of whom we may call 'common or unclean.' I fear that the Canadian churches have not yet been seized of the magnitude and import of this ever-growing problem.

J. W. SPARLING

Preface

What does the ordinary Canadian know about our immigrants? He classifies all men as white men and foreigners. The foreigners he thinks of as the men who dig the sewers and get into trouble at the police court. They are all supposed to dress in outlandish garb, to speak a barbarian tongue, and to smell abominably.

This little book is an attempt to introduce the motley crowd of immigrants to our Canadian people and to bring before our young people some of the problems of population with which we must deal in the very near future. It has no literary pretensions; its aim is entirely practical. Undertaken at the suggestion of Dr. F. C. Stephenson, Secretary of the Young People's Forward Movement, it has been written at odd times during a very busy winter.

We are glad to have had the co-operation of Mr. A. R. Ford, of the Winnipeg *Telegram,* who has written the chapters signed 'A.R.F.,' several of which have already appeared in the *Westminster.* The editing and illustrating have been done by the Young People's Forward Movement Department.

The book will accomplish its purpose, if it serves to stimulate an interest in important public problems, and to direct its readers to fuller sources of information. Much may be learned from the United States, where conditions similar to our own have existed for some years. We append a short list of books which have proved helpful in this study. In many of these books full bibliographies will be found.

J. S. WOODSWORTH
Winnipeg, June 1st, 1908

LIST OF BOOKS

Aliens or Americans. Howard B. Grose
Forward Movement Mission Study Course

Our People of Foreign Speech. Samuel McLanahan
A Handbook. Fleming H. Revell

Emigration and Immigration. Richmond Mayo-Smith
Charles Scribner's Sons

Immigration. Prescott Hall
Henry Holt & Co., New York

The Challenge of the City. Josiah Strong
Forward Movement Mission Study Course

How the Other Half Lives. Jacob Riis
Charles Scribner's Sons

Undistinguished Americans. Hamilton Holt
James Pott & Co., New York

The Russian Jew in the United States. Chas. S. Bernheimer
B. F. Black & Co., New York

The Italian in America. Eliot Lord
B. F. Black & Co., New York

Imported Americans. Broughton Brandenburg
F. A. Stokes, New York

The Slav Invasion. F. Julian Warner
J. B. Lippincott Co.

Chinese Immigration. George F. Seward
Charles Scribner's Sons

The Problem of the Immigrant. James D. Whelpley
Linden, Chapman and Hall

MAGAZINE ARTICLES

In *Chautauquan,* 1903-4, a series of articles on the 'Racial Composition of the American People,' by John R. Commons.

In the *Popular Science Monthly,* 1903-5, a comprehensive series on 'Immigration,' by Dr. Allan McLaughlin, of the U.S. Marine Hospital Service.

In *Charities,* 1904, several articles.

In the *North American Review,* the *Forum,* and *Political Science Quarterly* the question of restriction of immigration is discussed.

Nearly all the popular monthlies contain descriptive articles.

Coming Canadians — just arrived in Winnipeg

Immigration – a world problem

Out of the remote and little known region of northern, eastern, and southern Europe forever marches a vast and endless army. Nondescript and ever changing in personnel, without leaders or organization, this great force, moving at the rate of nearly 1,500,000 each year, is invading the civilized world.

Like a mighty stream, it finds its source in a hundred rivulets. The huts of the mountains and the hovels of the plains are the springs which feed; the fecundity of the races of the Old World the inexhaustible source. It is a march the like of which the world has never seen, and the moving columns are animated by but one idea — that of escaping from evils which have made existence intolerable, and of reaching the free air of countries where conditions are better shaped to the welfare of the masses of the people.

It is a vast procession of varied humanity. In tongue it is polyglot; in dress, all climes, from pole to equator, are indicated, and all religions and beliefs enlist their followers. There is no age limit, for young and old travel side by side. There is no sex limitation, for the women are as keen, if not more so, than the men; and babes in arms are here in no mean numbers.

The army carries its equipment on its back, but in no prescribed form. The allowance is meagre, it is true, but the household gods of a family sprung from the same soil as a hundred previous generations may possibly be contained in shapeless bags or bundles. Forever moving, always in the same direction, this marching army comes out of the shadow, converges to natural points of distribution, masses along the great international highways, and its vanguard disappears, absorbed when it finds a resting place.

Gaining in volume and momentum with each passing year, without apparent regard for the law of supply and demand, the pressure of this army has already made itself felt upon the communities in which it finds its destination. The cry of protest has gone up from those who find themselves crowded from their occupations and their homes by the new arrivals, and peoples are demanding of their Governments that some steps be taken to check this alien invasion.

Throughout Europe the word 'America' is synonymous in all languages with freedom, prosperity, and happiness. The desire to reach America is the first sign of awakened ambition, the first signal of revolt against harsh environment, the dream of age and youth alike. The countries of Western Europe receive the migratory element – the birds of passage – who help in the harvest, or furnish laborers for great undertakings, and then return to their homes richer for their season abroad. London absorbs into her mighty heart thousands of strange-looking human beings, talking gibberish languages, and quick to take advantage of her marvellous charities. South America, with the free-and-easy manner of that part of the world, accepts those rejected elsewhere.

Following the main columns of this army back to their beginnings, the real reason for its existence is soon discovered. The momentum is given at the source, and we find men pushing each other at the gang-planks of departing emigrant steamers to make their escape from inevitable political and economic wrongs. There is another reason, based upon the first, but none the less potent. The traffic in ocean passages has reached a stage of fierce competition, unscrupulousness, and even inhumanity inconceivable to those not familiar with its details. Men who profit by the march of these millions of people have a drag-net out over continental Europe so fine in its meshes as to let no man, woman, or child escape who has the price and the desire or need to go. Three great countries, Italy, Austria-Hungary, and Russia – where the masses of the people are low in the social scale, and where the percentage of illiteracy is discreditable to the twentieth century – are being drained of their human dregs through channels made easy by those seeking cargo for their ships.

WHELPLEY

Chapter 1

Who are we?

THE POPULATION OF CANADA

WITHIN the past decade Canada has risen from the status of a colony to that of a nation. A national consciousness has developed – that is, a nation has been born. A few years ago Canadian-born children described themselves as English, Irish, Scotch or French, according as their parents or ancestors had come from England, Ireland, Scotland or France. To-day our children boast themselves Canadians, and the latest arrivals from Austria or Russia help to swell the chorus, 'The Maple Leaf Forever.' There has not been sufficient time to develop a fixed Canadian type, but there is a certain indefinite *something* that at once unites us and distinguishes us from all the world besides. Our hearts all thrill in response to the magical phrase – 'This Canada of Ours!' We are Canadians. As yet we have not entered fully into our national privileges and responsibilities, but great national problems are already forcing themselves upon our attention. In grappling with and solving these we shall attain our national manhood.

'Strangers within our gates' – perhaps, in one sense, we are the strangers. Throughout the long years before the coming of the white man the Indian possessed the land. Then came the fierce frontier warfare in which the red man was driven back before the advance of the 'pale face.' Now his descendants have a place in our new nation.

In Eastern Canada the French came first. Soon began the bitter struggle for supremacy between French and English. Now we all proudly claim to be Canadian citizens and British subjects. Since then many nations have contributed to our population. To trace the causes that led to the coming of these early settlers, and their influence on the community, would be intensely intcresting, but cannot be attempted here. We seek merely a point of departure. Perhaps we cannot gain a better analysis of our population than that given by our last census.

Who are we, then, by birthplace, by race, and by religion?

In the Northwest Provinces a special census was taken in 1906. The following are figures for 1901 and 1906:

	1901	1906
Manitoba	255,211	365,688
Saskatchewan	91,279	257,763
Alberta	73,022	185,412
	419,512	808,863

'Figures talk!' Yes, if we study them and what they stand for. Let us look over these tables.

Surely we have come from the ends of the earth! We hardly knew we were so cosmopolitan. To see the nations of the world we need merely to journey through Canada. We would take the Grand Tour – then on to the most remote countries of Europe. After that, touching at Turkey and Syria we would pass on to India and back by China and Japan – and all without leaving our own shores.

Then if we wished to study comparative religions, what a field! We hardly knew there could be so many sects; and all of these are right – in their own eyes! What a theological training for our young people, if only they would find out the distinctive beliefs of each of these denominations, and then seek to give a reason for the faith that is in themselves!

We notice at a glance how rapidly the figures in the tables increase from left to right, and that at the right there are often figures when at the left there are only blanks. We are continually drawing on more and more countries for our population.

Note the sudden advance in the figures in the immigration from Russia during the last decade. Probably that tells the story of the coming of the strange Doukhobors. Again, see how Japan is represented in 1901. Expansion had begun in the little Island Empire, and Canada was known over the seas.

Or take one of the provinces – for example, Ontario – if only we could trace the various elements that constitute its people, that would be to write a history of Ontario.

We are not dealing with figures but with men, women and children – with their hopes and struggles, their victories and defeats. What idylls – what tragedies lie behind these figures. If only we knew *one life!*

Classes	1871	1881	1891	1901
By birthplace				
Canada	2,892,763	3,715,492	4,185,877	4,671,815
British Columbia		32,275	37,153	60,776
Manitoba		19,590	56,430	110,742
New Brunswick	245,068	288,265	300,621	317,062
Nova Scotia	360,832	420,088	433,696	442,898
Ontario	1,138,794	1,467,988	1,728,731	1,928,099
Prince Edward Island		101,047	106,103	105,629
Quebec	1,147,664	1,327,809	1,462,293	1,620,482
The Territories	405	58,430	60,850	65,784
Unorganized Territories				6,969
Not given				13,374
British Islands	486,376	470,906	477,735	390,019
England	144,999	169,504	219,688	201,285
Ireland	219,451	185,526	149,184	101,629
Scotland	121,074	115,062	107,594	83,631
Wales	*	*	*	2,518
Lesser Islands	852	814	1,269	956
British possessions	9,696	7,329	12,517	15,864
Australasia				991
India				1,076
Newfoundland	7,768	4,596	9,336	12,432
Other possessions	1,928	2,733	3,181	1,365
Austria-Hungary	102			28,407
Belgium and Holland				2,665
China			9,129	17,043
Denmark				2,075
France	2,899	4,389	5,381	7,944
Germany	24,162	25,328	27,752	27,300
Iceland				6,057
Italy	218	777	2,795	6,854
Japan				4,674
Norway and Sweden	588	2,076	7,827	10,256
Roumania				1,066
Russia	416	6,376	9,917	31,231
Switzerland				1,211
Turkey and Syria				1,579
United States	64,447	77,753	80,915	127,899
Other countries	1,836	7,670	9,582	2,188
At sea	430	380	321	339
Not given	1,828	6,334	3,491	14,829
By race or origin				
British	2,110,502	2,548,514		3,063,195
English	706,369	881,301		1,260,899
Irish	846,414	957,403		988,721
Scotch	549,946	699,863		800,154
Others	7,773	9,947		13,421
Austro-Hungarian				18,178
Chinese and Japanese		4,383		22,050
Dutch	29,662	30,412		33,845
French	1,082,940	1,298,929		1,649,371
German	202,991	254,319		310,501

	1871	1881	1901
Indian and half-breed	23,037	108,547	127,932
Italian	1,035	1,849	10,834
Jewish	125	667	16,131
Negro	21,496	21,394	17,437
Russian	607	1,227	28,621
Scandinavian	1,623	5,223	31,042
Other races	4,182	8,540	10,639
Not specified	7,561	40,806	31,539

By religion	Census, 1901		Census, 1901
Adventists	8,058	Latter Day Saints	
Agnostics (Atheists,		(Mormons)	6,891
Freethinkers, Infidels,		Lutherans	92,524
Secularists, Sceptics,		Mennonites	31,797
Unbelievers)	3,613	Methodists	916,886
Anglicans	680,620	Mohammedans	47
Baptists	292,189	New Church	
Baptists, Free	24,288	(Swedenborgians)	881
Brethren	8,014	Non-sectarian	215
Buddhists	10,407	No religion	4,810
Catholic Apostolic	400	Pagans	15,107
Christadelphians	1,030	Plymouth Brethren	2,774
Christians	6,900	Presbyterians	842,442
Christian Scientists	2,619	Protestants	11,612
Church of Christ	2,264	Reformed	
Church of God	351	Episcopalians	874
Confucians	5,115	Roman Catholics	2,229,600
Congregationalists	28,293	Salvation Army	10,308
Deists	78	Spiritualists	616
Disciples	14,900	Theosophists	107
Doukhobors	8,775	Tunkers	1,528
Evangelicals	10,193	Unitarians	1,934
Friends (Quakers)	4,100	United Brethren	4,701
Greek Church	15,630	Universalists	2,589
Holiness Movement		Unspecified	43,222
(Hornerites)	2,775	Various sects†	2,795
Jews	16,401	Zionists	42

*   Not given

†   Various sects

Assembly	Farrington Inde-	Millennial Dawnists
Believers	pendents	Nazarenes
Bethany Mission	Followers of Christ	Orthodox Catholics
Calvinists	Free Church	Re-Incarnationists
Carmelites	Gregorians	Reformed Church
Children of God	Gospel Workers	Saints of God
Christian Brethren	Gospel Army	Separated Catholics
Christian Brothers	Gospel Brethren	Trinitarians
Christian Catholics	Humanitarians	Unionists
Christian Workers	New and Later House	And 79 other sects with
Covenanters	of Israel	258 members
Daniel's Band	Messiahists	

Who are we in the various provinces? (1901)

	British Columbia	Manitoba	New Brunswick	Nova Scotia	Ontario	Prince Edward Island	Quebec	The Territories	Unorganized territories
Population	178,657	255,506	331,120	459,574	2,182,947	103,259	1,648,898	158,940	52,709
Birthplace									
Canada	99,612	180,859	313,178	435,172	1,858,787	99,006	1,560,190	91,535	33,476
British Islands	30,630	33,093	10,226	10,889	239,873	2,852	42,600	17,347	2,509
British Possessions	1,843	424	680	6,725	2,530	493	2,648	265	256
Austria-Hungary	1,151	11,570						13,407	193
China	14,576						1,043		164
Denmark			302	266		18			227
France	1,478	1,470	130	229		12	3,183	1,023	754
Germany		2,285			18,699		1,543	2,170	
Iceland		5,403						424	
Italy	1,470				3,301		1,549		112
Japan	4,515								
Norway and Sweden	2,742	1,772	182	218		6	2,670	2,093	1,268
Russia	1,007	8,854	215	230	3,373	6		14,585	294
Turkey and Syria			134	214		29			
United States	17,164	6,922	5,477	4,394	44,175	764	28,405	13,877	6,721
Other countries	2,007	1,925	317	726	7,365	25	3,880	1,402	344
At sea	38	23		32		2	15	28	
Not given	424	611	279	479	4,844	46	1,172	784	6,391

Chapter 2

The strangers

IMMIGRATION

'And Elisha prayed, and said, Jehovah, I pray thee open his eyes that he may see. And Jehovah opened the eyes of the young man, and he saw' (2 Kings vi. 17). Elisha's prayer is peculiarly fitting now. The first need of American Protestantism is for clear vision to discern the supreme issues involved in immigration, recognize the spiritual significance and divine providence in and behind this marvellous migration of people, and to see Christian obligation to rise to the mission of evangelizing these representatives of all nations gathered on American soil.

HOWARD B. GROSE

WE MUST now pass on to the latest arrivals – many of them from countries of which we have hardly heard. Possibly we dimly remember their being in the old geography at school. We must add these newcomers to the population which we have already considered. Some of 1900-1 are already included.

Through the great kindness of Mr. R. Fraser, Government Statistician, we are able to present a statement of immigration into Canada from July 1st, 1900, to December 31st, 1907, classified according to nationalities, and a statement of the declared destination of these immigrants during the same period. (It will be noted that in the first table the last two periods are of twelve and six months, and in the second table of nine months each. The grand total is the same.)

Instead of relegating these statistics to an appendix, we place them here at the first of our book. They should be studied, as they are full of interest and significance. If only we could read into these figures their real meaning!

During the past seven and a half years, of our total immigration over 28 per cent is non-English-speaking. Most numerous of these are the Galicians; then the Italians; third, the Hebrews; fourth, those from Russia.

During the six months ending December 31st, 1907, over 33⅓ per cent of the total immigration was non-English-speaking – one out of every three a foreigner. According to numbers they stand in this order: Japanese, Hebrews, Russians, Italians, Galicians, Hindus – three Oriental peoples, three from Southeast Europe. According to religion they are 'heathen,' Jew, Greek Catholic, Roman Catholic, Mohammedan. In the social scale they are all very near the bottom. Then we must remember that a number of our American immigrants are foreigners – or foreigners once removed. Also that quite a large percentage of the English immigrants come from the congested parts of the great cities. Surely here is 'food for thought!'

In 1901 the Austria-Hungarian people in Canada would have made a city of 28,407 – that is, a city larger than Vancouver was in 1901. Since 1901 there have come to Canada 6,261 Austrians, 512 Bohemians, 8,714 Bukowinians, 55,492 Galicians, 8,236 Hungarians, 982 Magyars, 1,399 Ruthenians, 761 Slovaks, 5,219 Poles; total 87,576. The greater number of these have come from Austria-Hungary. The Ruthenians and Poles included in this total who have come from Russia are more than offset by Germans and Jews, not

Total immigration to Canada from July 1, 1900, to December 31, 1907, by nationalities

Nationality	Fiscal year 1900-1	Fiscal year 1901-2	Fiscal year 1902-3	Fiscal year 1903-4	Fiscal year 1904-5	Fiscal year 1905-6	12 months ending June 30, 1907	6 months ending Dec. 31, 1907	Totals
English and Welsh	9,401	13,095	32,510	36,694	49,617	65,932	90,015	35,764	333,028
Scotch	1,476	2,853	7,046	10,552	11,744	15,846	23,864	7,912	81,293
Irish	933	1,311	2,236	3,128	3,998	5,018	6,900	2,574	26,098
Total British	11,810	17,259	41,792	50,374	65,359	86,796	120,779	46,250	440,419
South African				21	35	46	44	47	193
Australian	3	11	46	58	204	322	239	94	977
Austrian	228	320	781	516	837	1,324	1,426	829	6,261
Bohemian	9	3	16	91	107	110	134	42	512
Bukowinian	128	550	1,759	1,578	1,123	1,355	1,856	365	8,714
Croatian	65	59	1	16	27	226	293	77	764
Dalmatian					4	16	51	3	74
Galician	4,702	6,550	8,382	7,729	6,926	5,656	13,376	2,171	55,492
Hungarian	546	1,048	2,074	1,091	981	739	1,302	455	8,236
Magyar					5	324	504	149	982
Ruthenian					3	266	729	401	1,399
Slovak	14	27	82	116	47	154	240	81	761
Styrian					29				29
Belgian	132	223	303	858	796	1,106	1,256	468	5,142
Bulgarian		1	7	14	2	71	896	1,802	2,793
Brazilian				2	1	2	5	1	11
Chinese	7	2				18	439	1,144	1,610

Total immigration to Canada *continued*

Nationality	Fiscal year 1900-1	Fiscal year 1901-2	Fiscal year 1902-3	Fiscal year 1903-4	Fiscal year 1904-5	Fiscal year 1905-6	12 months ending June 30, 1907	6 months ending Dec. 31, 1907	Totals
Dutch	25	35	223	169	281	389	1,110	388	2,620
French	360	431	937	1,534	1,743	1,648	2,421	1,230	10,304
German	984	1,048	1,869	2,966	2,721	1,745	2,780	1,220	15,333
Alsatian						4	3		7
Bavarian						22	5	3	30
Prussian			5	11	28	23	13	4	84
Saxon			13	8	10	2			33
West Indian			17	52	69	171	109	79	497
Bermudian			6	3	8	11	39	11	78
Jamaican						12	23	93	128
Greek	81	161	193	191	98	254	875	685	2,538
Hebrew	2,765	1,015	2,066	3,727	7,715	7,127	8,426	4,752	37,593
Italian	4,710	3,828	3,371	4,445	3,473	7,959	12,771	2,656	43,213
Japanese	6				354	1,922	4,084	5,163	11,529
Newfoundlander			335	519	190	340	2,263	1,596	5,243
New Zealander			2	23	57	89	55	41	267
Portuguese					1	6	3	1	11
Polish	162	230	274	669	745	725	1,575	839	5,219
Persian		1	40	5	8	7	31	3	95
Roumanian	152	272	437	619	270	396	798	449	3,393
Moldavian		279	1						280
Russian	1,044	2,467	5,505	1,955	1,887	3,152	4,414	3,251	23,675
Finnish	682	1,292	1,734	845	1,323	1,103	1,573	637	9,189
Doukhobors		12			24	204			240

Total immigration to Canada *continued*

									Total
Mennonites		52	38	11					101
Spanish	14	1	7	5	10	12	55	27	131
Swiss	30	17	73	128	150	172	198	87	855
Servian	23		2	10	7	19	12	34	107
Danish	88	163	308	417	461	474	442	118	2,471
Icelandic	912	260	917	396	413	168	70	73	3,209
Swedish	485	1,013	2,477	2,151	1,847	1,802	2,128	981	12,884
Norwegian	265	1,015	1,746	1,239	1,397	1,415	1,769	575	9,421
Turks	37	17	43	29	30	357	488	208	1,209
Armenian	62	112	113	81	78	82	264	465	1,257
Egyptian	1	3	1	3	2	18	13	5	46
Syrian	464	1,066	847	369	630	336	399	594	4,705
Arabian	98	70	46	58	48	19	37	41	417
Maltese			2						2
Malay		5							5
Negro					5	42	151	90	288
Hindu					45	387	2,420	2,037	4,889
Total Continental, etc.	19,284	23,659	37,099	34,728	37,255	44,349	74,607	36,565	307,546
From the United States	18,055	26,461	49,473	45,229	43,652	57,919	56,652	25,142	322,583
Total immigration	49,149	67,379	128,364	130,331	146,266	189,064	252,038	107,957	1,070,548

Destination of immigrants from July 1, 1907, to December 31, 1907*

	Fiscal year 1900-1	Fiscal year 1901-2	Fiscal year 1902-3	Fiscal year 1903-4	Fiscal year 1904-5	Fiscal year 1905-6	Fiscal period 1906-7	9 months of fiscal year 1907-8	Totals
Maritime Provinces	2,144	2,312	5,821	5,448	4,128	6,381	6,510	8,870	41,614
Quebec	10,216	8,817	17,040	20,222	23,666	25,212	18,319	40,879	164,371
Ontario	6,203	9,798	14,854	21,266	35,811	32,746	32,654	70,080	243,417
Manitoba	11,254	17,422	39,535	34,911	35,387	35,648	20,273	36,516	230,946
Saskatchewan	14,160	22,199	43,898	40,397	39,289	28,728	15,307	26,515	299,949
Alberta	2,600	3,483	5,378	6,994	6,008	26,177	17,559	25,720	77,092
British Columbia	2,567	3,348	1,838	1,093	1,977	12,406	13,650	26,573	13,159
Not shown						1,766	395	175	
Totals	49,149	67,379	128,364	130,331	146,266	189,064	124,667	235,328	1,070,548

*The *declared* destination (as in this table) of the immigrants is often not their *final* destination. The estimates of the Commissioner of Immigration in Winnipeg show a much larger proportion to have settled in Western Canada. Many immigrants are booked to points in Eastern Canada, but after a few days or weeks find their way to the West. On this point accurate statistics are not available.

Churches of foreigners, Winnipeg
1 St Nicholas Greek Church
2 A Jewish Synagogue
3 St Joseph's German Catholic Institutional Church
4 Orthodox Greek Catholic

included, but who have come from Austria-Hungary. That means that we have now enough Austria-Hungarians to make three cities as large as Vancouver, Winnipeg and Halifax were in 1901. Or, take the Italians. In 1901 we had in Canada 5,854 'born in Italy' – the population of a town. Since then we have had 43,213 immigrants from Italy; they would now make a city the size of Hamilton (1901). Then the Orientals: In 1901 we had 17,043 Chinese and 4,674 Japanese – a little more than enough to fill the city of Victoria (1901). Since that time we have received 1,610 Chinese, 11,529 Japanese, and 4,889 Hindus – that is, almost another Victoria (1901).

In 1901 we had 127,899 people 'born in the United States.' Since then we have received 322,583, making a total of 450,482 – almost enough to make a combined (1901) Montreal and Toronto.

During the past seven and one-half years we have received from Great Britain 440,419 – more than enough to people the Northwest Provinces as they were in 1901 (419,512).

Our total immigration during this period has been sufficient to re-people (as in 1901) Nova Scotia and New Brunswick, Prince Edward Island and British Columbia.

Can we picture the rate at which we are growing – 252,038 added to our population through immigration in 1906-7? That is 690 a day all the year round. Try to imagine a great excursion train arriving every day with 690 passengers! One train load builds up several blocks in Montreal, the next settles a whole row of townships in Northern Ontario, and the third spreads out over miles of prairie. And on and on they come!

The immigration of 1906-7 was almost double that of 1903-4, and over five times that of 1900-1. Sir Wilfrid Laurier's prophecy that 2,300,000 people will have settled in Canada during the years 1901 to 1911 seems in a fair way to be fulfilled.

The following table shows the growth of our immigration for the last fifty years:

1851-1861	54,508
1861-1871	48,312
1871-1881	76,274
1881-1891	141,965
1891-1901	223,321
1901-1911 (estimated)	2,300,000

What a jump! We have entered a new era in our history. The immigrants are upon us! For good or ill, the great tide is turning our way, and is destined to continue to pour in upon us. Government policy may to a small extent quicken or direct the flow, but great economic laws rather than Government policy are responsible for the rise of the tide.

Chapter 3

With the immigrants

AN IMMIGRANT ship in mid-ocean — here is more of human interest to the cubic foot than is to be found anywhere else on the face of the globe. Alone on the rolling deep — shut off from all the world — a little world in itself — half way between the Old World and the New — what a history lies behind — what possibilities ahead!

That speck on the waters is a Noah's ark in which are all peoples after their kind — male and female of all flesh wherein is the breath of life. It is a seedpod being carried to unknown shores where the old life will be perpetuated with endless variations. Here we have the fruit of the ages — the germ of the time to be — an epitome of the older civilization — a prophecy of the coming days.

What a field for study! Does the artist seek picturesque groups, let him take passage in a west-bound Atlantic liner. Here they are — Galician peasants in their sheepskins — fair-haired, clear-skinned Swedes — dark-eyed, eager Italian children. Here a withered old Russian woman in her outlandish dress with her old-fashioned little grandchild — a diminutive copy of herself; there a bent-shouldered Jew; yonder a young Syrian pedlar. And what moods are developed during a sea voyage! The deck is the place alike for lovers and suicides. Our artist friend will find something more than forms and colors. He will find the lights and shadows, the gladness and tragedy of life.

Is a man interested in social life and social problems, let him study the first, second and third class decks. All classes and types are represented. You have only to go up or down a few steps to ascend or descend in the 'social scale.' The people have been sorted out by the money test. On top — here as everywhere — the well-to-do people. Below them, the people of more moderate circumstances. On the lower deck, the 'poorer classes.' One cannot but wonder if we have evolved a true principle of classification. Notice that weedy-looking young fellow with a cigarette, who has never done anything all his life. Why should he have every luxury while the men who tilled his father's lands are crowded together in the steerage below — leaving the old home for the sake of their children? Why, why, why? is the question that forces itself upon us at every turn.

Our theologians can here study to advantage all shades of creed and conduct. Our novelists could collect 'material' for more books than they will ever write. If only we could know the life-stories of our fellow passengers! To study a mixed group of immigrants is in itself a liberal education.

Most of our immigrants come second or third class. Let us give a list of our acquaintances during a recent trip. An English girl on her way to Winnipeg to try her fortune as 'lady's help.' She had no friends but was ambitious to 'do better' than she could 'at home.' An Englishman and his wife en route to the mines in British Columbia. He was born in India, educated in Scotland and England, had served in the army in Africa and Australia, and had been mining in Australia. An English girl on her way to join a sister in Ottawa; she would probably find a place in a shop or office. A young English girl who had been a cook, expecting to meet her brother in Western Ontario; he had sent her passage money. A Hollander bound for Winnipeg on a tour of inspection with a view to investing money in the West. A young English gardener with his bride on their way to start life near Montreal. An English woman with her baby; she was joining her husband who had a position in a departmental store in Winnipeg. A young woman from a seaport town in England, booked to Port Arthur, where she expected to marry a young man – if she liked him. An elderly Irish woman returning to Saskatchewan from a visit to Ireland, and taking with her a 'raal Oirish' niece. A middle-aged Englishman in the hotel business, who believes Canada a promising field. A young Englishman and his wife on their way to Edmonton. So we might go on. This will give an idea of the 'better class' of immigrants. In the third class some ships carry only English, German and Scandinavians. Others take all classes and conditions. What a mixed multitude! Watch them lying about the decks – propped against a sheltering wall – lounging on the great cables – gambling on the hatchways – the children rolling in the litter of the decks. What a filthy lot! Yes, the conditions are bad enough and worse than there is any need! But go among these people. Be one with them, and you will begin to sympathize with them – often to admire them – and ever after help them fight their battles. That family of Italians – undesirables, yes – and yet when we know them and their struggles – the long years of poverty, the good news that there was a land of promise, the hoarding that was necessary to send out the eldest boy, the glowing letters he sent home, the hope deferred, but now about to be realized – our hearts relent. We could hardly deny them admission. Here is a family of Poles; one child has 'weak eyes.' Of course, she must be deported. But do we think what it means – the shock to the family when they learn that their little one is to be sent back and they are to go on. Gladly they, too, would return, but they have no money. The poor have no choice. In spite of the father's and mother's grief the little girl is taken from them. Poor people! they will live in wretched rooms, on crusts till they can make enough money for the father to return to find and bring back his child. But, oh, the long months of waiting! But as yet out on the ocean they are unconscious of the trouble that awaits them. They are thinking only of the little home that they will have in the new land.

'Land!' Quickly the word goes round, and all is excitement. 'Land!' at all times, the most interesting moment in a voyage. What a thrill it brings now when it is land after the first voyage – and the New Land – the Promised Land – how eagerly the coast line is scanned! The lighthouses and fishing villages; and then the odd wooden painted houses, and the church spires. To the one who is coming home there is deep joy, mingled only with the vague fear of what may have happened in his absence. To the new arrival there is, after the first excitement, an overwhelming sense of strangeness and helplessness.

Fortunately, perhaps, the immigrant does not need to take the initiative, but finds himself carried along with the crowd. Management there must be, somewhere, and reason, doubtless, for all these tedious examinations, but he has no very clear idea as to the 'how' and 'why' of all that takes place during the long hours that elapse before he finds himself safely landed. His greatest anxiety is to look after his baggage. And what an assortment of boxes and bundles! No wonder that some pieces go astray!

First comes the medical examination. Then all must pass through the 'cattle pen' – a series of iron-barred rooms and passage ways. They must go in single file, and each pass before various officials who question them as to their nationality and destination, and the amount of money they have in their possession. All this is very necessary, but it is a weary, anxious time. No one can tell what will come next. Many fear they will be stopped. Some are turned back – one taken and the others left. Now, there is the customs examination. At last tickets are arranged for, baggage transferred, and the immigrants find themselves bundled into a colonist car. This is another new experience – not altogether a pleasant one either, since they are not accustomed to cooking and sleeping in such small quarters. Some have not made proper provision. After several days, all are glad to get off the train at one of the large distributing points. Here again are the Government officials who arrange everything. Within a few days they are sent out on some new branch line, and with their belongings set down at a little 'siding' on the prairie. They have some friends perhaps who drive them to their homestead, or who shelter them for a few weeks. Now begins the new life in the strange land.

The following extracts from an article written by L. M. Fortier, Chief Clerk of the Immigration Department, Ottawa, show the attitude of the Government officials, and also furnish illuminating incidents:

It is hard to sever the 'ties that bind'; to give up the old home occupied by the family, perhaps for generations — the old neighbors, friends and interests. The process of uprooting and transplanting is a painful one, but it is undergone by many a family to the great betterment of their prospects in life; and when the momentous decision has at last been bravely reached, the Canadian agent again steps in and renders assistance in the way of advice on transportation matters, 'what to take,' etc., besides offering various little attentions, which as a rule are gratefully received at such a time. At the port of embarkation the immigrants are met and seen safely on board ship with their belongings; sometimes they are accompanied across the ocean, and on reaching port in Canada they are always welcomed by Government officials, who direct them and see to their comfort in every possible way.

When fifty or more travel on one train there is an immigration officer to go with them on the railway journey, to attend to their wants and protect them against imposition, and assuming that they are going to the North-West, they find officials everywhere to give them useful direction. Comfortable accommodations are maintained at all distributing points, for the free temporary use of immigrants on their first arrival, and for a limited period afterwards while the men are looking for land and deciding where to settle. And so Canada gives no cold and niggardly reception to desirable settlers who seek her shores in response to her invitation. At the same time it is always well to have it understood that we fight shy of criminals and undesirables generally. Canada is not a healthful or inviting country for them to come to, and they are gently but firmly turned back, for their own good and ours.

The summer port of landing for all over-sea immigrants is Quebec, and the winter ports are Halifax and St. John. At these places comfortable and commodious buildings are maintained, in which the immigrants spend the waiting time between landing from the ship and entraining for the railway journey. The women and children have their own quarters and a matron and assistants to attend to them. If there is sickness, medical aid and comforts are at hand, and if a contagious disease should develop, the patient is promptly isolated and attended to. The men look after the baggage, the exchange of money and purchase of provisions, and when all is ready the journey westward by rail is begun, usually in 'colonist' cars, which are clean, and provided with facilities for cooking, eating, sleeping and spending the day in comparative comfort. But to spend a little time in a colonist car and witness the scenes there brings forcibly to one's mind Dickens' observations in *American Notes,* on the immigrants he saw travelling in Canada, concluding in these words:

'Looking round upon these people, far from home – weary with travel – and, seeing how patiently they nursed and tended their young children; how they consulted over their wants first, then half supplied their own; what gentle ministers of hope and faith the women were; how the men profited by their example; and how very, very seldom even a moment's petulance or harsh complaint broke out among them, I felt a stronger love and honor of my kind come glowing on my heart, and wished to God there had been many atheists in the better part of human nature there, to read this simple lesson in the book of life.'

Cheerfulness marks the progress of the journey to the far inland; helped out by many a practical joke and amusing incident. Only the other day one of the Government travelling agents had great difficulty in persuading a young fellow, before he started for the West, from investing some of his small capital in firearms and knives to kill the buffalo, wolves and other wild animals which his fellow passengers had persuaded him were to be encountered in the streets of Winnipeg. One day an immigrant train was brought to a sudden stop by an alarm from a Galician family that they had lost one of their children, a boy of eight, who had tumbled out of the window. All was interest and excitement, and the parents were loud in their expressions of dismay and grief, but as the train went slowly

backward the young hopeful was discovered walking along the
track and was finally picked up, quite unhurt, on perceiving which
the parents experienced a sudden revulsion of feeling, and gave
their offspring a vigorous whipping for the trouble he had caused
by his escapade.

On approaching Winnipeg the other day a party of Scotch immigrants were having their homesick feelings stirred up by singing the
old songs and somewhat sentimental speechifying; the women were
in tears, and the men were feeling 'lumpy about the throat,' when a
man at the other end of the car electrified the company and inspired
new hope and cheerfulness by shouting out, 'What are ye dreeing
aboot? Is't the poverty ye've left ahint? Think o' what's afore ye!'

Arrived at Winnipeg, all go into the Immigration Hall for rest and
refreshment, and from there in due time find their own place in the
new land. The majority are bent on farming, and those who have
means and experience to make an immediate start on their own
account are told about vacant lands, and helped to a decision upon
the momentous question of 'where to settle.' Others are directed to
employment of various kinds, and in various directions, and so party
succeeds party from day to day.

An article of this kind would be incomplete without some
reference to the North-West Mounted Police. Colonizing the
North-West would be a very different matter, both for the department and for the colonists, without the aid of this splendid organization. The country is so thoroughly taken care of by them that their
patrol map looks like a spider's web. A sharp lookout is kept for
smugglers, horse thieves, criminals, wandering Indians, and such like
gentry. Strangers are asked their business; note is taken of settlers'
complaints, the state of the crops, and the movement of cattle;
strayed horses are looked up and restored to their owners, with
every now and then a sharp ride for perhaps one hundred miles in
pursuit of horse thieves; prairie fires are watched for and put out, if
possible; the Indian reserves are visited, and note taken of the doings
there. Each patrol makes a written report, which, with the diary
kept at the outpost, is sent in weekly to the divisional headquarters.
In this way a general supervision is maintained, the police know all
the ins and outs of every district, and are in constant touch with the
people. All this is trying work, necessitating hard rides in all
weathers and much roughing of it.

When the great North-West Territory of Canada becomes what it promises to be, one of the greatest, richest and best-governed of lands, it will owe much to the work of this efficient and well-planned force.

As supplementing this we quote from an interview with J. Obed Smith, who for years was Immigration Commissioner in Winnipeg:

I believe that it is as much good business to look after the immigrant's welcome when he comes, as it is to secure him for the country. He becomes an advertising agent for us if he prospers. That is why the Government practically gives us *carte blanche,* and that is why it is possible to do all we do. Last winter, you may have heard, we sent out patrols into certain districts to see that the homesteaders did not starve because of the exceptional conditions. Some of these men were out fourteen days at a time, and in some extreme cases they sent whole families in to us, to tide them over the bad days. It was well that they did, for some, when discovered, were on 'the ragged edge,' and relief was sorely needed. This year we had to advance an enormous amount of seed grain to those farmers who were forced to use what they had during the winter.

We close this chapter with a cartoon with an explanatory paragraph by Ada Melville Shaw, Evanston:

Only an immigrant

A few months ago a swift-moving train, bringing its quota of immigrants to Chicago, collided with a freight train not far from the city. About fifty people were killed. The next morning McCutcheon, the *Chicago Tribune*'s great cartoonist, preached one of his most forceful, pathetic and timely sermons, without words, to this great cosmopolitan city.

There she stands, the mother with the unpronounceable name, the queer, shapeless garb, the coarse, work-worn hand. There are her babies, their round eyes bewitched at sight of the great ship. And there, one among the hundreds of steerage passengers — her 'one,' her 'man!' — is the husband, the father, the bread-winner, confidently setting out for great, generous, golden America. Before his clumsy fingers have thought of writing her a letter, before there is much to write of save his arrival in the strange land — he lies dead, 'only an immigrant.' Whoever wrote the report of that horror for the *Tribune* had a heart, and the reader felt somehow that the owners of names ending in 'stein,' 'nski,' 'owitz,' 'zak,' were after all men, women and little children not merely immigrants!

THE STORY OF AN IMMIGRANT AS TOLD BY HIMSELF
The following letter was written as a composition exercise in February, 1908, by one of the boys in the night school at All Peoples' Mission; we have made only slight corrections:

It was the '03-'04 winter in Russia. I, in a business school, and my brother, in a technical school, were living ten miles from our parents who lived in a small country town where my father had kept a general store for eight years. (This was three months before the Russian-Japan war.) When we came to our home for Christmas vacation we found our father thinking to exchange his form of life. None of us liked store-keeping. For a long time we had thought of farming. A year and a half before my father had written to the Government of Russia asking permission to buy some land. (The Hebrews have not liberty to buy land in Russia.) The reply came in the negative. Then my father thought to emigrate to Palestine — the Holy Land of Zion. But this was not so easy. It required a large sum of money. Then we thought about the Argentine where the Jewish Colonization Association had founded some colonies. To obtain information my father went to another city to a

man who came from Argentine. He explained that it is a fair country
where there is a lot of good land, and there is a company which sells
it on credit. My father came back thinking to emigrate in the spring
to Argentine. But a little later he decided to exchange Argentine for
Canada, because the latter is a more educated country, and Englishmen are much better than Spaniards. We were all glad to leave Russia
and emigrate to Canada.

On the 13th of June my father went to Fort Qu'Appelle, Sask.,
where there was a Roumanian Jewish colony two years old. There
were a few Russian Jews who came a couple of months before my
father. My father's letters were very favorable. They were full of
poetry; the green grass, the fresh air, the woods, the ponds, the
birds — and one hundred and sixty acres for ten dollars. He did not
tell us about the poverty of the farmers, or about their very cold
houses; so we thought that the farmers lived a very comfortable life
in their new colony.

We had to sell two stores on the town market, and a house
communicating with a two hundred dollar grocery store, situated on
the other side of the town. As the town was small we could not get
rid of the stock till the middle of '05 winter. Then came a great
disaster. Our house was burned. We had to rent a house to live in till
spring when we expected to go to our father. We did not write to
him about the fire. A month later we gave my uncle fifty dollars to
help him to go to Canada, too. After this we sent father one hundred
dollars. Then we had some payments to make, and three hundred
dollars to collect. Of this we did not collect one-third. We thought
by selling the property to have enough money for the journey. But
in a small country town in war time it is not so easy to sell properties. We remained till the 18th of June. Not being able to sell the
properties we left Russia with only one hundred and fifty dollars
(three hundred Russian roubles). A man lent us one hundred dollars.
By the time we had reached Canada he had sold the stores, but
would not mind to send us the difference money.

We expected to get cheap tickets from London, but to our
dismay we did not find any society with cheap tickets for poor
immigrants. We were obliged to stay in London nine weeks till my
father had sold his cattle and sent us one hundred and fifty dollars.

In London we had a very bad time. I will never forget the
wretched journey. In the three days' train ride from Quebec to

Qu'Appelle we had nothing to eat. It was very hard on my dear
mother, because it is the worst time for a mother when her children
are hungry. Only one day, we thought, and we will be at our new
home with our dear father! But we had to wait more than a day for
we found that the colony is forty miles from Qu'Appelle. In
Qu'Appelle we met a Hebrew boy who lent us two dollars. Oh,
glorious moment! After a fast we enjoyed our dinner! Next day we
engaged a man who took us to the colony. But there we did not find
what we expected. We thought a colony would be as in Russia — two
to four hundred houses together. Here we found a small shack,
occupied by a Hebrew farmer, who explained to us what the
colonies are in Canada. He had no place for us for the night, but he
directed us to another farmer one mile further. We went, and to our
delight found he was a friend from the Old Country. He explained to
us that our father was working for a farmer, and that all farmers
were poor enough yet. So we had to wait a week more till our father
came to see us. It was the 30th of October, 1905.

The winter of '05-'06 we lived in another farmer's house, because
ours was not ready for the winter. My work was to feed five head of
cattle, cut wood, bring in wood, water or snow. So I was busy all
day at home, and my father and brother in the bush, because we had
no other income to keep us alive. It was a hard time. Four dollars a
week cannot keep well a family of eight. But we did not care much
for it. We were very glad to be in Canada, and have a farm.

In the spring of '06 we moved to our farm where we had a two-
story lumber house which we had to plaster. On the farm we had
two good cows, and so had more to eat, and our life was more
comfortable. The plastering of the house was very hard work for us,
as we were not used to such work. We mixed clay and water, and put
it on the walls. But we did our work well, and we have a very comfortable house. Just as hard was the bush work in summer, or the
building or plastering of the big stable. But we always did our work
with pleasure. The best work was our garden. We planted it carefully, and for our labor had quite a lot of vegetables. My mother and
sister were busy with the chickens. In the middle of July we started
the nice haytime. It was very agreeable work to cut hay around the
ponds. In the autumn we gathered our vegetables down the cellar.
Our autumn work was to get wood for the winter and for sale. Every
day my father and I went to the bush, and came back with a large

load. After autumn came the severe '06-'07 winter. To keep us alive
my father or brother used to go twice a week to town with wood or
hay. I had the same kind of work as the winter before – to feed
eight head of cattle and cut the wood, and carry water and snow.
But everything has an end, and that strong winter ended.

Living on the farm I had no chance to learn English as I wanted
to do. In the free time I used to copy from an old primer, but I did
not understand the meaning of the words. At last I asked my parents
to go to Winnipeg to work and to learn. They let me go. With thirty-
five cents in my pocket I went to Winnipeg, but arrived without a
black cent. This was the 24th of April, 1907. I had an uncle here. He
found me some work in a factory where I worked for a short time.
Then I started to work in a grocery store where I worked till the
10th of November. Now I am working in the G.N.W. as a messenger
boy. I did not have any lessons in English till I started to your
school. To it, I am obliged for whatever I know of the English
language.

This may be taken as a typical story of the experiences of a
family of immigrants – the dissatisfaction in the old land – the
dreams and plans about the new – the father going first to prospect
and prepare – the sacrifice made in leaving the old home – the
anxieties and hardships of the journey – the hopes that buoyed
them – the disappointment in reaching the land of their
dreams – the struggles to gain a foothold – the privations of the
first few months or years – the gradual making of the home – the
move of the young men to the city – their struggles. How much one
can read between the lines! With variations, this is the experience of
immigrants from all countries. Thousands of families scattered all
over the prairies can tell such tales.

Such stories give us hope for the future. Such courage – such
endurance – such struggles cannot but develop a high type of
character. Compare such experiences with the easy-going, self-
satisfied, narrow, unprogressive lives of many who are hardly holding
what their fathers gained! These latter, with their little round of
petty pleasures, despise the poorly clad 'foreigner' with his broken
English and strange ways; but the odds are largely on the side of the
immigrant. It required no little decision of character to undertake to
change the whole course of his life. It required no little management

to carry this through successfully. Then what an experience in the long journey and in the coming to a new land! A year in Europe is sometimes considered, by the wealthy, a liberal education. These immigrants have that kind of liberal education which can come only by experiencing two very different kinds of life, and really entering into the second. We must also think of the powers of adaptation that are necessary in fitting one's self to the new conditions. In this again the immigrant has the advantage. Of course, there is the other side — the long, hard struggle for life that crowds out many of the things that make life worth living — the uprooting of lifelong associations, and the difficulty of taking root again in a strange soil — the sudden emergence into freedom unknown before, and the difficulty of training the children for the new life — the strain of rising in a few short years through degrees of well-being that ordinarily would take generations. Such are the trials. How wisely should we care for the immigrant! What will become of this Jewish boy who has told us his story? Full of the highest possibilities he runs most serious risks. His ambition will save him from many evils. Will he become a money-making sceptic? Or will he become a man of high ideals and noble life? That depends — well, upon what?

Chapter 4

Immigrants from Great Britain

DURING the past few years very large numbers of immigrants have been coming to us from the British Isles. For the last seven and one-half years the figures are as follows: English and Welsh, 333,028; Scotch, 81,293; Irish, 26,098; total, 440,419. Almost half a million have migrated to this part of the Greater Britain beyond the seas. The majority of these have readily taken their places in the life of the new land and are among our best citizens. In India, it is said that English regiments are necessary to 'stiffen' the native army. We need more of our own blood to assist us to maintain in Canada our British traditions and to mould the incoming armies of foreigners into loyal British subjects.

As a rule the British immigrants are scattered throughout the country and do not form distinct colonies. There have, however, been a number of interesting experiments in colonization. In 1903, Rev. I. M. Barr organized an 'All British colony,' and settled a large district in which is now located the town of Lloydminster. Two thousand Britishers were brought out in a chartered ship, and transported overland from Saskatoon to the site of the new colony. They endured great hardships. There was serious mismanagement and much dissatisfaction. Many, after great privations and heavy financial loss, became discouraged and returned to England. Others showed great pluck, and are now on the road to success.

Other interesting colonies were the Scotch crofters and the Welsh from Patagonia. Both classes were wretchedly poor, and not specially adapted to the country. At first they suffered many hardships, but the majority succeeded in getting a start and now will be able to make their way.

Generally speaking, the Scotch, Irish and Welsh have done well. The greater number of failures have been among the English. This is due partly to a national characteristic which is at once a strength and a weakness – lack of adaptability. Someone has said that 'the English are the least readily assimilated of the English-speaking nationalities.' But the trouble has been largely with the *class* of immigrants who have come. Canada has needed farmers and laborers, and these should be resourceful and enterprising. England has sent us largely the failures of the cities. The demand for artisans in our cities is limited. In any case many of the immigrants are culls from English factories and shops. These cannot compete with other English-speaking people and often not with non-English, despite the latter's

The harvest and the laborers
1 The wealth of the western prairies — gathering the harvest
2 In Winnipeg Station on the way to the western harvest fields

disadvantage in not knowing the language. On many western farms, certain Englishmen have proved so useless that when help is needed 'no Englishman need apply.' Even on Ontario farms where there are more 'chores' to be done the Englishman is not at a premium. The following extracts from a crop bulletin, issued by the Ontario Department of Agriculture show the Eastern opinion of farm labor:

Most farmers have to do their own work; wages are so high that they cannot pay them. The help that may be obtainable at times is without any knowledge of farming.

We exchange time and labor with each other, and so are masters and servants by turns.

We have good farm hands, but three-fourths of them are of no use. They don't know and they don't seem to 'want to learn.'

Many of the young men who have been placed with farmers have left, and have gone into the shops in the cities.

A good Canadian can get anything he asks, but men from the Old Country get about $18 per month for the summer months.

The number of farm laborers has been sufficient, but it has been of poor quality. Many of them are not worth their board, and yet there are so many complaints; good men can command any wages they like.

We have a lot of useless immigrants, and more are coming; something should be done to stop this dumping business.

Many of the Old Country men seem actually helpless on a farm.

The supply of labor is not what it should be because nearly all Englishmen are itinerants; they want to be on the move.

Such people are really townspeople, and drift back to the cities where they form a serious problem.

The following is a list of immigrants taken at random from the books of the Government Labor Bureau at Winnipeg. They are all applicants for work on farms. They represent a good class of immigrants but what wonder if they are not all adapted to the work Canada has to offer:

English farmer, English quarryman, English laborer, Welsh farmer, Scotch farmer, English hotelman, Scotch gardener, Irish farmer, English draughtsman, Scotch clerk, English jockey, English painter,

English chemist, Scotch brakesman, Scotch miner, Irish laborer, English clerk, Scotch farmer, English gymnast, English druggist, English metal-worker, Scotch laborer, English soldier, English electrician, Irish laborer, English brickmaker, Scotch tailor, English engineer.

Let us analyze our English immigration. The majority are those who are anxious to better their condition or to give their children a better chance, and so seek the advantages of a new country. These are quickly absorbed by Canadian society; they form no separate class. Their children are Canadian as our fathers were English.

But there are several classes that stand out more prominently and whose record is less favorable. These are the 'younger sons' and remittance men, and ne'er-do-weels, who are shipped to Canada to 'learn farming' – or because they can live here more cheaply – or that they may reform – or in plain English, to be got rid of. Useless at home, they are worse than useless here. The saloon gains most largely by their presence.

Mr. Bruce Walker, Immigration Commissioner, tells a story of an English magistrate who was reprimanding a youthful criminal. 'You have broken your mother's heart, you have brought down your father's gray hairs in sorrow to the grave. You are a disgrace to your country. Why don't you go to Canada?'

Then we have the assisted immigrants. Statistics compiled from the immigration arrivals in Canada of a year ago show that 12,260 immigrants were sent to Canada by organizations whose aims have been entirely good, but the results of whose endeavors have been looked upon with more or less disfavor by the immigration authorities, both in Canada and Great Britain. The work of these societies in sending out this number of immigrants is classified as follows: Salvation Army, 406; East End Immigration Fund, 6,096; Self-Help Emigration Society, 506; Church Army, 1,519; Church Emigration Society, 663; Central Unemployed Body, 2,842; Central Emigration Board, 228.

The majority of these are from the slums of the great cities – a people described by the Archbishop of Canterbury as 'a suffering population which can hardly exist, hanging on the sharp edge of illness and hunger, and in full sight of abundance, luxury and waste.'

Let us look at the problems of poverty from an Old Country standpoint. We quote from John A. Hobson: 'Considerations of space will compel us to confine our attention to such figures as will serve to mark the extent and meaning of city poverty in London. But though, as will be seen, the industrial causes of London poverty are in some respects peculiar, there is every reason to believe that the extent and nature of poverty does not widely differ in all large centres of population.'

The area which Mr. Booth places under microscopic observation covers Shoreditch, Bethnal Green, Whitechapel, St. George's in the East, Stepney, Mile End, Old Town, Poplar, Hackney, and comprises a population of 891,539. Of these no less than 316,000 or 35 per cent, belong to families whose weekly earnings amount to less than twenty-one shillings. This 35 per cent composes the 'poor,' according to the estimate of Mr. Booth, and it is worth while to note the social elements which constitute this class. The 'poor' are divided into four classes or strata, marked A, B, C, D. At the bottom comes A, a body of some 11,000, or 1¼ per cent, of hopeless, helpless city savages who can be said only by courtesy to belong to the 'working-classes.' Their life is the life of savages, with vicissitudes of extreme hardship and occasional excesses. Their food is of the coarsest description, and their only luxury is drink. It is not easy to say how they live; the living is picked up ... They render no useful service; they create no wealth; more often they destroy it.

Next comes B, a thicker stratum of some 100,000, or 11½ per cent, composed largely of shiftless, broken-down men, widows, deserted women and their families. Most of them are incapable of regular, effective work, and are therefore dependent upon casual earnings, usually less than eighteen shillings per week. Most of the wreckage of city life is deposited in this stratum, which presents the problem of poverty in its most perplexing and darkest forms. For this class hangs as a burden on the shoulders of the more capable classes which stand just above ...

Class C consists of 75,000, or 8 per cent, subsisting on intermittent earnings of from eighteen to twenty-one shillings for a moderate-sized family. Low-skilled laborers, poorer artisans, street sellers, small shop-keepers, largely constitute this class. The curse of their life is not so much low wages as irregularity of employment, and the moral and physical degradation caused thereby.

Above these forming the top stratum of the 'poor' comes a large class, numbering 129,000, or 14½ per cent, dependent upon small, regular earnings of from eighteen to twenty-one shillings. This class includes many dock and waterside laborers, factory and warehouse hands, carmen, messengers, porters, etc. What they have comes in regularly, and except in times of sickness in the family, actual want rarely presses unless the wife drinks.

Mr. Booth, in confining the title 'poor' to this 35 per cent of the population of London, takes, perhaps for sufficient reasons, a somewhat narrow interpretation of the term. For in the same district no less than 377,000, or over 42 per cent of the inhabitants, live upon earnings varying from twenty-one to thirty shillings per week. We can only say that when they are fortunate they stand above the line of physical destitution. The whole of this 77 per cent of East London may without impropriety be included under the designation of 'the poor.'

Let me give two cases of England's poor transplanted to Canada.

Richard Carter was a dyer in Whitechapel; his wife had been a lace-maker. They had two children — a boy of four and a girl of two. A charity organization sent them to Canada to farm. They never got beyond Winnipeg. The man was not strong enough physically to farm, and his eyesight was defective. Before many months the wife was in the courts accusing her husband of assault. The children were sickly; after about a year it was discovered that the little boy was weak-minded. The 'home' was a copy of the homes in the slums of East London.

John Hobbs, his wife and four children had their passage paid by a clergyman in a village in the South of England. They arrived in Canada with one pound, supplied them by the kind-hearted clergyman. But five dollars does not go far in starting a home. They sought the help of a clergyman here. He interested some friends who secured work for the man, and bought a stove and a few articles to furnish a room in a tenement. The husband was 'no good,' and 'couldn't keep a job.' The immigration hall supplied five dollars' worth of groceries. Another job was found for the man; clothes were given to the children; and so they are being 'carried' by the community.

We sympathize with these poor people, but we are glad that the Canadian Government is taking steps to prevent the 'dumping' of these unfortunates into Canada.

Another large class are the juvenile immigrants. 'An average of 2,000 children is annually emigrated to Canada in organized bands.'

'During the past five and thirty years it is estimated that at least 50,000 children of Anglo-Saxon origin have been sent to Canada under the auspices of organized societies and accredited agencies.' 'From 1867 to June 30th, 1904, Dr. Barnardo's organization has sent to Canada a total of 15,609 juveniles.' The following table shows the number of juvenile immigrants who arrived in Canada during the past five years, together with the number of applications received by the various agencies during that period:

	Arrivals	Applications
1900-1901	977	5,783
1901-1902	1,540	8,587
1902-1903	1,979	14,219
1903-1904	2,212	16,573
1904-1905	2,814	17,833
1905-1906	3,258	19,369
	12,780	82,364

Such are the statements made by Mr. Bogue Smart, Chief Inspector of British Immigrant Children and Receiving Homes in Canada. Mr.. Smart, an enthusiast in his work, tells of the life of the children in the large cities:

Although perhaps not unfamiliar with stories of misery and neglect in the Old Land, it was not until now that I was able to appreciate the true significance of the words 'poverty' and 'wretchedness.' It was plainly to be seen in many of these overburdened and over-crowded homes that real family life was an unknown quantity. No one could help seeing danger ahead for these youthful subjects unless they were removed from their prejudicial surroundings at an early age. I saw children with only a miserable apology for a home. One of the saddest pictures I witnessed during my travels was that of a girl about fourteen years of age wearing an ordinary salt sack with the end cut out, for a dress, fastened about her waist with a cord. Such sights, however, soon became familiar. In the over-populated districts, there are narrow streets which lead one into dark court-yards, where there are rows of tenement houses. Some of these

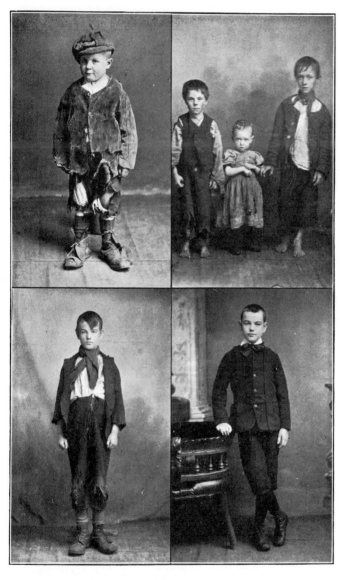

Juvenile immigrants from Great Britain
1 His best and only suit 2 Neglected and half-starved

A boy who was given a chance
3 Taken August 1st, 1902 4 Taken February 5th, 1903

houses were once the residences of merchant princes and other
leading citizens, but long since abandoned, and are now in a state of
dilapidation. I walked through these thoroughfares to one such
house, a four-story building which I found to be occupied by eight
families. To each family was assigned a single room. The interior was
quite dark, and we were obliged to light matches in order to see our
way up the stairs. Having reached the top flat, I entered a small,
dark, cheerless room, the occupants of which I learned were a man,
his wife and two children. There was no furniture in the room save a
small table with a few dishes on it. I looked about to find where the
family slept, and in one corner I found a bundle of rags encased in a
mattress ...

A few hours after my arrival in Liverpool, I witnessed a sight
unique to a Canadian, a procession of two hundred and fifty (by
actual count of heads) ragged, shoeless and hatless children, 50 per
cent of whom were bright, healthy and alert, *and good types for
immigration from a Canadian point of view.*

We venture to dissent from Mr. Bogue Smart's conclusion. Children from such surroundings with inherited tendencies to evil are a
very doubtful acquisition to Canada.

We do not doubt that the change is generally good for the children. We do not deny that many have succeeded; we would not
refuse to help the needy. But we must express the fear that any large
immigration of this class must lead to degeneration of our Canadian
people.

Dr. Barnardo tells the story of the rescue of a waif and his success
in Canada:

Eighteen months or so ago a lad was brought before the magistrates
in a Western town — Falmouth. He was charged with vagrancy,
sleeping out, and having no visible means of subsistence. This was
the third time he had been so charged, and he was only about sixteen years of age. The magistrates did not know what to do with
him. Kind-hearted, they did not like to send him to prison. What
could they do? They sent him to the workhouse for a while. But
when the time was up he was turned adrift again, and was very soon
once more before the bench. But this time he was charged with
attempting to commit suicide. They asked him why he had dared to

think of doing so dreadful a thing. Poor chap! He stood up and replied in a broken voice: 'No one cares whether I starve or not. No one will give me work. I am starving. I thought I had better end it.'

Then they thought of me. When the lad reached me I spoke somewhat roughly to him, just to test him. 'What good can I do you?' I said; 'you're lazy, you won't work.' 'Won't I,' he replied; 'you try me, sir.'

Well, we sent him to our labor home, and soon he was reported as industrious, decent and honest. He went to Canada. And here is a letter which says of him: 'He is a fine fellow, doing well and greatly respected.'

Now you have it in a nutshell; eighteen months ago he was starving and attempting suicide, and no one would give him work. Now he is greatly respected. What may he not now become?

Who would not give a chance to such a boy? Yet as we think of the 'home' boys and girls whom we have known, we cannot but admit that often their past is too great a handicap. All honor to those who win out!

The following description, written by Mr. A. R. Ford, introduces us to the better class of English immigrants as they are approaching their destination:

'Fourteen hundred British immigrants arrived in Winnipeg last night bound for points in the west.'

You read that item in the morning paper. It is nothing to you; you pass on to see if the Ottawa solons are still in session; if Willie Jones has won the school prize. Yet every one of these 1,400 immigrants represents a story. And what a story! A story of home ties broken, of loved ones left in the old land, of hopes and ambitions in the new land.

It was a weary, homesick, tired-looking lot I found as I climbed aboard a British immigrant train, westward bound, at some unheard-of station on the C.P.R., somewhere between Fort William and Kenora. Still, they were a jolly, cheerful crowd. Oh, how hopeful! How they looked forward to the new land, the Eldorado of their dreams. It was an optimism that made you sad, when you knew all the hardships they were to endure, the hard knocks they would have to stand, and the setbacks that were sure to come. They were so innocently hopeful, so unsophisticated in their enthusiasm over the outlook. Yet they were not quite as jolly a crowd as they appeared, when one got behind that English mask. Everything that they had learned to love for years in that tight little island of theirs had been left behind. Many a man had left behind his wife and kiddies while he came to make a home for them in the new land.

The immigrants on the train I had boarded represented probably the best class of immigrants from the old land.

Most of them had come over with the Salvation Army on the steamer *Kensington,* though some had had a stormy trip on the *Virginian.* They came from all classes; every industry was represented. They all told the same story. Thousands out of work in England; hundreds upon hundreds of laboring men, who had had good positions, were walking the streets. They had all come to the Dominion for work. It was all they asked. Canada, they said, was in everyone's mouth. Everyone was talking Canada, and you couldn't get away from the advertisements. They were in every paper, they were posted at every railway station and in every post-office. It was Canada, Canada, Canada.

Sitting in front of me was a well-dressed, likely-looking man of forty. He seemed tired and worried, and was rather unkempt from a two weeks' rough voyage, but a man who you were sure would make good in this new country. I made some excuse to sit down beside him.

'Why have I come to Canada? Well, that is easy. To get work. I haven't earned a penny since Christmas. I have walked twenty miles a day looking for a job. For every position that is open there are hundreds of applicants. They actually have to call out the police. I had been in one position twenty-eight years looking after the stud of a wealthy man. The governor died. The stables were sold. Every man of us was discharged; some there forty years, too. It was tough, I can tell you. I have been looking for work ever since. There is none to be had. There are hundreds of thousands out of employment. Conditions are awful. It's my opinion England is going down hill — that England has had her day. Everybody is talking Canada. You hear Canada every place. There are advertisements in every railroad station, in every post-office.

'Do you think I can get work? I have booked to Winnipeg. I have letters to men there. But I don't care what it is. All I want is work, and the right to make a living.

'Am I married? Yes, the wife and three kiddies are left in Old London.' I could see the lower lip start to tremble. 'I hope soon to bring them out if I can only get a job.' The tears welled big in his eyes. He tried hard to hide them, but they would come to the surface. 'I beg your pardon, sir, but you don't know what a bitter pill it is to come so far, and leave the wife and kiddies behind with scarcely any money, and not knowing what is ahead of you. But do you think it will be easy to get work?'

With all it was the same story. Out of work, no work to be had. What was to be done? Canada talked about, advertised everywhere; so off they come to the Dominion, full of hope of what the new land will offer them.

Thomas Bagloile, with the customary English tweed cap, and his scarf jerked about his neck, looked as if he might be worth interviewing. I had heard him conversing with his chum and knew he was a cockney. I passed the time of day and remarked on the weather, and when he saw I was disposed to be friendly he slipped over and made room for me in his seat.

'I am booked for Carnduff. How much further is it anyway?' He drew out a note of introduction to a Thos. Jones, Carnduff, from the Salvation Army. 'Did I ever farm? I should say not. I've lived in London all my life. I'm a railroad man. If I can't make farming go, perhaps I can get on the railroad. They say there are lots of railroad jobs. I was on the London and Southwestern. I was firing, but I went into the shops cleaning boilers. Then last fall they cut down their men. I was let out. I haven't been able to get anything to do since. I thought I had better pop out to Canada before my money was all gone.'

'Are you a Salvationist?' I enquired, when he said he had come over on the *Kensington*. He laughed.

'No, but they are the most convenient way to come. Then they have a labor bureau, and get you a job. I say, how is our Premier?' he enquired, the interviewed suddenly turning interviewer. 'I haven't seen a paper since we left Liverpool.'

I informed him that Campbell-Bannerman was not dead, but that he had resigned, and Asquith was Premier.

''E won't last long,' he added, in that determined English fashion. 'The Liberals will soon be defeated. It's 'em as has messed up the country. Pity Joe Chamberlain is used up. 'E's the boy.'

There was a pink-cheeked, fair-haired, blue-eyed young Saxon pacing the platform at Kenora, waiting for the train to start again.

He had that indescribable air of refinement which marks the man of family and education the world over.

'Cold,' I ventured as we passed each other.

He nodded assent, drawing his ulster closer around him and emphasizing his opinion of Canadian weather in a few unlawful phrases. The ice was broken.

He was bound for Edmonton. 'I have some chums there,' he explained. 'They have been anxious for me to come to Canada. Then my profession is overcrowded in England. There is no chance for a young fellow.'

I nodded an encouraging 'Yes.'

'I am an electrical engineer. What do you think are the chances for a job?' he shot at me.

'My home? Oh, I'm from Warwickshire. My father is a parson. This is Kenora, isn't it? I have an uncle here.'

I mildly enquired about his uncle. But he looked at me suspiciously, gave another twist to his ulster, drew into his English stolidness, and climbed on board, inprecating again the beastly weather.

I passed into another car. A group of four or five young fellows were arguing vehemently over the value of some Canadian money received as exchange at Kenora. My services were called in as arbitrator.

'I say,' with that peculiar accent on the say, which no Canadian can affect, asked one fellow, 'can you tell me the result of the English football tie?'

I was forced to confess ignorance, and he was crestfallen. He brightened up again; his blue eyes sparkled.

'Who won the boat race?'

I remembered seeing it played up large on the front pages of the papers.

'Cambridge, I believe.'

'Good, I thought they would win. What did I tell you, George? That's one on you. I say, you have a jolly big country here. We thought we had a long ride from Paddington to Liverpool, six hours, but we have been going since Tuesday. Where the deuce does it end?'

I sat down, for he was one of those likeable chaps — one of those attractive fellows one runs across in odd corners and in the most out-of-the-way places the world over. He was really a handsome chap. He had a great shock of yellow, curly hair that wandered all over his forehead, a well-moulded face, and a chin that stuck out in a most aggressive way. You couldn't get away from that twinkle in his eyes. And the laugh he had — it came from a pair of deep, strong lungs. It rolled through the whole car. It kept everyone from getting blue. Even the sullen-looking Russian women, in one lonely end of the car, gave a hint of a smile when he bellowed out laughing. I could scarcely believe it when he told me he had been looking after horses all his life. You pictured something big and brave for such a handsome giant.

'Whatever is bringing you to Canada?' I queried, and a dozen fellows crowded around our seats.

'The same thing that is bringing all the boys,' was the answer. 'We want work,' and he roared out laughing, as if it was a great joke. 'That's right, isn't it?' and the boys all echoed, 'It was work.' 'We can't get it in England, and we are coming to Canada to start all over again. I have been out of work for three months. I was getting too hard up. I had to do something. Canada has been preached to us on every hand, so I decided to try my luck. I've walked hundreds of miles looking for work. For every position there were scores of applicants. I had the best of references, but it was no go. I applied for one job. When I got there one hundred and fifty were standing in line. I sidled up to the porter. "Get in line," he tells me. "I say, governor," I asks him, "how many have been in already?" "About twice as many." I decided to look for another job,' and that gay infectious laugh of his again echoed through the car. 'What's the chance of a job?' he asked. 'The Salvation Army has directed me to Heward. They say it is a ranch. I don't care what it is. All I want is work, and enough to be able to bring out the girl and the little one. You know I am married,' and as he turned to me, I knew the smile was forced, this time. 'The handsomest girl in London, and the kid — you should see him. Nearly two years old.' It was a sad smile now. 'But I don't care if I never see England again if they can only come out,' and he was cheerful once more. 'I have come out to be a Canadian.'

His optimism, his interest in everything, his delight at the least change in the monotonous scenery through which we were travelling, his interest in Canada, the pleasure he took in hunting up Heward in his greasy, thumbed time-table and then locating it on the map was refreshing. It was infectious. I hope Fred, as he was known, gets a job.

He was the leader in the car. They all looked to him. He kept
everybody in good humor. He never got downhearted. They were a
jolly crowd of good fellows. There was one chap who had been in
the British navy for eight years. He had been all over the earth, and
was one of those inveterate globe wanderers — one of the restless
kind Robert Service sings about, who had the wanderlust in his
blood. He was booked for Holland, Manitoba, to enter service with a
farmer. 'Never farmed in my life, but if they want to climb anything,
here's the boy who can do it. I don't know how long I'll stay. Until I
get more money, I suppose.'

There were a couple of Lancashire lads, stalwart, sturdy, silent
chaps — clams would be loquacious beside them — with a dialect it
will take four generations to lose.

There were a couple of London clerks, pale-faced chaps, but
anxious to make their way. 'I'll starve before I'll ever go back, and
have them say, "I told you so! He couldn't make good." I've come
out to be a Canadian. I'll do as Canadians do, even if they tell me to
work standing on my head.' He will make good. He had the right
kind of grit in him. He and his friend were going through to Fillmore,
where the Salvation Army had sent them, but Edmonton was their
ambition. They will make their way, but I feel sorry for them and
for that farmer, for what they didn't know about farming was a
caution.

Then there were two Sussex yeomen, both of them farm laborers.
One was going to Deloraine where he had friends. The other had a
ticket for Caron. They were stocky-built chaps, but on their faces
was the stamp of generations of toilers for others on the land. They
had the same story to tell — no work, or irregular work with small
pay. They had heard Canada talked by everyone, they had read the
advertisements in the papers. One was a teetotaler, and didn't mind
proclaiming the fact to the world at large. The other had an over-
powering thirst from having travelled two weeks on a Salvation
Army boat and train. He had rested only once in his trip, at Halifax,
where they had spent Sunday. How he cursed that Sunday! At
intervals these two men engaged in the most heated arguments. The
teetotaler brought up the most gruesome examples of wife-beating
and destitution amongst drunkards, and painted his picture in
splashes of the darkest hues; his bibulous friend failed to see why he
should be deprived of his pint of beer, because some man once beat

his wife. They told me the argument had been in progress the whole two weeks.

But they grew tired being interviewed, and started to interview. How they fired the questions at me! They wanted to know everything about Canada, from how far it was to some flag station on a jerkwater railway branch in farthest Alberta, to what were the provisions of the Homestead Act. I was bombarded from the right, from the left, from the centre, from behind. Even the query editor would have thrown up his hands and asked for mercy. I turned the subject to politics, by asking what was the cause of the defeat of the Liberals in Peckham. They were off. That had precipitated a debate in which even the quiet Salvation Army captain, who was on board, joined. As I slipped off into another car I could hear above the roar and the pound of the train, the merry laugh of my cheerful friend, Fred, clinching one of his arguments. When I returned later they were still arguing.

As we neared Winnipeg they grew more and more boisterous. 'Let's have a song, boys,' one cried, and the car reverberated with one of England's exultant songs of the sea, which mostly tells what will be done to the enemy, how it will be done and who are the boys to do it. Salvation Army songs, like "Roll the Old Chariot Along,' and the latest London music hall hits were interlarded in a most irrelevant manner.

Then the Baby Elephant sang a song in Dutch, and was encored and re-encored until the Baby Elephant pleaded in his broken English that he could sing no more. The Baby Elephant was a great giant of a Hollander, who had been an Amsterdam policeman. He was like a boy let out of school. He played the most innocent pranks. He let the children romp all over him. He enjoyed everything. When he joined the *Kensington* at Liverpool he could not speak a word of English. Now he could make himself understood fairly well. He was improving every minute. He went from article to article asking, 'What makes that in English?' Someone had christened him the 'Baby Elephant,' though he was perfectly innocent as to the meaning of his nickname. He took an interest in everything with almost a childish enthusiasm. For the children he would crow like a rooster, baa-baa like a sheep, and do a hundred and one things to delight a child's heart. He had even learned enough English to join in the songs.

Then a young Salvation Army captain struck up, 'We'll Roll the Old Chariot Along.' How they shouted out the chorus! When they came to the line, 'If the devil's in the road we will run right over him,' they fairly screeched it. It would have gone hard with his Satanic Majesty if he had been lurking around that car just then.

But the favorite song was the latest music hall hit, and the boys roared it over and over again. As I left and shook hands with them, and they gathered up their luggage to slip up and down the stretches of the great West, to be lost in its activities and the whirl of its industry, it was echoing through my ears. Still I can hear those hopeful voices singing it. It ran like this:

'Is London like it used to be?
    Is the Strand still there?
Do the boys still stroll up the west
In its glitter, and its glare?
Are the girls as fair and beautiful?
    Are my friends all right?
What would I give to be with them
    In the old town to-night!'

Chapter 5

Immigrants from the United States

THE IMMIGRANTS themselves are very desirable, and they bring
with them an ample supply of capital and energy. The value of the
settlers' outfits these American families bring is not less than $1,000
a family, and often as high as $8,000, besides money. From North
Portal to Moose Jaw there is plain evidence of prosperity; what was a
few years ago a treeless prairie is now so closely settled that the
farmers are erecting newer and larger farm buildings, and very largely
increasing their area under cultivation. All the towns on the line of
the railway are increasing in size and importance, plainly indicating
that the settlers are there to stay.

Vegreville, Alta. — Forty-two car-loads of settlers' effects arrived
here. It is estimated between 800 and 1,200 settlers arrived in the
district, many of them taking up homesteads. The settlers are a good
class, mostly Canadian and American, or those born in foreign
countries who have lived in the United States for years.

Carstairs, Alta. — The class of immigrants arriving consists of the
most progressive Canadian and American type, who have disposed of
their property in their old homes for large figures, and can well
afford to buy the best farms in the neighborhood.

Milestone, Sask. — Two hundred and thirty-six cars of settlers'
effects were unloaded at Milestone station, some coming from as far
east as Nova Scotia and Massachusetts, and from as far south as
Kentucky, but the majority come from Iowa, Illinois, Minnesota and
North Dakota.

Such are the District Reports of the Immigration officials; they
give a very fair idea of the way in which the American settlers are
coming in, and the Canadian estimate of their value. This 'American
invasion' is a most remarkable movement. During the past seven
years over 300,000 people have come to us from the United States.
Some of them are Canadians who moved to the Western States
twenty-five years ago. They are returning with their families, and
with their flocks and herds, and the possessions they have accumu-
lated during that time. Many are German or Scandinavian Americans, whose farms have become too small for their large families of
growing children. They are able to sell their land in Iowa or

Nebraska or Illinois, and buy just as good land in the Canadian West at one-quarter the price. Shrewd, generally successful, the American has been shown the possibilities of Canada and has come to share in the general prosperity. Government agents who are operating in 'practically every state from Maine to Oregon, and from the Dakotas to Oklahoma,' and the representatives of land companies are responsible for the great northern 'trek.' At a score of points the railroads are joining hands across the border, and we may look for increasingly frequent intercourse with our southern neighbors.

Desirable settlers? Yes. Most of them are 'well-to-do' when they come, and are bound to 'make things go.' The majority of them average up pretty well with our own Canadians. Of course, they are not British subjects, and some of them rather object to acknowledging allegiance to King Edward VII. But the King lives away in England. They soon become good Canadian citizens. Their children will be loyal British subjects.

There are some respects in which we much prefer our Canadian to the American type. But we must remember that many of the same forces that moulded the American people are moulding our own nation, and that only the most strenuous efforts on our part can prevent us sharing those evils which the best Americans so deeply deplore.

While we welcome most of our American cousins, there are some who are coming from across the line who are far from desirable. One class is so numerous as to require special treatment – the Mormons.

THE MORMONS
In 1880, Bishop Lunt laid down the programme of the Mormon 'Church.'

Like a grain of mustard seed was the truth planted in Zion; and it was destined to spread through all the world. Our church has been organized only fifty years, and yet behold its wealth and power. This is our year of jubilee. We look forward with perfect confidence to the day when we will hold the reins of the United States Government. That is our present temporal aim; after that we expect to control the continent ... We intend to have Utah recognized as a State. To-day we hold the balance of political power in Idaho. We rule Utah absolutely, and in a very short time we will hold the

balance of power in Arizona and Wyoming. A few months ago
President Snow, of St. George, set out with a band of priests for an
extensive tour through Colorado, New Mexico, Wyoming, Montana,
Idaho and Arizona, to proselytize. We also expect to send missionaries to some parts of Nevada, and we design to plant colonies in
Washington Territory. In the past six months we have sent more
than 3,000 of our people down through Sevier Valley to settle in
Arizona, and the movement still progresses. All this will build up for
us a political power, which will in time compel the homage of the
demagogues of the country. Our vote is solid and will remain so. It
will be thrown where the most good will be accomplished for the
church. Then, in some political crisis, the two present political
parties will bid for our support, Utah will then be admitted as a
polygamous State, and the other territories we have peacefully
subjugated will be admitted also. We will then hold the balance of
power, and will dictate to the country. In time our principles, which
are of sacred origin, will spread throughout the United States: We
possess the ability to turn the political scale in any particular
community we desire. Our people are obedient. When they are called
by the church they promptly obey. They sell their houses, lands and
stock, and remove to any part of the country to which the church
may direct them. You can imagine the results which wisdom may
bring about with the assistance of a church organization like ours.

Ten years ago Dr. Josiah Strong wrote: 'The Mormon Church
to-day virtually controls Utah, Idaho, Wyoming and Arizona, and
holds the balance of power in other great Empires of the West. Utah
has become a sovereign State, as Bishop Lunt anticipated; and
though not admitted as a polygamous State, it has become such in
the sense that polygamy is now practised there with entire
impunity.'

During the past ten years this octopus of Mormonism has
stretched a long arm across the border, and now the large Mormon
colony (about 15,000) is almost strong enough to hold the balance
of power in Southern Alberta.

The Mormons started to come to Alberta about twenty years ago.
The Patriarch, Ora Card, was the pioneer; his wife, 'Aunt Tina,' is a
daughter of Brigham Young. Their son is now principal of Cardston
Public School.

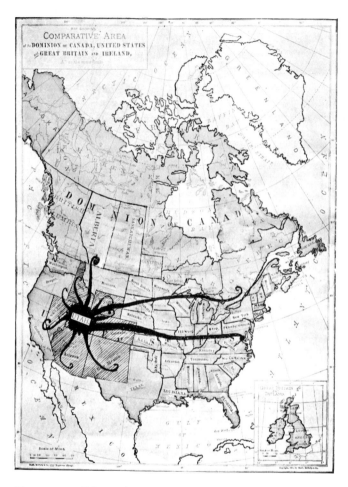

The octopus of Mormonism

The colony has grown rapidly and prospered. They have large grain farms and cattle ranches, and are entering extensively on dairy-ing, fruit farming and sugar refining. In their enterprise they compare favorably with other American settlers. Indeed, a casual visitor sees little to distinguish a Mormon community from the ordinary settlement in the Western States. The home life is much the same. Polygamy is not practised – at least, not openly, though some-times the presence of an unattached 'cousin' may make a suspicious Gentile wonder if these Latter Day Saints have entirely abandoned their cherished beliefs. One thing is noticeable – the large number of children. An important convention was held in Cardston a few years ago, at which the principal speakers were Joseph Smith, the Presi-dent of the Church; Senator Reed Smoot, and John W. Taylor, the first Apostle. President Smith did not advocate polygamy, but he told with pride how by his six wives he had forty-eight children, and exhorted his followers to increase and multiply and replenish the earth. His programme was that they were the first to occupy the eastern slope of the Rockies – and their colonies now extend from Mexico to Canada – and they were to inherit the whole of the North American Continent.

Most of the 'saints' are of Northern European extraction, and are rather below the average in intelligence. The children are being educated in the Public Schools, and as rapidly as possible the Mormons are training their young people as teachers. Religious exercises are held on Thursday and Friday of each week for half an hour after school.

The Mormon organization is most complete. Zion is divided into 'stakes,' and each stake is divided into 'wards.' Over each stake is appointed a President, and over each ward a Bishop. There are already three stakes in Southern Alberta.

The 'Bishop' is the most influential man in each community. He is one of the people, and when appointed still carries on his own ordinary secular work. His duties are various and arduous. He pre-sides at meetings, solemnizes marriages and transmits the tithes or their cash value to headquarters.

The Mormons are most scrupulous as to their tithes, giving in kind one-tenth of all their produce. In come the loads of hay and grain and young cattle and vegetables; these the Bishop must sell to the best advantage, so he is a sort of local commission agent – only, as the work is for the good of the church, his honorarium is very small.

Although the Bishop solemnizes marriages, these are not valid in heaven unless they are ratified in the temple by the Secret Mystic Rites. Hundreds of people have travelled from Canada to Salt Lake City to pass through the temple. Now a temple has been erected in Alberta, and the solemn rites may be performed on Canadian soil.

The ordinary services are very simple. The Bishop presides with a first and second councillor on each side. The minutes of every meeting are carefully recorded. First comes an observance of the Lord's Supper in which bread and water are used. Then follow hymns, and readings from the Bible and the Book of Mormon. There is no professional preacher, but one is selected at random — sometimes two or three. The sermon is thus entirely impromptu. Sometimes it is moral or spiritual in tone; sometimes entirely worldly-wise, dealing with the most practical affairs. A few obtain a great reputation as speakers, and are in demand, especially at funerals where their eloquence finds full scope. Others go out regularly each Sunday to conduct services in the surrounding district — 'local preachers.' Indeed here lies no small part of the power of the Mormon Church — the people all have a share. Thousands of self-supporting missionaries go throughout America and Europe making tens of thousands of converts.

Sunday Schools are organized much after the usual style. The Bible is taught in the morning and the Book of Mormon in the afternoon, and the children receive a very thorough drill in their catechism.

The social life resembles very closely that of other communities. Naturally Mormons and Gentiles are not closely associated. The Mormons preach much against the oppression of the Gentiles, but are not adverse to intermarriage, as this affords an opportunity for converting the unbelieving wife or husband.

Within the community everyone is brother or sister. As in every class, there are good and bad. Intemperance and gambling are discouraged. Dancing is almost part of their religion, the dances being opened and closed with prayer.

The Mormons form a part of our United States immigration. But though Americans, they are in no true sense American, and their presence is a serious menace to our Western civilization. No one doubts their industry — they have made the desert to rejoice and blossom as the rose. But of greater importance to our country than material development are freedom and morality and true religion, and to these the system of Mormon is antagonistic.

An exposition and exposé are given in a series of leaflets issued by the League for Social Service. These are our authority for the following brief statement of the history and doctrines of the Mormon Church.

In 1827, Joseph Smith claims to have discovered the Book of Mormon buried in a stone vault near Palmyra in New York State. It consisted of a number of engraved plates which he professed to translate. He soon became associated with one Sydney Rigdon, and together they founded the Mormon Church. The church grew rapidly, but wherever Smith went there were charges against him of immorality and dishonesty. Wherever he went he appropriated property and wives 'for spiritual purposes.' Finally he was arrested, but an infuriated mob broke into the jail and lynched him. Brigham Young succeeded Smith as prophet, and established the great Mormon colony in Utah. Here for many years he had his own way unmolested. A special revelation was received making polygamy a condition of exaltation to the next world. Gradually civilization moved westward. At first the Mormons massacred 'the Gentiles' who invaded their territory, but finally they were forced to admit 'people of other faiths.' Various modifications have since taken place in their teaching and practice. A reform party has organized a new church from which the most obnoxious features have been excluded. But all still cling to the Book of Mormon.

Now, what is this book? As a matter of fact, it seems to be pretty well established that it was an unpublished novel of a Rev. Solomon Sydney Spaulding. When a pastor in Pittsburg, Sydney Rigdon found the manuscript in the publishing house of Patterson and Lamdin, and Joseph Smith for a time lived in the same house as Mr. Spaulding's widow. Just how the scheme was concocted no one knows. Eleven men testified to having seen the plates, but none of them could read the writing. Only five of these eleven joined the organization. One of these was turned out of the church, lived the life of a libertine, and died a drunkard. Another was subsequently declared by Smith not to be fit for decent people to notice. Two more, years afterwards, were sent to jail and there killed by a mob. The history of the fifth is not recorded, so probably he died a consistent Mormon.

How large numbers of people can base their faith on such a foundation is passing strange. Yet in more recent years, and among a more enlightened class, such men as Dowie have been able to propound the most remarkable doctrines, and yet retain their hold on a large following. There seems to be in these systems sufficient truth to give at least a semblance of reason to the teaching. This, coupled with the appeal to lower motives or human weaknesses, may perhaps in part explain the conversion of so many.

The following are some of the Mormon doctrines:

1 The 'Book of Mormon' and the 'Book of Doctrine and Covenants' are on a par with the Bible.
2 Salvation and exaltation are found only in the church organized by Joseph Smith. Belief in the person and mission of Joseph Smith as a prophet of God is an essential article of faith.
3 Faith in the Mormon priesthood and submission to the same is essential to man's future blessedness.
4 A plurality of gods. Adam is God. Men became gods by practising plural or celestial marriage and the other Mormon principles.
5 God is a polygamist — the natural father of all intelligent beings in heaven and earth and hell. Jesus was a polygamist. The doctrine of polygamy is both sacred and fundamental.

These doctrines are obviously inconsistent with the teaching of Christianity, and are directly inimical to the welfare of the State. The practice of polygamy will subvert our most cherished institutions. But more dangerous even than polygamy is the utter surrender of personal liberty, and the acknowledgment of the absolute authority of the priesthood. This means the end of all free government, and is the confessed aim of the leaders of the Mormon Church.

Can we as Canadians remain inactive while this 'politico-ecclesiastical' system is fastening itself upon our Western territory?

Chapter 6

The Scandinavians

THE SCANDINAVIANS, by A.R.F.

'A gathering of the Western Canadian Swedish farmers has always impressed me as if it were a meeting of Scotch settlers. Attend a Swedish church assembly, and you would imagine, if it were not for the language, that you were in the midst of a gathering of Presbyterian elders. Serious, thoughtful, sober, determined and possibly a little bit obstinate, the Swedes are astonishingly like the Scotch.' This was the compliment paid to the Swedish settlers of the Canadian West by one of the superintendents of Baptist Missions, a man who travels among them and knows them. 'In their severely religious trend of mind,' he went on, 'in their purity of life, and in their general temperament, they are for all the world like the sons of the heather. I have no hesitation in saying we have no better settlers.'

During the past few years there has been an astonishingly large influx of Scandinavian people to the Canadian West. Hardly an immigrant train rolls into the Winnipeg depot that has not its quota of Swedes and Norwegians – the men, big, brawny, broad-shouldered, fair-haired giants; the women, pretty, healthy, clear-featured and rosy-cheeked, with great masses of golden hair. It is estimated that in Western Canada there are of Swedes, Norwegians, Finns and Danes about 50,000, scattered from Fort William to the Coast. The Swedes are placed roughly at 25,000, Norwegians at 15,000, the Finns at 10,000, and the Danes at 5,000.

We include the Finns with the Scandinavians. Racially they are more closely connected with the Magyars and Lapps, but long residence near the Scandinavian peoples has influenced them greatly. Many of those from the coast – the district from which most of our immigrants come – can hardly be distinguished from Swedes. The attempted 'Russification of Finland' has met with great opposition from this intelligent, sturdy people. Many of them prefer to leave their homes rather than sacrifice their independence. In Finland, as in the Scandinavian countries, the living is often poor, and the people are attracted to a country where they are certain to receive better returns for their hard, constant labor.

The majority of the Swedes eventually drift into farming, but most of those from the old land have little funds, and have to start at first at rough laboring, often at railway and construction work. At Fort William there are 1,200 Scandinavians, mostly working on the

Farmhouses of our newcomers from Europe
1 Swedish   2 Polish   3, 4 Typical Doukhobor homes

railways. At Kenora there is a large settlement, while every construction camp between Fort William and the Rockies has its quota of men, who through their alertness and intelligence soon occupy the better positions, such as foremen, time-keepers, etc. Winnipeg has a Swedish colony of probably 3,000, while every Western city has its proportion of Scandinavians.

They easily assimilate with the Anglo-Saxon peoples and readily intermarry, so that they do not form isolated colonies as do other European immigrants. Where they have formed settlements, they quickly learn English, and intermingle with the families of Canadian farmers, while the younger prople drift off to the towns and cities.

Outside of Winnipeg there are in Manitoba no large colonies of Swedes, Norwegians, or Finns, the largest settlement being at Scandinavia, north of Minnedosa. A number also have settled at Merryfield, near Estevan. Passing to Saskatchewan they are settled in large numbers at Harrowby and Langenburg, while along the main line of the Canadian Northern there are a great number around Buchanan and Wadena. In the Duck Mountains there are many Scandinavians, and there is another colony at Fort Pelly.

Of the three prairie provinces Alberta has by far the largest share of Scandinavians. It is estimated that in the Sunny Province there are some 20,000, practically all farmers, and as prosperous, as wealthy and as successful farmers as the province possesses. The great proportion of Swedes and Norwegians in Alberta are not from the old land, but have migrated to the last West from the Northern States, particularly Minnesota, attracted by the inducements of cheap land and big profits.

They understand Western farming, have come in with money, and have readily adapted themselves to Canadian institutions and Canadian ways. It is no wonder they are as well-to-do farmers as can be found. While scattered throughout the length of the province from Claresholm on the south to Edmonton on the north, they are most thickly settled east and west of Wetaskiwin. In the fertile Crooked Lake district, and along the Battle River, the Scandinavians have settled in large numbers. They are not confining themselves merely to the growing of wheat, but are teaching their Canadian neighbors a much-needed lesson by devoting their attention to dairying and mixed farming.

As a rule, throughout the whole of the West the Norwegians and Swedes are to be found in the same settlements, though occasional localities will have only one of these peoples. At Camrose and Killam in Alberta are large Norwegian colonies. Swedish Finns are to be found in all Swedish settlements, though particularly in Alberta.

British Columbia likewise has its share of Scandinavians, many of them farming in the valleys, and numbers working in the lumber camps, where many have acquired large interests. In the Nelson district they are very numerous, while in Vancouver and all along the Fraser River are to be found many Swedes and Norwegians.

The Scandinavians are very ambitious, are anxious to become Canadian citizens, and readily adapt themselves to Canadian ways. Although after they have passed the stage of laboring men the greater number go into farming, yet some are to be found in every calling. An encouraging sign of their progressiveness and of the ambition of their youth is found in the fact that a dozen Scandinavian students are enrolled this year at the Brandon Baptist College.

The Swedes are naturally a religious people, practically all of them being Protestants. The Lutheran Church is the strongest. A number belong to the Mission Friends and to the Baptist Church, and some to the Methodist Church. In this country the Baptists are particularly enterprising among the Swedes, having some fifteen churches scattered from Fort William on the east to Golden, British Columbia, on the west.

The Scandinavians are a very sociable people, and wherever they are settled in large enough numbers, have their social and political clubs. They are natural politicians, and, as in Minnesota where they are the dominating element, they are bound to be a strong factor in the future of the West. There are several Swedish papers, and one Norwegian, in the Canadian West.

Taken all in all there is no class of immigrants that are as certain of making their way in the Canadian West as the people of the peninsula of Scandinavia. Accustomed to the rigors of a northern climate, clean-blooded, thrifty, ambitious and hard-working, they will be certain of success in this pioneer country, where the strong, not the weak, are wanted.

THE ICELANDERS, by A.R.F.

'Why shouldn't we go to Canada? Didn't we first discover this country?' was the answer flung back at me by an Icelandic citizen of Winnipeg, when I asked him why his people emigrated to the Dominion.

And he was quite correct, for it was the bold navigators of the isolated northern island who first set foot on the Continent of America, and who, centuries before the days of Columbus, explored the Atlantic coast, and even endeavored to plant colonies. It is the descendants of these same Viking sea-rovers who are making their way in the Canadian West, and who are becoming in their adopted land a potent influence.

From 15,000 to 20,000 Icelanders are to be found scattered through the four provinces of Manitoba, Saskatchewan, Alberta and British Columbia, and it is doubtful if any class of immigrants has been more successful. There are Icelanders in our legislative halls and in our municipal chambers. In our schools and universities they carry off prizes and scholarships. They are doctors, lawyers, editors, merchants, business men, farmers; in short they are taking a leading part in the development of the West.

It was in 1872 that, owing to the depression in Iceland and the political dissatisfaction over the status with Denmark, the first stray settlers found their way to the Dominion. It was not, however, until 1874 that the real movement took place. In that year some 500 Icelanders left their native shores. It was a long and weary trip for the adventurous voyagers. From Iceland they went to Leith, Scotland, thence to Glasgow, and from there crossed the Atlantic. Some of these settled in Nova Scotia, near Halifax and Lockeport. The majority, however, went first to Ontario and located at Kinmount, north of Toronto. They were not satisfied, however, and in 1875 a delegation was sent to Manitoba to spy out the land. Only one of the members of that delegation is at present residing in Manitoba, Captain S. Jonason, of Gimli, who at the last election was elected as Liberal member for his home constituency. The deputation finally selected Lake Manitoba as the most likely spot for the new colony, and in the fall of 1875 the band of pilgrims forsook Ontario and journeyed to the West. It was a long trip in those days. They went by boat from Collingwood to Duluth, and thence by rail to St. Paul and Fisher's Landing. Red River boats took the newcomers to Winnipeg, and the rest of the journey was made in flat-bottomed boats.

The following year the Dominion Government sent Captain Jonason to Iceland, and as a result of his missionary trip some 1,600 immigrants left their native shores to join the Gimli colony. But the troubles of the settlement had only begun. Bad seasons, poor crops and sickness followed, until finally many lost heart. A number of the colonists decided to form a new settlement and located at Glenboro, while a large party crossed the boundary line and pitched their tents at the Pembina, North Dakota.

Since 1880 there has been a steady stream of immigration to Canada, although recently, owing to the prosperity of Iceland, it has diminished in volume. Within the past few years the principal Icelandic emigration to Western Canada has been from the Northern States, the largest settlements being in Saskatchewan and Alberta. In Manitoba, in addition to the older settlements at Gimli and Glenboro, there are colonies south of Morden, one at Little Shoal Lake and another on the east side of Lake Manitoba, between the Narrows and Lundyville. On the other side of Lake Manitoba, also, there is a small settlement at Westbourne. Then north of Swan River there is a prosperous colony, while on the Arcola branch of the Canadian Pacific Railway, near Sinclair, are to be found a few Icelanders.

The oldest Icelandic settlement in Saskatchewan is probably that at Churchbridge, which was established by some of the original Gimli colonists. At Tantallon on the Canadian Pacific Railway, Kirkella branch, is to be found a flourishing settlement, most of the homesteaders being from North Dakota. The fertile Quill Lake plains have also a large number of Icelanders, who are rapidly becoming wealthy. They have been in the district some six years, and have proved themselves excellent citizens.

Alberta also has its quota of Icelanders. They are scattered all along the Calgary-Edmonton line of the C.P.R. There is a particularly large number settled between Innisfail and Red Deer.

Very few of the newcomers when they left Iceland had more than $100, now there is no other class of settlers so well-to-do. They were without means, did not understand the English language, and had never seen a plow or any of the regular modern farm implements. That they have prospered as they have, and have so readily adapted themselves to Western methods is a remarkable testimony to this industrious people.

In British Columbia, also, there are to be found large settlements of Icelanders, particularly in the cities, where they have representatives in every industry and profession. In the various mountain valleys there are a number who are engaged in farming and fruit raising.

The Icelanders are natural politicians, and a few years after their arrival in this country are to be found actively participating in Canadian elections. Liberal and Conservative clubs flourish in every large settlement. Born students, serious-minded as a race, they take their politics in earnest, and can debate and discuss problems of the Dominion with an astonishing amount of intelligence. At the present time there are two Icelandic members in the Manitoba Legislature.

Like most of the northern peoples the Icelanders are very religiously inclined. Practically all of them are Lutherans, members of the State Church in Iceland. Since coming to this country a number have become Unitarians, and organized separate churches.

There are a number of Icelandic papers in the West, the two principal ones being the *Heimskringla,* Conservative, and *Lagberg,* Liberal, both weeklies, published in Winnipeg. The Lutheran Church has a periodical, while a monthly magazine was recently established in Winnipeg. At Gimli, also, there is an Icelandic paper, established in the early days of the settlement.

The Icelanders have taken their place in the development of the country, and have become a powerful influence in the social and political life of the three prairie provinces. Sober, industrious and thrifty, they are in every way excellent citizens.

Chapter 7

The Germans

FEW of our German immigrants come from Germany. The great majority are from Austria and Russia. As to numbers it is exceedingly difficult to obtain reliable figures. The official statistics show an annual immigration of only about 2,000. How many of those classed as Austrians and Russians are Germans it is impossible to say. Then the Mennonites are classified as a distinct nationality. In addition to these are the American Germans, many of whom have lived only a few years in the United States, and are only legally 'naturalized.' A German immigration official, familiar with the country, stated that he thought there were 75,000 in Western Canada. Possibly his figures ought to be cut down very considerably.

About a century ago large numbers of Germans were induced to emigrate to Russia. They were most desirable as agriculturists, and were granted special privileges. They were successful, but they maintained their own language, their nationality and their religion. During the past twenty-five years there has been much unrest among the Russian Germans. Their privileges were withdrawn, and they found themselves placed under serious disabilities. They simply refused to be dominated by the Russians. Many of them preferred to sell their farms and emigrate. We have numbers from this class. They have not been greatly influenced by their Russian environment. They are the same independent, thrifty people though perhaps a little poorer, and not so well educated as their brethren from the 'Vaterland.'

The Germans from Austria come to improve their condition. Most of them have owned small farms; these they have sold, and so have a little capital with which to start in the new land. In the cities we get more of the poorer class — some of them just escaping from a hard existence; others who are content with the life of a laborer in the city. But the great majority of the Germans are farmers.

On the main line of the Canadian Pacific Railway there are German settlements from Qu'Appelle to Regina, and from Herbert to Swift Current, then from Wetaskiwin to Edmonton, and away east at Battleford, Humboldt, Rosthern and Lemberg. Solid 'colonies' are not formed, but scattered all through the country are districts in which German settlers predominate. In Manitoba, outside the Mennonites, the Germans are chiefly in Winnipeg or east at Beausejour and Whitemouth.

Though there are German societies and German newspapers, and there may be the 'German vote, 'the Germans do not form any very

Germans from southern Russia in southern Russian costume

distinct class. Even those who detest 'foreigners' make an exception of Germans, whom they classify as 'white people like ourselves.' The German is a hardworking, successful farmer. He soon takes his part in the life of the district in which he lives. He establishes his own churches and endeavors to maintain his own language, but the younger people soon learn English and often leave the German churches for those in which English is spoken, and where most of their associates attend. The majority of the people are Lutherans. A large number are Roman Catholics. The remainder is divided into a number of sects, Reformed, Baptist, Evangelical, Evangelical Association, Moravians, Adventists, etc. On account of their peculiarities a special section is given to the Mennonites. The Stundists from Russia, of whom we have a few, also form a most interesting study.

Of the Germans, as a whole it need hardly be said that they are among our best immigrants. In one sense they are 'easily assimilated,' and yet in the long run it would seem as if it is often the others who are Germanized. Englishmen are good colonizers. America is an English-speaking country, and yet some declare that America is more German than it is English. However this may be, and notwithstanding some faults, we welcome the German.

Much may be said of the Hollanders, of whom we have several thousand. The 'patient Hollanders' and 'sturdy Germans' possess those qualities which form the foundation of enduring success.

THE MENNONITES

'Are there many Catholics among the Mennonites?' Such was the question gravely asked by a minister occupying a prominent position in his church. Such is our ignorance of the people about us! He might as well have asked, are there many Catholics among the Lutherans? The name Mennonite has no more to do with nationality than the name Lutheran. It denotes a religious body whose adherents might almost be called Baptist-Quakers. In Manitoba the majority of them are Germans; in the West, Germans from Russia.

The Mennonite Church is really a branch of the great Reformation Movement. The views now held by the Mennonites were advocated in Zurich, Switzerland, as early as 1525. They soon spread to the surrounding countries. In Holland, Menno Simons, a Roman Catholic priest dissatisfied with the Church, espoused and expounded the new teaching. A community of his followers was

formed, and came to be known as Mennonites, just as later the
followers of Wesley were called Wesleyans.

Their chief doctrines were:

1 Baptism only on confession of faith
2 The separation of Church and State
3 Refusal to take oaths or to fight
4 A strict life and a primitive church organization

The new sect was bitterly persecuted in Holland. Many fled to the
new colony then being founded by William Penn, which afterwards
became Pennsylvania. Others migrated to Prussia to join their
German co-religionists. But here again, trouble arose. Military service
was required; this was contrary to their conscience, and they
endured great persecution.

Then came the German emigration to Russia. The Empress
Catherine ii offered most liberal inducements in order to obtain
German colonists for Southern Russia — free land, loans, exemption
from taxation for a number of years, exemption from military
service, their own schools and religious liberty. In 1783-8 communities of Mennonites trekked to Russia, and entered upon a century of
peace and plenty.

Who, then, are the Mennonites in Canada? The census of 1901
gives the Mennonite population as 31,797. Of these 12,208 are in
Ontario, 15,246 in Manitoba and 4,273 in the Territories.

In Ontario, the majority are the descendants of those who came
from Pennsylvania over a century ago. They are located in Western
Ontario in the vicinity of Berlin, Brussels and Waterloo, where they
are closely associated with the 'Pennsylvania Dutch,' and with them
form some of the most thrifty and prosperous communities in
Ontario. They have ceased to be strangers, and now are an integral
part of the Canadian people.

The Mennonites of Southern Manitoba and Saskatchewan came
from Russia thirty years ago. In 1870 the Russian bureaucracy,
disregarding the promise of Catherine, withdrew the special privileges granted to the Mennonites. Again they were required to render
military service, and again they sought a new home. A colony was
established in Kansas, another in Southern Manitoba.

The Canadian Government modified the regular homestead
regulations, and guaranteed a loan of $75,000 made by Ontario

Mennonites, which was repaid within twenty years. Further they
granted exemption from military service, and the right to affirm
instead of taking an oath. Two reserves containing 720 square miles,
were set apart, the larger now the Municipality of Rhineland, and
the smaller east of the Red River. This open prairie had hitherto
been shunned by the pioneers, but was in reality one of the richest
sections of the country.

The following brief descriptive sketch, published in 1880, graphi-
cally describes the coming of the Mennonites: 'In '75 the few settlers
at Pembina Mountain fondly hoped that in the course of fifteen or
twenty years this plain would become settled, notwithstanding the
absence of timber. Before the summer was over, a large line of camp
fires, extending for miles and miles, announced one evening to the
lonely settlers that six thousand Mennonites had located on
seventeen townships.'

Of course, there were difficulties and discouragements. There
were the small beginnings, and the locusts and the frosts and the
'hard years'; but the people were inured to hardships, thrifty and
persevering, and to-day are among the wealthiest farmers in
Manitoba.

At first they settled in villages after the Russian fashion. In fact,
the Dutch-German-Russian village was simply transferred to
Canadian soil — quaint houses with high-pitched, thatched roofs,
ancient flour mills with huge arms and sails, ungainly churches, all
higgledy-piggledy along the roadside. Soon the bright flowers and
trees appeared, and once more the wanderers had a home. Some of
the names of the villages are of interest: Rosenfeld (field of roses),
Rosengart (garden of roses), Rosenthal (dale of roses), Blumenist
(place of flowers), etc. At one time there were sixty-two of these
villages.

In Castell Hopkins' Canadian Encyclopedia is an interesting description of the Mennonite villages, by Miss Cora E. Hind:

The earliest houses of these settlers were built of mud and sticks,
thatched with straw or hay. Some of the oldest are still standing.
The walls are a delicate lilac, the window sashes a dull red, the shut-
ters gray. Wind and rain and sun have stained the thatches a deep
brown. A village of these houses, seen when flooded with mellow
October sunshine and against a background of yellow stubble fields,

presents a wonderful harmony of color, and is more suggestive of
Holland, in the sixteenth, than Manitoba in the nineteenth, century.

These village communities were modelled after those from which
the settlers had come. The village was in the centre of a block of
land. Each man had a Government grant of 160 acres. But this was
distributed according to the old system — a village plot, a strip of
good land, and a portion of hay land more remote from the village.
Each village had its own church and school; elected its own 'head
man,' and governed itself in accordance with traditional custom.
Whole villages had 'moved out' together, the richer helping the
poorer, so social conditions were almost exactly reproduced. At first
the houses were poor mud-and-stick structures with sand floors and
thatched roofs, and if one mistook the door he might find himself in
the stable.

The people wore the garb of the European peasant — a sheepskin
smock with the skin side out.

But thirty years have worked a wonderful change. Now, well-
dressed men and women entertain in comfortable modern houses.
The homes compare well with those of the older settlers in other
parts of Manitoba. In this short time the Mennonites have attained a
position very similar to that of their co-religionists in Western
Ontario. This development forms one of the most interesting chapters in the history of the West.

Now the village community is almost a thing of the past, the
majority having built homes on their own homesteads, which they
farm in much the same way as their Canadian neighbors. The affairs
of the community are administered according to the Canadian
municipal system.

Accompanying these material changes there has come a development in the religious beliefs and practice of the people. There has
been a breaking away from the narrowness and exclusiveness of
former years. One of the fundamental principles of the Mennonite
Church is 'Separation of the church and the world.' This was inter-
preted to mean absolute withdrawal from every kind of public life, a
'closed' settlement, refusal to attend Public Schools, or to intermarry with those outside their own community. Many conservatives
— especially in the reserve east of the Red River — still hold to the
good old ways. But the younger generation is less strict. The

Mennonite vote is now not to be despised; indeed, in Alberta a Mennonite sits in the legislature.

Public Schools are now found throughout the whole Mennonite settlement. Marriages between Mennonites and those of other denominations are not infrequent. Large numbers of the younger generation are leaving the mother colony, and are taking up homesteads throughout Saskatchewan. New colonies are located at Rosthern and Hague.

Upon three points of doctrine all insist — baptism only on confession of faith, exemption from military service and refusal to take oath. On minor points, such, for instance, as those connected with baptism or the Lord's Supper; there are endless differences of opinion. The 'New Mennonite' church represents the more liberal section of the community. The church government is very simple. In each community there is what might be called a 'presiding elder,' who alone has the right to baptize, and several preachers — all elected by the community from among themselves. This might be called a 'circuit,' in the older Methodist sense, and services are conducted according to a 'circuit plan.' Each of these large 'circuits' is self-governing, and often neighboring circuits differ very decidedly in doctrine. In some the old custom of feet-washing is maintained. The conference for the whole of America was held this year at Langham, Saskatchewan.

Perhaps it is along educational lines that the Mennonites have made the most rapid development. This is owing, to no small extent, to the untiring efforts of Rev. H. H. Ewert, of Gretna. For years he has been the inspector of schools, and Principal of the Mennonite Educational Institute. Not only is excellent work being done in the Public Schools, but increasing numbers are making their way into our colleges. It is rather a remarkable fact that the first graduate of Wesley College to find a place on the staff of his Alma Mater is a Mennonite. Many are taking prominent positions in professional life. From a material, a social, an educational or a religious standpoint, the Mennonites will contribute no small share in the making of the Canadian West.

Chapter 8

The French

THE PICTURESQUE figure of the Habitant is inseparable from Canadian life. It is only in recent years, however, that the peasants from France and Belgium were to be met with in Canada. Now, in some districts, one may almost imagine himself in the land of Breton and Millet. Here we have the same group at work in the fields, or in procession to the little church – bits of France transferred to Canada; the same simple life and yet something more and something less. The new land gives a different background. The rustic has wandered into the city square.

In 1901 there were nearly 10,000 French and Belgian people in Canada. Since that time about 10,000 have come from France and 5,000 from Belgium. Some of the Belgians speak Flemish, but they all live much the same life as French peasants, and in this country are generally found in the same districts. Up to the present time the French immigrants have formed no large colonies. Generally a number of families secure land together; these little settlements are scattered all over the West. These immigrants are reported as thrifty and successful. Farming operations are on rather a small scale, and methods are often decidedly primitive; but there is a tendency to adopt the habits of their Canadian neighbors.

In the larger districts Separate Schools are maintained, and here the French priests exercise almost unlimited authority. Speaking the tongue of the people, they are in more sympathetic relation with them than in the other foreign settlements. Indeed, the parish priest is almost father to the community. But this paternal relationship, so charming in theory and art, has its disadvantages, as the people are less apt to learn to think and act for themselves. Throughout the greater part of the West the children attend the Public Schools. They are bright and eager to learn.

The coming of these immigrants creates no new problem. Naturally the French language and the Roman Catholic religion unite them more closely with the French-Canadians than with any other class in Canada. Their development is bound up with that of our French-speaking Canadian.

The Swiss immigration is very small, and hardly forms a class by itself.

Chapter 9

Southeastern Europe

RUSSIA, THE DOUKHOBORS, THE LITHUANIANS

WHEN we pass to Southeastern Europe we enter what is to most of us a *terra incognita.* We plunge into an apparently inextricable tangle of nations, races, languages, and religions. On what principle are we to adopt a working classification – geographical situation, political allegiances, national ties, racial characteristics, linguistic affinities, religious beliefs, social distinctions, or some group of these? In a book of this kind, not intended for the technical student, it will be found unwise, if not impossible, to adhere closely to any one principle of classification. Generally speaking, we take language as our basal principle, but vary from this as convenience of treatment may demand. A careful study of the accompanying table of European languages, taken from the *Encyclopaedia Britannica* (vol. VIII, p. 699), may throw some light upon the various divisions of the people, and at the same time will reveal the complexity of the problem which confronts the serious student:

Although language is no test of race, it is the best evidence for present or past community of social or political life; and nothing is better fitted to give a true impression of the position and relative importance of the peoples of Europe than a survey of their linguistic differences and affinities. The following table contains the names of the various languages which are still spoken on the Continent, as well as of those which, though now extinct, can be clearly traced in other forms. Two asterisks are employed to mark those which are emphatically dead languages, while one indicates those which have a kind of artificial life in ecclesiastical or literary usage:

I *Aryan* (Indo-Germanic, Indo-European, Celto-Germanic)

1 Indic branch, represented by	Gipsy dialects
2 Iranic branch, represented by	1 Ossetian 2 Armenian
3 Hellenic branch, represented by	1 Greek* 2 Romanic 3 Neo-Hellenic

4	Italic branch, represented by	1 Latin
		2 Oscan**
		3 Umbrian, etc.**
	(*a*) Neo Latin	4 French
		5 Walloon
		6 Provencal
		7 Italian
		8 Ladin (Rumonsh, Rumansh, Rheto-Romance)
		9 Spanish
		10 Portuguese
		11 Roumanian
5	Celtic branch, represented by	1 Irish
		2 Erse or Gaelic
		3 Manx
		4 Welsh
		5 Cornish**
		6 Low Breton
6	Teutonic branch, represented by	1 Gothic**
	(*a*) Scandinavian	2 Norse or Old Norse**
		3 Icelandic and Faroese
		4 Norwegian
		5 Swedish
		6 Danish
	(*b*) Low German	7 Saxon, Anglo-Saxon or First English**
		8 English
		9 Old Saxon**
		10 Platt-Deutsch or Low German
		11 Flemish — Netherlandish

Low German	12	Dutch-Netherlandish
	13	Frisic
(c) High German	14	Old High German**
	15	Middle High German
	16	New High or Literary German

7 Slavonic branch, represented by	1	Church Slavonic*
(a) Southeastern	2	Russian
	3	Ruthenian, Rusniak or Little Russian
	4	White Russian or Bielo-Russian
	5	Bulgarian
	6	Servo-Croatian
	7	Slovenian
(b) Western	8	Czech (Bohemian)
	9	Slovakian
	10	Polish
	11	Sorbian (Wendic, Lusatian)
	12	Polabian*
8 Lettic branch, represented by	1	Old Prussian**
	2	Lettish
	3	Lithuanian
9 Unattached	1	Old Dacian**
	2	Albanian

II *Semitic*

1 Canaanitic branch, represented by	1	Hebrew*
	2	Phoenician or Punic**
2 Arabic branch, represented by	1	Arabic**
	2	Mosarabic**
	3	Maltese

III *Finno-Tataric* (Turanian, Uralo-Altaic, etc.)

1	Samoyedic branch or group, represented by	1	Yurak

2	Finnic or Ugrian, represented by	1	Finnish Proper or Suonic
		2	Karleian
		3	Tchudic
		4	Vepsic
		5	Votick
		6	Crewinian
		7	Esthonian
		8	Livonian
		9	Lapponic
		10	Tcheremissian
		11	Mordvinian
		12	Permian
		13	Votiak
		14	Siryenian
		15	Magyar or Hungarian

3	Turkish or Tartar group, represented by	1	Kazak Khirghiz
		2	Nogairic
		3	Tchuvak
		4	Turkish

4	Unattached		Basque

RUSSIA

Most of our immigrants from Russia are not Russians. Many of them are Germans or Jews; others are Lithuanians and Poles. Those who stoutly maintain that they are 'Russ' are 'Little Russians.'

Russians, generally, may be classified thus: (*a*) 'Great' Russians (in the north); (*b*) 'White' Russians (in the west); (*c*) 'Little' Russians (in the south).

Usage varies, but in Russia the Little Russians are often called 'Red' Russians. They are very closely allied to the Rusniaks or Ruthenians of Galicia and Bukowina.

Practically none of the Great Russians or Russians proper are among our immigrants. Most of them are Little Russians. They may be classed with the Galicians, and hardly require separate treatment. The languages are cognate, and the social conditions much the same.

Two peoples from Russia demand special attention – the Doukhobors and the Lithuanians. The former have come in large numbers, and form a class by themselves. The latter are not Slavs, but are so closely related that they may best be placed here.

THE DOUKHOBORS, by A.R.F.

The various, rather strange, and picturesque pilgrimages of the Doukhobors in Western Canada have managed to keep these peaceful but interesting people as prominently before the public as any class of immigrants in the Dominion. At the time of their coming to Canada their cause was championed by Count Leo Tolstoy and Prince Kropotkin. The untiring efforts of these noble sympathizers aroused the interest of the Society of Friends and of a group of English and American *literati*, who did much to create general interest in their peculiar mode of life. Since their settlement in Eastern Saskatchewan the occasional vagaries of a few of the more ardent and their decided aversion to Western civilization have not allowed the people of the Dominion to forget their presence.

The Doukhobors have been eulogized in the highest terms by enthusiastic idealists and sympathizers; they have been condemned in language equally fervid as ignorant, unprogressive and immoral. As a matter of fact, no one exactly understands this peculiar people. They are actually some seven hundred years behind the times. Their customs, their mode of thought, their whole spirit is that of the thirteenth century rather than the twentieth. In their pilgrimages, so inexplicable to a man of this day, they are moved by the same stirrings of the heart and prompted by the same feelings which set thousands on their heroically useless marches to the Holy Land.

The term Doukhobor is a mere nickname, meaning Spirit Wrestlers, applied in derision, as was the name Methodist originally. The sect seems to have started in a village on the southern frontier of Russia in the eighteenth century. Their doctrines spread until they attracted the attention of the Russian Government and the Orthodox Church. For some fifty years they were not seriously disturbed by the authorities; but as their numbers increased and their doctrines spread, the Russian Government, in its usual autocratic manner, set to work to crush out the iniquitous beliefs they preached and

Doukhobor pilgrims
1 On the march
2 Resting in front of 'Ralph Connor's' Church, Winnipeg

practised, the principal one to which St. Petersburg objected being their refusal to render military service. They were subjected to repeated banishment to Siberia, and their prosperous communities were again and again broken up. In 1840 and in 1850 they were banished to Trans-Caucasia, near the Turkish frontier. Up to the year 1887 the conscription laws were not rigidly enforced. From 1887 onward, as a consequence of Russia's military ambitions, a new policy was enforced, and the authorities began to carry out the conscription laws with greater stringency. Then began a series of vigorous persecutions, the Doukhobors bearing the brunt of the Government's displeasure. This went on for some ten years, until the peasants could endure it no longer. They grew restless. Advantage was taken by the Doukhobors and their sympathizers of a visit to the Caucasus by the mother of the Czar, Empress Maria, to put their case before her. It is understood the Dowager Empress enlisted the sympathy of the Czar; anyway, permission was given them to leave the country. This was granted in February, 1898, and assiduous enquiries were at once started as to a suitable place for a colony. Cyprus first attracted attention, and a number of Doukhobor families moved to the Mediterranean island. The southern climate was, however, scarcely suitable. Argentine, Brazil, and the United States were spoken of. Finally, an article in the *Nineteenth Century*, by Prince Kropotkin, on Western Canada and the success of the Mennonites, attracted the attention of one of the members of the committee of English Friends who were aiding the Doukhobors in their search for a new home. Prince Kropotkin was communicated with, and advised in favor of the Dominion. After an inspection of various districts of the West, it was decided to migrate to Western Canada. No time was lost, as the Doukhobors were anxious to leave Russia before the fickle-minded authorities cancelled the permit. On December 22nd, 1898, the first contingent, 1,822 strong, set sail from Batoum to Canada, on the Beaver Line steamer *Lake Huron*. Other shiploads followed fast, in all some 8,000 to 8,500 of these oppressed people coming to the Dominion.

The newcomers were located in Saskatchewan, where there are three colonies – the Thunder Hill colony, west of Swan River; the Yorkton colony, near Yorkton, which is by far the largest; and the Rosthern colony, in the Prince Albert district. The life of the Doukhobors in these settlements is exceedingly interesting, though it is difficult to secure accurate information owing to the suspicion of the leaders towards strangers and the crass ignorance of the great majority. Peter Veregin, who at the time of their migration to Canada was an exile in Siberia, and has since joined them in this country, is their recognized leader. Whatever his qualities may be, he is undoubtedly a strong and able man, and exercises a remarkable influence over his people. He rules as an autocrat, and seems to be their religious as well as their political head. His headquarters are near a little station off the main line of the Canadian Northern, called after himself, Veregin. The morality of his domestic life has been often called in question. Two or three times a year he makes a state pilgrimage through the settlements, where his coming is a great event.

Outside of a few independents, the principle of communism prevails. Everything is supposed to be owned in common, though Veregin practically has all things in his control. He acts as banker for all his people; he buys all provisions wholesale, looks after securing railway contracts, purchases threshing outfits, and superintends generally the business of the settlements. That the Doukhobors have prospered under his rule cannot be denied, and during the past few years, under his shrewd guidance, they have increased wonderfully in material wealth.

The Doukhobors live in small, communistic villages, consisting of from 150 to 200 people each. When they came to Canada they were given the privilege of taking land without the regular homestead duties; they were also granted exemption from military service. Recently they have been given land on the basis of fifteen acres to each member of the family. As the Doukhobors are not troubled with race suicide, this means a liberal allowance. This land is owned and tilled in common, while all live in the little villages. The government of these villages follows the general Russian custom. There is a head man, appointed in this case by Veregin and responsible to him alone, who is advised by a council of elders. While they deal with all minor questions of administration, nothing of importance is done without consultation with Veregin.

The life in these communities is simple – in one way almost idealistic. The men are detailed for work, one band going to the fields, another remaining at home to look after the chores, etc. The women pursue the same plan. It is a common sight to see one woman minding ten to fifteen babies, swinging in hammocks strung along the cottage roof; the hammocks are connected by one rope, so that she can swing all at the same time and still look after her knitting — a delightful plan that might be adopted in city tenement houses or apartments. The mothers, in the meantime, will be out raking hay or weeding their gardens. The work is periodically shifted around; the woman who looks after the babies to-day may to-morrow be working in the fields. The whole plan has its idealistic side, and there is supposed to be a basis of equality for one and all. However, as in all such communistic colonies, there is also the darker viewpoint. There are to be found the drones who shirk their work and attempt to live on the labor of their neighbors, though such are generally dealt with sternly. Then, again, the elders are sometimes accused of partiality in dividing the stores and the work, and of favoring their friends in the division of labor and profits.

A story has been published widespread, and generally believed, to the effect that the Doukhobors object to using horses, and commandeer their women. This, in justice, it must be said, has very slight foundation. The tale is believed to have originated from the fact that on one or two occasions the women did assist in plowing while the men and horses were away on contract labor. It was time to start farm work. The women themselves suggested that they act as horses; harness was improvised, and, with eight to ten women, all more or less enjoying the fun, the work was accomplished.

The Doukhobors have no schools, and practically nine-tenths of them are illiterate. Attempts by the Society of Friends and other sympathizers to educate them have signally failed. The leaders have discouraged all such efforts. Veregin himself says that in due course schools will be established, but hitherto his promise remains unfulfilled. However, the policy of those who direct their affairs seems to be to keep the people in ignorance. They are discouraged from associating with English-speaking people, and any progressive ambitions on the part of the youth are promptly suppressed. There have been dark stories — stories that will not down — of the strange disappearance of those who have shown a disposition to be independent and to adopt Western civilization. There is a constant impression among those familiar with the Doukhobors, of dark deeds, and there are persistent tales of persecution and ostracism for recalcitrants. Through the ignorance of these people and their fear of trouble it is almost impossible to verify such stories.

They have no priests, no churches, yet through the whole warp and woof of their lives religion is interwoven. Their praiseworthy qualities and their shortcomings are alike the outcome of their firm beliefs and their dogged persistence in clinging to these beliefs. They are not religious fanatics; they have a few elementary dogmas, and to these they cling with something of the heroic spirit of the early Christian martyrs. When the first band of fatigued wanderers on the latest pilgrimage tramped into Winnipeg, they, by their simple, child-like faith and their straightforward answers to all questions, non-plussed and even won over as enthusiastic sympathizers the rather sceptical reporters sent out to interview them. In their villages they have no regular religious services; their sole worship seems to consist of peculiar chants, half sung in a weird, melodious sort of monotone – chants handed down from generation to generation. Veregin is their religious head, and to him reverential homage is paid. His visit to a village is looked upon as a wonderful event. A sacramental table is spread in the village street. As Veregin passes along in state, all bow low while he distributes the communion.

Loose ideas seem to prevail as to social life and marriage. There is apparently no formal ceremony. A promise is simply made in the presence of relatives, and the dissolution of the marriage tie is often reported.

Whatever may be said about the Doukhobors, they have two redeeming qualities for which credit must be given, namely, cleanliness and industry. They are hard workers, and there are few idlers, though occasionally a man will be found who takes advantage of the communistic scheme.

That the Doukhobors have in them the elements which will, in time, make of them good citizens seems to be the unanimous opinion of those who have come in contact with them. They are a strong race physically – far from degenerates. They are sober, industrious, and thrifty. What apparently is needed more than any-thing else is education, and an opportunity to get away from the narrow round of their mediaeval life. They are still as illiterate as when they left the steppes of Russia ten years ago. A thorough investigation of the whole problem should be made. The real status of Veregin, his influence, the stories of persecution, immorality, and dark deeds, should be thoroughly investigated.

THE LITHUANIANS

The Lithuanians are neither Teutons nor Slavs, but belong to a separate branch of the Aryan race. Their language is very old and primitive, and closely resembles Sanscrit. Probably they were the first of the Aryan races to settle in Europe, when, in the tenth century, they became divided into three branches – the Borussians, the Letts, and the Samoghitians. The Borussians, who occupied what is now East Prussia, soon fell under German influence and lost their political existence, leaving only their name corrupted into Prussia. The Letts occupied the country now known as the Baltic Provinces of Russia. The Samoghitians, or Lithuanians proper, occupied territory south of the Baltic Provinces. In the fourteenth century the King of Lithuania ruled the territory occupied to-day by Poles, Lithuanians, and White Russians. In 1569 came a union with Poland. From that time the history of Lithuania has been the history of Poland. The inaccessibility of the country has helped to preserve the racial characteristics of this people. A typical Lithuanian is tall and well proportioned. He has the features of a Greek and the complexion of a Norseman.

About 200,000 Lithuanians have come to the United States during the last thirty or forty years, and now quite a number are commencing to find their way to Canada. In their own country they are almost all engaged in agriculture. In the United States almost half of them are in the mines in Pennsylvania, the remainder being chiefly laborers. In Canada they are closely associated with the Slavs, and are generally employed in construction work.

In religion they are devout Roman Catholics. They are industrious and good-natured, but, like their Slavic neighbors, are addicted to drunken sprees.

H. Holt tells the story of a young Lithuanian immigrant. Away in Russia he heard of a wonderful country where there were free papers and prayer books, and free meetings where men could speak as they liked. When the time came for military service, his father arranged to send him to America. He tells of his journey:

It is against the law to sell tickets to America, but my father saw the secret agent in the village, and he got a ticket for Germany and found us a guide. I had bread and cheese and honey and vodka (Russian whiskey), and clothes in my bag. Some of the neighbors

Beginning life in the new land
1 Ruthenian wedding group
2 Lithuanian wedding group

walked a few miles and said good-bye, and then went back. My father and my younger brother walked on all night with the guide and me. At daylight we came to the house of a man the guide knew. We slept there, and that night I left my father and young brother. My father gave me $50, besides my ticket. The next morning, before light, we were going through the woods, and we came to the frontier. Three roads ran along the frontier; on the first road there is a soldier every mile, who stands there all night; on the second road is a soldier every half-mile; and on the third road is a soldier every quarter of a mile. The guide went ahead through the woods, while I hid with my bag behind a bush, and whenever he raised his hand I sneaked along. I felt cold all over, and sometimes hot. He told me that sometimes he took twenty emigrants together, all without passports; and that, as he could not pass the soldiers, he paid a soldier he knew a dollar a head to let them by. He said the soldier was very strict, and counted them to see that he was not being cheated. So I was in Germany; two days after that we reached Tilsit, and the guide took me to the railroad man. This man had a crowd of emigrants in a room, and we started that night on the railroad — fourth class. We were very slow in the stations, when we changed trains, and the railroad man used to shout at us then; one old German man, who spoke Lithuanian, told me what the man was calling us. When he told me this, I hurried, and so did the others, and we began to learn to be quicker. It took three days to get to Hamburg. There we were put in a big house called a barracks, and waited a week. The old German man told me that the barracks men were cheating us. They kept us there till our money was half spent on food. The boat was the biggest boat I had ever seen; the machine that made it go was very big, and so was the horn that blew in a fog. I felt everything get bigger and go quicker every day.

We have talked with many Russian immigrants who can tell of similar experiences through which they have passed. That is the one end of the journey. Then, on this side come the bewildering and often painful experiences of the new life — the ignorance of the language, the struggle for work, the contact with the roughest side of Canadian life. 'One hundred men killed in rockcuts on the Transcontinental.' One or two will be unknown Lithuanians; next day their places are filled by new hands. Who cares? A family in far-off Russia waits for word that never comes.

Chapter 10

Austria-Hungary

BOHEMIANS, SLOVAKS, RUTHENIANS, POLES, HUNGARIANS

A RECENT writer in the *World's Work* has written of Austria: 'The word "nation" has no application to Austria and very little to Hungary ... It is the variegated contradictoriness of Austria-Hungary ... a Tower of Babel erected into a system of government; a geographical expression – nothing really Austrian in Austria; no Austrian interests, no Austrian nationality, no Austrian standard of civilization – nothing except the Emperor and the army and the cockpit of Reichsrath that the races share in common.'

Let us see if it is possible in any degree to straighten out the tangle. First comes a lesson in political geography:

I *Austria:* composed of 17 lands or crown lands

Kingdoms	Bohemia
	Galicia and Lodomeria
	Dalmatia
Archduchies	Lower Austria
	Upper Austria
Duchies	Salzburg
	Styria
	Carinthia
	Carniola
	Silesia
	Bukowina
Principalities	Görz-Grdiska*
	Tirol**
March countries	Moravia
	Istria*
Land	Voraalberg**
Special crown land	Trieste*

II *Lands of St. Stephen's Crown (Hungary)*
Kingdom of Hungary (including Transylvania and part of the Military frontier)
Kingdom of Croatia – Slavonia
Fiume (town and district)

---

*   Included in same administrative territory.
** Included in same administrative territory.

III *Bosnia and Herzegovina*
Principalities under the suzerainty of Turkey, administered by
Austria-Hungary.

Now we pass to a classification of the people. The different races,
as determined by the different languages spoken, were represented as
follows:

In Austria proper, in 1890 (per cent)

Germans	36.05
Bohemians, Moravians, Slovaks	23.31
Poles	15.84
Ruthenians	13.23
Slovenes	5.01
Servians and Croats	2.75
Italians and Ladini	2.88
Roumanians	0.89
Magyars	0.04

In Hungary proper, in 1901 (per cent)

Hungarian Magyars	51.38
Germans	11.88
Slovaks	11.88
Roumanians	16.62
Ruthenians	2.52
Croatians	1.17
Servians	2.60
Others	1.95

John R. Commons gives a splendid idea of the general situation:

Not only are there in Austro-Hungary five grand divisions of the
human family — the German, the Slav, the Magyar, the Latin and the
Jew — but these are again divided. In the northern mountainous and
hilly sections are 13,000,000 Slavic peoples — the Czechs, or Bohemians, with their closely related Moravians, and the Slavic Slovaks,
Poles, and Ruthenians, or Rusniaks; while in the southern hills and

along the Adriatic are another 4,000,000 Slavs — the Croatians, Servians, Dalmatians, and Slovenians.

Between these divisions, on the fertile plains, 6,000,000 Magyars and 10,000,000 Germans have thrust themselves as the dominant races. To the southwest are nearly a million Italians, and in the far East 2,500,000 Roumanians speaking a Latin language. The Slavs and Latins are in general the conquered peoples, with a German and Magyar nobility owning their land, making their laws, and managing their administration ... Totally unrepresented in government are the Jews, numbering two per cent to four per cent of the population in Bohemia and Hungary, and fully ten per cent in the Polish and Rusniak areas (*Chautauquan*, vol. 38, p. 433).

Keeping these general conditions in view, we may now proceed to the study of the various peoples who come to us from this part of the world (see race table, p. 107).

BOHEMIANS

The most intelligent and progressive of the Slavic races are the Czechs, or Bohemians. A few hundred have already found their way to Canada, where they are making rapid progress.

Mr. Nan Mashek (in *Charities*, 1904) gives the following interesting summary of their history:

For two hundred and fifty years they have been oppressed by a pitilessly despotic rule. In the day of their independence, before 1620, they were Protestants, and the most glorious and memorable events of their history are connected with their struggle for the faith. The history of their church is the history of their nation, for on the one hand was Protestantism and independence, on the other Catholicism and political subjection. For two centuries Bohemia was a bloody battleground of Protestant reform. Under the spiritual and military leadership of such men as Jerome of Prague, John Huss, and Liska, the Bohemians fought their good fight and lost. After the Battle of White Mountains, in 1620, national independence was completely lost, and Catholicism was forcibly imposed upon the country. All Protestant Bibles, books, and songs were burned, thus depriving the nation of a large and rich literature. Men who still clung to their faith publicly were banished, their property becoming forfeited to the State. After one hundred and fifty years, when Emperor Joseph II of Austria gave back to the Protestants some measure of their former freedom, many of the churches were re-established; but Protestantism had lost much of its strength. The political revolution of 1848 led to new subjugation, and emigration was the result. Large numbers left the country in quest of freedom, and some of these found their way to America.

Most of the Bohemians who come to us are Roman Catholics. In Bohemia a few have come under the influence of Protestant missionaries, and here they are the most accessible of the Slavic peoples. But the great tendency seems to be toward scepticism and withdrawal from all church organizations.

The Bohemians are chiefly engaged in manufacturing. They constitute no peculiar 'problem,' as they readily adapt themselves to American or Canadian conditions.

SLOVAKS

Closely akin to the Bohemians are the Slovaks of Northern Hungary. But they are distinctly a lower grade. One-quarter of the immigrants are illiterate; and, while some are skilled artisans, many are fitted only for rough labor. In the United States the majority are in the mining districts, though many have commenced farming, an occupation to which they had been accustomed in the Old Country.

In Canada we have several Slovak colonies in the West, and a few Slovaks are found in all the larger cities. As yet they are hardly distinguishable from other Slavic peoples with whom they are closely associated. In the United States they have made remarkable progress, and their children are being given educational advantages.

One Slovak name we all know – Kossuth. Let us become familiar with such national heroes; thus we can best understand the history and ideals of these people, and come to know them. Those mud-bespattered fellows in the workingman's car – they, too, have their dreams.

RUTHENIANS, by A.R.F.

'Three killed in an explosion,' was the news brought in by the excited cub reporter of a Winnipeg daily.

'Who are they?' coolly enquired the city editor.

'Galicians.'

'Cut it down to a stick and a half; they are only Galicians,' was the city editor's curt reply.

This attitude of the newspaperman is only a crystallization of the feeling of the general public throughout the whole of the West towards this class of immigrants, who during recent years have been crowding to our shores. In so low an estimation are they held that the word Galician is almost a term of reproach. Their unpronounceable names appear so often in police court news, they figure so frequently in crimes of violence that they have created anything but a favorable impression.

However, whichever side one takes in the controversies which are waged as to their general desirability and as to their likelihood of becoming good citizens, the cold fact is that we have some 125,000 in the Dominion, principally in Western Canada. Manitoba has some 40,000, so that one in every nine or ten of the inhabitants of this province is a Galician; Saskatchewan has about 50,000 Galicians, or one in every six of the inhabitants; and Alberta some 30,000, or about the same proportion. No more figures are needed to show what an important factor the Galicians are in the West, and how difficult is the problem of Canadianizing them, even without the influx of another immigrant.

Who are the Galicians, or the Ruthenians, as they are more properly called? The Ruthenians are a Slavic people, who live in the Austrian Provinces of Galicia and Bukowina. They are closely allied to the Little Russians of Southern Russia. The majority of Ruthenians in this country are from Galicia, though there are from 20,000 to 25,000 Bukowinians. Illiterate and ignorant as are the Galicians, the Bukowinians are even more so; only a very small percentage can read or write. It is probable that if an analysis were made of the nationality of those charged with crimes, the result would show a far greater number of Bukowinians than Galicians.

Much of the rough work of nation-building in Western Canada is being done by the despised Galician. The unskilled labor for which contractors and railway builders have been loudly calling is supplied principally by the Galician. In the cities and towns, where new works are being pushed to rapid completion, or out on the farthest stretches of the prairie, where the steel is being laid for the coming settler, can be found the grimy, stolid Galician, puffing his

Foreigners build our railways
1 A construction gang – foreigners do most of the rough work
2 Foreign workmen unloading the first car of steel on the Grand Trunk Pacific

ever-present cigarette and working with a physical endurance bred of centuries of peasant life and an indifference to hardships that seems characteristic of the Slav. But the Galicians are not all to be found herded together in the cities or working in contract gangs; an astonishingly large number have taken to the land. In Manitoba there are large colonies at Gimli, Sifton, Starbuck, and Broken Head. By far the largest settlement is to be found in the Shoal Lake district, where there are some 5,000. At Stuartburn there is also a large settlement, though principally of Bukowinians. In Saskatchewan there are Ruthenian settlements at Rosthern, Canora, and Beaver Hills. In Alberta the largest settlement stretches away northeast from Edmonton past Star and Pakan. British Columbia has probably not more than a few hundreds.

As farmers they are not particularly enterprising, and yet their worst enemies must admit that since coming to Canada they have made progress, and that to a considerable degree. They have in many cases settled in the poorest districts, where they have succeeded in making their way, despite their disadvantages. They are purchasing modern machinery, and are gradually adopting Western methods. Those of the younger generation are adopting our customs, and are beginning to intermingle with the peoples of other nationalities. The young men often find their way into the towns, while the girls, as a rule, make good domestics.

The Galician figures, disproportionately to his numbers, in the police court and penitentiary. Centuries of poverty and oppression have, to some extent, animalized him. Drunk, he is quarrelsome and dangerous. The flowers of courtesy and refinement are not abundant in the first generation of immigrants. But he is a patient and industrious workman. He is ambitious. He is eager to become Canadianized. He does not cling to a language which is rich in words that express sorrow and despondency and misery, and meagre in those that express aspiration and joy and hope. Above all, he yearns to get on the land and to own some acres of his own. A Roman Catholic priest tells of conducting a Galician and his wife to a quarter section he had helped them to secure for homesteading. The man could hardly believe that the land on which he stood was, on certain conditions, to be actually his own. When he was assured that such it might be, he knelt down and kissed the sod.

The great majority of Ruthenians, when they come to this country, are members of what is known as the Uniat Church. It is the Roman Catholic Church, with some of the doctrines and rites of the Greek Orthodox Church preserved. The Ruthenians were all originally Greek Catholics, but when they came under the sway of the Roman Catholic sovereigns, centuries ago, an attempt was made to impose upon them the Roman Church. The higher bishops acknowledged the Pope's authority; the lower clergy stood by the old religion. The result was a compromise. The Pope's authority was acknowledged, but the priests were allowed to marry, while many of the rites of the Greek Church were maintained. This union was effected as long ago as 1596. The followers of the new church were known as Uniats.

The first sign of the leaven of Western civilization at work upon the mind of the Ruthenian immigrant has been shown in the development of a spirit of religious independence. The freedom of the new world has revealed itself in a disposition to renounce the authority of the Pope, which they have so long been forced to acknowledge. The Greek Independent Church has been the result, and through the aid of the Presbyterian Church of Canada, is gaining in strength in the Dominion, so that there are now a number of Greek Independent churches in the Canadian West. When the subject of breaking away from the old church was first broached, the authorities of the Presbyterian Church were approached for advice. They decided to lend all the financial and other aid possible to the movement, while still allowing the new church to retain its old rites, ceremonies, and even beliefs. They hoped in this way to more easily reach the Ruthenian people. The foresight of the policy which was adopted with vague fears is now evident.

The Greek Independent Church is becoming more and more evangelical in tone, and students for the priesthood are actually attending Manitoba College. But, although the Greek Independent Church is making rapid progress, a large proportion of the Ruthenians in this country are still within the fold of the Roman Catholic Church, though termed the Greek Catholic United Church (Uniat Church). How strong they are is shown by the fact that the church in North Winnipeg has a membership of over four thousand, although Winnipeg's Ruthenian population is not more than 8,000 to 10,000. A number of Basilian monks were brought to Canada to work with the Ruthenians, but it is understood there are only three left; although it is said that a number of priests are at present in Galicia studying particularly for the Canadian work. There are a few Orthodox Greek churches, especially among the Bukowinians. These are under the jurisdiction of the bishops in the United States.

From an educational standpoint the Galicians are making remarkable progress. Scores of schools have been established among them. The Government of Manitoba has established, at Brandon, a school for the training of Ruthenian teachers for the Galician colonies. Proper distribution and education seem the two most important factors in transforming these Slavs into Canadians.

THE POLES IN WESTERN CANADA, by A.R.F.

Poles and police courts seem to be invariably connected in this country, and it is difficult for us to think of the people of this nationality other than in that vague class of undesirable citizens. Yet we would perhaps have a little more sympathy and a little more appreciation for the Poles if we stop to think of the contributions which Poland has made to the science, literature, music, and art of the world. Among the great names of our own time are Paderewski, Modjeska, Sienkiewicz, and Munkacsy; while Poland of old developed such men as Sobieski, the conqueror of the Turks; Mickiewicz, the great national poet; and Copernicus, the astronomer. A race which has produced such genius, which is so artistic in its temperament, which has struggled so stubbornly for freedom, and which has preserved, despite its division amongst three empires, its national patriotism, cannot surely be judged by the fighting brawlers who figure too often in our police records.

It is only within the past few years that there has been immigration to any extent into the Dominion by Polanders. Recently they have been crowding in through our open doors, until it is estimated there are from 10,000 to 12,000 now in Canada, principally in Manitoba and Saskatchewan. Of this 10,000 odd, from two to three thousand are located in Winnipeg. In Western Canada, as in the United States, they crowd principally into the cities, and every little Western town has its Polish colony. In Manitoba there are a number of small colonies in the vicinity of Winnipeg. In Saskatchewan there are two farm settlements — one at Canora and the other at Beaver Hills. They are both, however, of such recent formation that it is too early yet to give an opinion as to their probable success. As the Polanders are industrious and thrifty farmers in Europe, there seems no reason why they should not be equally successful, even under the vastly altered New World conditions.

Most of the Poles who reach this country are peasants, or workingmen from the cities and towns — far from the best class. They are poor, illiterate, and with a code of morals none too high. It is not altogether to be wondered at that when they suddenly find themselves in a land of freedom they sometimes swing into excesses and figure with astonishing frequency in the police courts. Without money, without education, the only work they can turn to is unskilled labor; they join with the Galicians in doing the rough work of empire-building in Western Canada. Yet all the Poles in Western Canada are not uneducated laborers; there are to be found occasionally university-trained men, cultured and refined, who have come to the New World to escape Russian tyranny. There are several Polish lawyers in Winnipeg, while last year a Pole, with the characteristic name of Marcarski, ran for alderman. One of the most encouraging signs is the tendency the Poles have shown during the past couple of years to take to the land. The two colonies in Saskatchewan show that they are not entirely wedded to city life, with its unhealthy atmosphere, and there is apparently a willingness, as soon as sufficient capital has been collected, to go homesteading.

The Poles are practically all Catholics, and usually Catholics of a fanatical type. However, since coming to America a feeling of restlessness and a spirit of revolt have developed. As a result, there has sprung up the Polish Independent Church. Practically all the ritual and the services of the Roman Catholic Church are followed; the authority of the Pope, however, is not acknowledged. The first independent church was organized in Chicago; now in every important Polish centre one is to be found. The movement has spread to Winnipeg, and on Burrows Avenue is an independent church. The very establishment of such a church, the willingness to break away from Rome which they have acknowledged since time immemorial, shows that the leaven of Western enlightenment is at work.

As their long and unfortunate history manifestly shows, the Polanders are intensely patriotic. In this new land they still cherish

their love for poor Poland, and Polish national societies foster the
traditions and keep alive the memories of the homeland in the hearts
of the immigrants and the immigrants' children. The strongest
organizations are the Polish Alliance and the Polish Turners (athletic
societies); of the former there are several branches in Winnipeg.

That the Poles are beginning to realize the necessity of education
is shown by the fact that but a short time ago a large deputation
waited upon the Manitoba Government, asking for a Polish training
school for teachers. At present the majority of the Polish children
attend the Separate Schools of the Catholic Church, though a fair
proportion are in attendance at the Winnipeg Public Schools.

THE HUNGARIANS

'Slavs and Hungarians – all the same.' So said an immigration
inspector. 'All peasants; all agriculturists in Austria; all do the same
work here; all Catholics.'

In a general way, perhaps, this estimate is true. All the peasants of
Southeastern Europe have much in common; but those who are
most familiar with these peoples find many differences. The Slavs
and the Hungarians themselves certainly think they are very
decidedly different.

The Hungarians, or Magyars, are, on the whole, probably more
progressive than the majority of the Slavs. Someone has said that
they are 'more intelligent and less industrious.' They are more
ambitious, and more readily rise above the heavy plodding kinds of
work in which both are at first engaged.

About 10,000 Hungarians have come to Canada, the majority of
them having gone directly to the prairies. In Winnipeg there are
probably about 1,500, and every city has its share; but the great
majority remain in the city only long enough to 'get a start' – to
save sufficient money to take up a homestead. Their ambition seems
to be to own their own land. A race of farmers, they easily adapt
themselves to conditions on the prairie, where they soon make a
home and become prosperous settlers.

In Manitoba, outside those in the city and those in construction
work, the majority are located at Huns Valley, northwest of
Neepawa. In Saskatchewan they are pretty well distributed. There
are settlements at Yorkton, Canora, Touchwood Hills, McDonald
Hills, south of Humboldt, at Esterhazy and west to Grayson. The

The foreign women help in market gardening
1 Tomatoes gathered by Galician women
2 Polish and Ruthenian women, Canadian overseer

largest colonies are in the vicinity of Rosthern, where they are very prosperous, and have contributed much to the fame of that district as a wheat-growing country. In Alberta and British Columbia the majority are engaged in coal mining, although there are in Alberta scattered colonies from Lethbridge to Edmonton, the largest being near Wetaskiwin.

The Hungarians are inclined to be clannish. They form clubs of their own, and seem content to live largely to themselves.

In religion the majority are Roman Catholic. The Reformed Church, closely associated with the Presbyterian Church, is growing in numbers. On the part of the Roman Catholics, there seems to be a tendency to break away from the authority of the bishops and French priests.

The Hungarians are better educated than the Slavs. They have a newspaper in Winnipeg – the *Kanadi Magyarsag* ('Canadian Hungarian'). They are intensely patriotic, but, since they have decided to make Canada their home, are taking a great interest in our politics. In time they ought to make good citizens.

Chapter 11

The Balkan states

BY A. R. F.

EMIGRATION to Canada from the Balkan States, from Turkey in Europe and from Greece, is far from large in volume and is not yet regarded seriously. However, during the past few years there has been considerable influx from this region, and the outlook is that it will grow yearly; so that it is a problem well worth a little study.

How much do you know about the Balkan States and far Eastern Europe? Just take stock for a few minutes, and the probabilities are that you will be forced to the conclusion that there are few civilized portions of the globe concerning which you know so little. The Balkan peninsula and the states which comprise it have had as stormy a history as any country in Europe, while they are peopled by an almost inextricable tangle of races. Since the remotest days the Balkan peninsula has formed the battle-ground between the east and the west; it has been the buffer between Europe, and Asia with its westward sweeping hordes.

The present political divisions of the southern and eastern corner of Europe are as follows:

1 Independent kingdoms: (*a*) Montenegro, (*b*) Servia, (*c*) Roumania
2 Autonomous principalities, subject to Turkey: (*a*) Bulgaria, (*b*) East Roumelia
3 Turkey in Europe
4 Greece

Montenegro is the smallest of the Balkan States – a mere toy nation. It is but half the size of Wales, and would make only a decent-sized county in Canada. It is an absolute hereditary monarchy. The country is extremely mountainous, and the people are simple-living, freedom-loving mountaineers. They are nearly all of Servian descent – a branch of the great Slav race.* The State church of Montenegro is Greek Catholic, and while the great mass of the people belong to this church there are a few Roman Catholics and Mohammedans.

Servia is in many ways the most backward of the three Balkan States. Education is at a very low stage, although there is supposed to be a school in every commune. The people generally are illiterate and superstitious. The main industry is agriculture, and the people

* See race table, Chapter 9.

live a very simple and primitive life. They are mainly Serbs, another race of Slavic origin. Servia is a constitutional kingdom. The executive power is in the hands of ministers responsible to the King and to the national assembly, the latter consisting of 130 members. The State church of Servia is Greek Orthodox, the head of the church being the Archbishop of Belgrade. Practically all the people are Greek Catholics, as religious tolerance is a thing unknown.

Roumania, the largest of the three independent Balkan kingdoms, has a popultion of from five to six million people. It became independent in 1881, and is formed by the union of the two ancient principalities of Wallachia and Moldavia, the union having taken place in 1859. It is probably the most enlightened, the most progressive and the most democratic of the three states. The Government is a limited monarchy. The executive consists of a council of eight ministers. The legislative power is vested in a Chamber of Deputies, composed of 180 members, elected for four years, and in a Senate of 120 members elected for eight years, one-half retiring after four years.

The Wallachians are a Latin race and boast of being descendants of the ancient Romans. The province was undoubtedly first settled by Roman soldiers of the legions of the Emperor Trajan and by colonists from Italy, yet the country was so overswept, times out of number, by successive hordes of Huns, Goths, Avars and Magyars, that they are now a heterogeneous people, though the language is Latin. The Moldavians are of Slavic origin. Nine-tenths of the people are Greek Catholics, though there are probably 400,000 Jews, and a few Mohammedans and Protestants.

Bulgaria consists of two provinces – Bulgaria, north of the Balkans, and East Roumelia, south of the Balkans. By a popular movement they were united in 1885 into a single state. By the Berlin Treaty of 1878, which attempted to settle the whole of the vexatious Eastern problem, Bulgaria was constituted an autonomous principality, subject to the authority of the Sultan, but with a Christian governor and an autonomous administration.

The population of Bulgaria is a jumble of races. About 75 per cent are Bulgarians, descendants of the ancient hordes of Finnish extraction, who overran the peninsula in the seventh century. Turks, Roumanians, Gypsies, Jews, Armenians, Russians and Servians form the remainder of the population. The language is fundamentally

Slavonic, with a large mixture of foreign words in which Turkish, Russian, Greek, Italian and Persian elements abound. The State church is the Greek Catholic, but there is religious toleration. The clergy are deplorably ignorant and education is in a very backward state.

Turkey in Europe is likewise a medley of ancient races and historic provinces. The population consists of Albanians, Turks, Greeks, Macedonians, Bulgarians and Latins.

It is only within the last couple of years that there has been any immigration to speak of from the Balkan peninsula though, as the immigration restrictions grow tighter in the United States, and as Canada becomes better known in Eastern Europe it will undoubtedly grow in volume. Nearly all the immigrants have remained in Eastern Canada – in Montreal and Toronto. Of the various races from far Eastern Europe there are from 1,000 to 2,000 in Toronto, the majority being Bulgarians from Macedonia. Only a small proportion of them are skilled workmen; they are nearly all laborers, and with practically no money when they arrive. There have been many stories far from creditable regarding them. They are said to refuse work, and to prefer to starve rather than labor. They have been defrauded and deceived so often by fake employment bureaus, generally run, it is true, by their own countrymen, that they are naturally suspicious, while their ignorance of Canadian customs and the English language has added to the difficulties. They are a simple, sluggish people, who have been oppressed and down-trodden for ages; therefore, it can scarcely be expected that they can land in this country, and at once fall in with our peculiar ways, and understand or appreciate our institutions.

Chapter 12

The Hebrews

Israel shall be a proverb and a byword among all people.
I KINGS ix. 7

What advantage then hath the Jew? or what profit is there of circum-
cision? Much every way.
ROM. iii. I.

A people with restless energy, shrewd insight, breadth of view, in-
tense intellectual initiative, moral strength, spiritual power – some
of the qualities latent because of lack of opportunity – are thrown
into an atmosphere in America for which they are well fitted, and in
which they would make great advance if they had not to struggle at
first with severe economic necessity. The struggle is fierce in certain
quarters, and during the struggle some untoward results follow.
Coming here hampered and trying to adjust themselves, they must
strive in a way which those long settled here cannot appreciate. It is
our business to improve the conditions surrounding them, and to
whatever extent we help them they will profit. They are bound to
rise no matter how great the difficulties. All who know the stuff of
which they are made have no fear but that from the grinding process
there will rise men and women of the highest types of citizenship,
business and professional men of high grade, poets, scholars, scientific workers in many fields.
BERNHEIMER

'OUT OF a total of 10,000 children under the Protestant School Commission of Montreal 3,500 are Jews. Within a few years it would seem as if the Jewish children will be in the majority.' This statement brings home to us very forcibly the rapid increase in our Jewish population.

In Canada in 1881 we had only 667 Jews; in 1901, 16,131. Since that time the official figures show nearly 38,000 Jewish immigrants. But probably there are many more who have been classified as Russians. In Montreal there are 25,000 to 30,000 Jews; in Toronto, 12,000 to 15,000; in Winnipeg, 5,000 to 6,000, and each city or town of any size has quite a large contingent. There are several fairly prosperous farm colonies in Saskatchewan. The largest are at Wapella and Hirsch. Most of our immigrants come from Russia, Austria or Roumania; some of them having spent some time in England. Many of them have been assisted to emigrate by their wealthy co-religionists. The Rothschilds and Baron Hirsch have devoted immense sums to aid their suffering brethren. We subjoin an extract from a report* which will show the countries from which our Jewish immigrants come, as well as their distribution throughout Canada:

Labor Bureau — During the year just completed the arrivals from Europe, who were handled by this branch of our activity in conjunction with the Relief Committee, numbered as follows: Men, 2,412; women, 468; children, 785; total, 3,665.

The nationalities of the new arrivals were:

	Men	Women	Children
Roumanians	39	12	23
Austro-Hungarians	26	9	19
Turkey and Palestine	11	1	
Germans	14		
English (through B. of G. and R. J. Com.)	108	19	27
English (unassisted)	43	14	39
French	3		
Russians	2,168	413	677
Total	2,412	468	785

*   Forty-third Annual Report for year ending October, 1906. Baron de Hirsch Institute and Hebrew Benevolent Society, Montreal.

The people were distributed as follows:

Toronto, Ont.	133	New Liskeard, Ont.	22
Liverpool, N.S.	30	Cobourg, Ont.	10
Port Arthur, Ont.	19	Farnham, Que.	34
Sudbury, Ont.	14	Saint Therese, Que.	15
Port Hope, Ont.	22	Sydney, N.S.	94
Brantford, Ont.	26	Winnipeg, Man.	60
Algoma, Ont.	26	Woodstock, Ont.	5
Lachine, Que.	64	North Bay, Ont.	5
C.P. Railway		Guelph, Ont.	18
Construction	15	Hyslop, Ont.	34
Collingwood, Ont.	52	Rossland, B.C.	10
Shelburne, N.S.	56	St. Anne's, Que.	23
Sault Ste Marie, Ont.	47	(Left to join relations	
Black Lake, Que.	27	in United States)	160
Carleton, Ont.	24	Total	1,045

The remainder who were able to work have been placed in different occupations in this city (Montreal).

What brings the Jews in such large numbers to Canada, for this migration is only the latest of a long series? We must briefly trace their history and condition in Europe — sufferance the badge of all their tribe — driven from one country to another.

England was the first to expel the Jews (1290), France followed a century later (1395), and Spain and Portugal two centuries later (1492 and 1495). But in Germany and Russia they found no rest, and were forced to flee to Poland. The division of Poland again placed the majority of them in Russian territory. In 1881 began the terrible persecutions which have again driven them forth in search of a home.

Hall thus summarizes conditions in Europe:

The general policy of Russia is to restrict the Jews within a circum-scribed territory, including what was formerly the kingdom of Poland and certain contiguous western provinces. This, known as the Jewish pale, was first established in 1786. In 1897 the number of Jews in the Russian Empire, according to the census, was 5,189,401; of these 1,316,576 were in Poland, and 3,607,373 were in Russia. A

few specially favored classes, amounting to a small percentage of the
total, are allowed to reside outside the pale. Under the 'May Laws,'
often mentioned in this connection, enacted in 1882, all the Jews,
except those who could prove a right to residence in small towns and
villages, were obliged to move into the large towns. The 'May Laws'
have thus created the Ghetto conditions in Russia, and have caused
much of the Hebrew emigration since they were passed. The con-
gestion in the cities and large towns has resulted not only in disease,
but in overcrowding industries and lowering the standard of living.
These results are intensified by the fact that only a few occupations
are open to the Jews, and that public works, including transportation and its branches, are entirely closed to them. Roumania was
created a kingdom by the Treaty of Berlin, which especially stipu-
lated for the complete civil and religious liberty of the Jews. The
Roumanian Government, however, has since surpassed even the
Russian in its oppressive laws.

'Oppressive laws.' Think what they mean! 'In Russia to-day the
Jew is not permitted to foreclose a mortage, or to lease or purchase
land. He cannot do business on Sundays or Christian holidays; he
cannot worship nor assemble without police permit; he must serve in
the army but cannot become an officer; he is excluded from schools
and universities; he is fined for conducting manufacturing and
commerce; he is almost prohibited from the learned professions –
the Government and the army join with the peasants in what is
truly a national uprising.' *Hall.*

In one sense a Jew is a Jew all the world over, yet Jews differ
widely. Through the long centuries they have been greatly influenced by their environment and intercourse with other peoples. A
Spanish, a German and a Polish Jew might be thought to belong to
entirely different races.

That which makes the Jew a peculiar people is not the purity of his
blood, but persecution, devotion to his religion, and careful training
of his children. Among the Jews from Eastern Europe there are
marked intellectual and moral differences. The Hungarian Jew, who
emigrated earliest, is adventurous and speculative; the Southern
Russian, upon whom the riot first broke in 1881, keeps none of the
religious observances, is the most intellectual and socialistic, and

most inclined to the life of a wage-earner; the Western Russian is
orthodox and emotional, saves money, becomes a contractor and
retail merchant; the Galician Jew is the poorest, his conditions at
home were the hardest, and he begins American life as a pedlar.
These are the main characteristics as recognized by the Eastern Jews
themselves. That which unites them all as a single people is their
religious training and common language. *Dr. Allan McLaughlin.*

In view of such differences we must be on our guard against
making general statements, or regarding them as of universal
application; yet the large majority of Jews possess many characteristics in common.

First of all, perhaps, is the power of 'getting on.' They come here
wretchedly poor, and yet in some way they exist and make money.
They are not strong physically, yet the death rate among them is
low. They are often housed in crowded tenements, and yet observe
certain sanitary precautions that save them from many of the
diseases that attack others. The majority are disinclined to do hard
manual labor, yet are most industrious and make a living where
others would starve. They may be miserly along some lines, and yet
they are most generous in helping one another. There are few Jewish
applicants for public charity. They care for their poor through their
own charitable organizations. It is a far cry from the Jewish pedlars
or sweatshop tailors to the money-barons who control the world's
finances, yet the same keen business instincts are common to both,
and to all the grades that lie between. Though, economically, largely
non-producers they are by no means parasites, but are destined to
play a prominent part in our commercial life.

Again, they are an intellectual people; many of them are not well
educated, but this has been their misfortune, for no people more
highly value an education. The great majority of the men, at least,
read Hebrew, which is the written language. Often this has been
taught by father to son. Many have a good knowledge of the Hebrew
Scriptures and of the Talmud. The greater number speak Yiddish, 'a
jargon without syntax, conjugation or declension.' Its basis is
sixteenth century German with the addition of Polish and Hebrew
words and suffixes.

The first task on arriving in the new land is to acquire a
knowledge of English. This they quickly accomplish as they are

wonderful linguists. It is almost pathetic to see old men, after their day's work, coming to night school to read from children's primers; and this is not merely that they may do business, for at once they plunge into all kinds of intellectual activities. They are omnivorous readers. Our librarians tell us that the young Jewish people patronize the public libraries more than any other class. They establish literary societies, social and dramatic clubs and political associations. They glory in their literary traditions. The following extract from a recent Jewish lecture, given in Toronto, recalls to our minds the place of the Jewish people in the world's history, as well as reveals to us the ideals which they constantly keep before them:

We cannot realize what the Jews have done for the progress and the enlightenment of the world until we imagine their work taken away, and know the vacuum that would be left. Science would become bald and ragged, some of the brightest jewels would drop from the crown of literature, and the fairest garments would be shed from the shoulders of art.

The Jewish race has given the brilliant Halevy and the versatile Heine to poetry, Maimonides and Spinoza to philosophy, Mendelssohn and Meyerbeer to music, Israels and Mosier to painting, Antokolski and Ezekiel to sculpture, D'Israeli and Zangwill to literature, Marx and DeBloch to political economy, Lombrosi and Nordau to sociology, Sylvester and Jacobi to mathematics, Goldschmidt and Herschel to astronomy, Benfey and Ollendorf to philosophy, Neander and Edersheim to history, and thousands of others who by their genius in every walk of life and every field of human endeavor have elevated and ennobled humanity while reflecting lustre on themselves.

Many of our immigrants from Russia and Roumania are Socialists, some of them of the most extreme type. This seems rather strange, as naturally the Jew is individualistic. But the intolerable conditions that exist in Eastern Europe have driven them almost to despair. Socialism has come as a gospel, and they have welcomed it with almost religious devotion. Some of them have preached anarchy. But here, conditions are so different that the extremists cannot secure a large following, and the general tendency seems to be to adapt themselves to actual conditions and take an active part in the political life of the country.

In religion there have been great changes, and greater are anticipated. The first synagogue in Canada was organized in Montreal in 1768. The members of the congregation were descendants of the exiles from Spain and Portugal. Later came English and German Jews, who now predominate, but the ritual used is still the Portuguese. In 1846 German and Polish synagogues were established. In Toronto, the Holy Blossom Synagogue was established in 1865, and has become the centre of numerous benevolent and literary associations. Synagogues are now found in nearly all the cities of Canada. These organizations are nominally under the jurisdiction of the Chief Rabbi in England, but in many ways they are quite independent. In different synagogues not only does the ritual differ greatly, but the teaching is almost as diverse as that in various Christian churches. Among the Jews, as among others, there are the conservatives and the progressives. The tendency in Canada and in the United States is toward liberalism. In many ways the Christian Church is influencing the Jewish synagogue. Many Jews bemoan the fact that the young people are drifting away from the synagogues; they are not becoming Christians, but atheists or secularists. Too often the situation is summed up in the remark of a Jew, 'My father prays every day, I pray once a week, my son never prays.'

Alas, this is the most serious danger which besets our immigrants — the loss of the old faith in the new land.

Naturally, religious, temperate, home-loving, intelligent, industrious and ambitious, the Jew is bound to succeed.

Chapter 13

The Italians

NORTH AND SOUTH

AN ITALIAN! The figure that flashes before the mind's eye is probably that of an organ-grinder with his monkey. That was the impression we first received, and it is difficult to substitute another. Italian immigrants! The figure of the organ man fades away, and we see dark, uncertain figures, and someone whispers, 'The Mafia – the Black Hand.'

Soft Italian airs, Italian landscapes! Not for a moment do we connect such ideas with Italians. Garibaldi and Mazzini – what have they to do with 'dirty Dagos'? Of few peoples have we so many unreconciled, detached ideas. Rome, Naples, Venice, Milan – these cities we know, but their citizens are strangers; and yet there is no people whom we should know better. More Italians are coming to the United States than any other class of immigrants. In Canada, of all our non-English immigrants the Italians stand second. Surely we cannot afford to remain ignorant concerning them. In 1901 there were only about 10,000 Italians in Canada. Now there are 50,000, and the stream is only starting to flow in our direction. Two hundred thousand a year leave Italy, yet so prolific is the race that the population continues to increase rapidly. With the tightening of immigration restrictions by the United States, there will be a tendency for the Italians to crowd more and more into Canada.

To understand the Italian we should remember his history – Ancient Rome, the Holy Roman Empire, Mediaeval Italy, the decadent Italian states, and now, Modern Italy arising from its ashes with new life. No one can visit Italy or study its conditions without being impressed with its wonderful vitality and the remarkable progress that has been made in recent years. Italy is by no means a nation of the past; her people have not yet entered into their own.

Here, again, we must distinguish between Italians of various districts. Dr. Allan McLaughlin says:

In considering Italian immigrants it is necessary to recognize the differences existing between Northern and Southern Italians. The Northern Italian is taller, often of lighter complexion, and is usually in a more prosperous condition than his brother from the south. The Northern Italian is intelligent, can nearly always read and write, and very often is skilled in some trade or occupation. He compares favorably with the Scandinavian, or German, and his desirability as an immigrant is seldom questioned. He usually leaves Italy through the representations of friends in this country, and therefore comes here with a definite purpose, and is not at the mercy of a 'padrone.' On the other hand, the Southern Italian, short of stature, very dark in complexion, usually lands here almost destitute. His intelligence is not higher than one could imagine in the descendant of peasantry illiterate for centuries. He can seldom read and write, and invariably is an unskilled farm laborer. He has little money, often has no definite purpose, and naturally must depend on someone who speaks his language. In this way he falls into the hands of the 'padrone.'

The padrone, it may be said, is a sort of middleman who acts as contractor and banker, and often contrives to 'fleece' his poor, ignorant fellow-countryman. The padrone system has been broken up in the United States, but it is said that the employment agents and others often take advantage of the newly-arrived immigrant.

The Southern Italians should again be divided into several classes, with fairly well-defined characteristics. Brandenburg says that dishonesty is the prevailing feature of the 'Neapolitan zone.' Most of the diseased and criminal Italians, who have given their compatriots such an unenviable reputation in America, have been shipped from Naples by the police authorities. In the 'Roman zone' the Church and the State, as institutions, have dominated everything. The people are now reacting against the evils of these systems. 'Political and religious scepticism is growing to be as dangerously common among the poor people, in and about Rome, as it was in France early last century.' In the 'Heel and Toe' — or extreme south — poverty and taxes almost sum up the situation. In Sicily, Brandenburg finds an almost ideal picture of rural life.

In Canada we have immigrants from all parts of Italy. The majority come from the south; many of these from Sicily. We have no carefully classified statistics, but what is true of the United States is probably, in a general way, true of our immigrants. Over 80 per cent are from the south; over 80 per cent are between the ages of 14 and 45; almost 80 per cent are males, and 80 per cent are unskilled laborers. The Italian laborer represents the Italians who are coming to Canada. Many have been accustomed to fruit-farming at home, and take up some kind of fruit business here. Few go into farming, though they have often excellent gardens. In the cities there are a few barbers, tailors, stonecutters, etc., but the great majority belong to the pick and shovel brigade, and are doing rough work in the new land. But the Italians are quick to learn, and many soon find places in factories and business establishments.

In Montreal there are 12,000 Italians; in Toronto, 6,000; in Winnipeg, probably 2,000. Great numbers are employed on railway construction. When we ride in comfort over our great transcontinental lines we sometimes forget that many a poor, unknown Italian lies buried in the 'dump.' The most serious difficulties with the Italians are found in the congested districts of the cities; here they help to create slum conditions. They are miserably poor when they arrive; the majority are anxious to save money to send home to bring their families. High rentals drive them into crowded, unsanitary tenements. Many Italians, unaccustomed to city life, do not know how to make the most of the poor accommodations they have; so there come filth, disease and crime. Too much, perhaps, has been made of the criminal instincts of this people. A few crimes of violence have given a false estimate of the character of the Italian. Jacob Riis says:

With all his conspicuous faults, the swarthy Italian immigrant has big redeeming traits. He is as honest as he is hotheaded. There are no Italian burglars in the Rogues' Gallery; the 'ex-brigand' toils peacefully with pick-axe and shovel on American ground. He may occasionally show, as a pickpocket, the results of his training with the toughs of the Sixth Ward slums. The only criminal business to which the 'father' occasionally lends his hand, outside of murder, is a bunco game, of which his confiding countrymen, returning with their hoard to their native land, are the victims. The women are faithful wives and devoted mothers. Their vivid and picturesque costumes lend a tinge of color to the otherwise dull monotony of the slums they inhabit. The Italian is gay, light-hearted, and, if his fur is not stroked the wrong way, inoffensive as a child. His worst offence is that he keeps the stale beer dives.

The Italians are industrious, and rarely become a charge on the public. They are temperate, though they are in danger of substituting beer for the light wines to which they are accustomed. Family morality is high. They sometimes think lightly of truth, and yet rarely tell deliberate lies.

Sixty per cent are illiterate, but the children are quick and ambitious. The following bit of conversation, overheard and recorded by Brandenburg, illustrates the Americanizing process and its dangers: 'Said the mother in very forcible Tuscan: "You *shall* speak Italian, and nothing else, if I must kill you; for what will your grandmother say when you go back to the old country, if you talk this pigs' English?" "Aw, gwan! Youse tink I'm going to talk Dago 'n' be called a guinea? Not on your life! I'm 'n American, I am, 'n' you go way back 'n' sit down." ' Incidentally, it may be said that such an attitude is too common on the part of immigrant children. They grow to despise their parents who cannot speak English and who maintain their old-fashioned garb and customs. The ensuing loss of parental control is responsible for much of the juvenile crime among foreign children.

So far the Italians have taken little interest in political affairs, though many of them have become naturalized. Their dominant idea is to make money. They are far from clannish. Indeed, they have little *esprit de corps*, and jealousy often divides Italian communities. On the other hand, they are open to good influences. Institutional work in the Italian quarter has generally been successful.

The Italians are nominally Roman Catholics. The women occasionally attend church, but the men have escaped from its influence. The whole tendency is toward absolute religious indifference. With the young people this passes into scepticism.

So far most of our Italian immigrants have come through the United States. It is very probable that direct communication between Canada and Italian ports will soon be established. Then, as information about Canada is being widely circulated, we may expect a still larger influx.

Chapter 14

Levantine races

GREEKS, TURKS, ARMENIANS, SYRIANS, PERSIANS

THERE ARE probably nearly 10,000 people who come from the shores of the Eastern Mediterranean. Most of them have come to us within the last few years, and they constitute one of the least desirable classes of our immigrants.

First, we have a few Greeks. They generally keep restaurants or fruit stalls or boot blacking establishments. Even in Canada, it is said, they are often under the control of padroni – that is, men who have brought them over and control their earnings.

More numerous are the Turks, 1,200 of whom have come during the past seven years. They are mostly pedlars or shop keepers, selling rugs and Eastern fancy goods and trinkets.

About the same number of Armenians have come to Canada, and are engaged in similar work. A few are more independent and ambitious, and push out into other lines, but they are physically incapable of hard manual labor. This people belong to a primitive branch of the Christian Church, and are glad to escape the oppressions of a government that is little better than organized robbery, and permits, if it does not encourage, the most horrible atrocities.

Most numerous of all are the Syrians, of whom there must now be six or seven thousand in Canada. The majority of them have come from Mount Lebanon, a little independent territory which the Christian powers protect against the 'unspeakable Turk.' The greater number belong to the Greek Church, or the Maronite branch of the Roman Catholic Church, though many of them have come under the influence of Protestant missionaries. By occupation they are chiefly small traders and pedlars. Many of them become quite wealthy. Recently, in Winnipeg, we have had the formation of a Syrian Liberal Club and a Syrian Conservative Club.

Whelpley says of the Syrians and Armenians: 'In the country of their adoption they usually become itinerant merchants or factory hands. They are generally of a most undesirable class; and, while not vicious, their intellectual level is low. There are exceptions to this rule, but not in sufficient numbers to remove from this immigration movement the bad reputation it has attained among those brought into contact with it. The most dangerous feature is the general prevalence of contagious and loathsome diseases, some of which are difficult of detection, any one of which constitutes a serious threat to foreign communities into which these aliens are absorbed.'

Dr. Allan McLaughlin is even more emphatic in his disapproval of these immigrants:

The mental processes of these people have an Oriental subtlety. Centuries of subjection, where existence was only possible through intrigue, deceit, and servility, have left their mark, and, through force of habit, they lie most naturally and by preference, and only tell the truth when it will serve their purpose best. Their wits are sharpened by generations of commercial dealing, and their business acumen is marvellous. With all due admiration for the mental qualities and trading skill of these parasites from the near East, it cannot be said that they are anything in the vocations they follow but detrimental and burdensome. These people, in addition, because of their miserable physique and tendency to communicable disease, are a distinct menace, in their crowded, unsanitary quarters, to the health of the community. In their habits of life, their business methods, and their inability to perform labor or become producers, they do not compare favorably even with the Chinese, and the most consoling feature of their coming has been that they form a comparatively small part of our total immigration.

In this connection, perhaps, we ought to mention the Persians. A few are scattered through our cities, and near Battleford a farm colony was established a few years ago by Dr. Adams, a missionary. They come to escape religious persecution. It seems improbable that colonization on any large scale will be carried out, as these people are manifestly not fitted for life in Western Canada.

Chapter 15

The Orientals

CHINESE, JAPANESE, HINDUS

BRITISH COLUMBIA has an immigration problem peculiarly its own, and a perplexing problem it is – the Oriental question. It is difficult for the rest of Canada to really appreciate the seriousness of the problem, although it was realized to some extent when the news of the Vancouver riots of some months ago was flashed over the wires. Then, for the first time, did the East understand that there was a question in the Coast Province that could not be argued away by politicians. As long as immigration from the Orient was confined to a few odd Chinamen a year, who were quite content to do work distasteful to a white man, no particular objections were raised. It was when the Japanese and Hindus started pouring into British Columbia by the thousands that the trouble arose. During the last year and a half nearly ten thousand Japanese and from four to five thousand Hindus have entered the Coast Province.* When it is considered that the population of British Columbia is only 250,000 – not even the population of Toronto – it is not to be wondered at that the people of that province, especially white labor, took alarm at the hordes pouring in by the steamer load. If this were to continue, the millions of the far East would soon swamp the country west of the mountains. If the cities of Montreal and Toronto were to see a thousand Japanese a week landing on their docks, they would probably have more sympathy with the people of the far Canadian West.

The Oriental problem is not a new one in Canada. The Chinese, in any numbers, were first brought in when the Canadian Pacific Railway was being built, in order to work on the construction of that line when it was next to impossible to secure white labor. When the road was completed the Chinese still continued to flock in, and so a head tax of $100 was imposed. This has since been raised to $500. In 1901 there were about 20,000 Chinese in Canada. Since that time less than two thousand are reported as immigrants. Most of them come from the populous Province of Kwang-tung, in which the city of Canton is situated; they are principally of the coolie class.

In the Eastern provinces the Chinaman is generally in the laundry business. There are about a thousand in Toronto, nearly that many in Montreal, and about seven hundred in Winnipeg, while nearly all the towns have a few of these 'Celestials.' In British Columbia they

---

*   See Table, pp.24-5.

Our Woman's Missionary Society's work for Chinese girls in Victoria
1 Mending day in the Chinese Girls' Home
2 The New Home Building, erected 1908

are engaged in almost every kind of work, though they are found particularly in the fishing and lumbering industries. Large numbers work on the 'ranches,' or fruit and vegetable farms, and they do much of the domestic work of the province.

We append a description of Chinatown, a chapter from a splendid little book, *The Story of China in Canada*, by the Rev. J. C. Speer:

CHINATOWN

Some one has said that it is not necessary to go out of our own country to visit China, for one can take a trip through Chinatown, as found in any of the Coast cities of this Dominion, and pass in the distance of a couple of blocks into conditions which are practically identical with what one would find in any of the larger or smaller cities in China proper. It is a remarkable fact that some of these quarters are situated in the very heart of the English-speaking cities, a condition which is due to the fact that the Chinese came in at a time when the early residents were about to look for new quarters, their first buildings having become either too cramped or too dilapidated for the growing and up-to-date demands of modern times. The average Chinaman comes to this country with no intention of remaining longer than the time when he can save a little cash, and therefore, as it is with many others when settling but for a brief period of time, the Chinese are in no way particular as to the locality or the character of the dwelling. The result is that while Chinatown is generally in the heart of the city it is the most unattractive, squalid and forlorn of all places one can find.

The people who have a laudable ambition to advance and beautify their city have their patience greatly tried by this eyesore, which is often surrounded by the modern buildings of business centres. On the other hand, the landlords who can rent these ramshackle places are much more difficult to move than the Chinese merchants. This condition of affairs places the Chinese who come to us at a view-point which is most unfavorable. Those who have visited China will bear testimony that art in architecture is one of the things in which China can have not a little pride, and one may well believe that but for the fact that they are here for only a brief period of time there would be a much better showing. If the people of Chinatown are not pressed by the city authorities they will take little or no interest in keeping their streets in order, so that often in dry weather the dust is blinding, and in wet the mud is thick and deep. But while on this point it may as well be said that the Chinese, as a class, are not a whit worse than many other foreigners, and we are not aware that they have suffered from diseases which are incident to insanitary conditions more than any other class of people who have come to us from European countries.

One of the things which is striking to the visitor is the absence of women and children. A few there are, it is true, but for the most part the Chinese are transients, and such as these do not bring their families to our shores. This is a most serious matter, and one of the sound objections which may be raised to the coming in large numbers of these people. It is always a disaster for men to congregate together, whether for a longer or shorter period without the blessed influences of a home in which there are women and children. This is true of thousands who spend their years in the lumber-camps, and in the mines of the far North and West. It is a poor home indeed that is totally void of some uplifting influence, and as for the most part these Chinamen leave their wives and children in China, they are in a most dangerous and degrading environment. There are a few who have brought their families to this country — men who after they were here for a time either felt that they could not get rich in a day, or who found that this land was a better place to live in than the one from which they came. The laws, until of late, were not such as to deter a man who had lived under Chinese rule, and the earning power of two pair of hands were much greater in Canada than amidst the swarming millions of the home-land. Those who have thus settled down to live with us have shown themselves to be good citizens, or at least as good as they know how to be.

Passing through the streets one sees the children (for there are some) at play with all the enjoyment of our own little ones. The little child has not the dull, stolid countenance of the father, but with bright, black, sparkling eyes they scurry out of the way of the white visitor, showing thus early that they have learned the bitter lesson that they are strangers in a strange land. It is pleasing to hear words of our own tongue from these little strangers, and one is reminded that some of them are as much Canadian as are we of Anglo-Saxon speech. Here and there one meets the tottering form of a woman, picking her way to the house of a neighbor. She is the victim of a custom which has been an unmitigated curse to millions

of little children and women in the Celestial Empire — that of foot-
binding. These women are dressed most artistically, according to the
ideals of the fashion-plates of the Chinese; tiny shoes, most beauti-
fully embroidered, with the sole tapering almost to a point, so that
the foot rolls as on a rocker as the wearer walks on the solid sidewalk, the lower limbs encased in silk leggings, a short skirt and a silk
quilted smock complete the costume.

The Chinese ladies wear no head covering, but seem to find their
chief pleasure in the most elaborate toilet. Their blue-black hair is
done up so that it will remain for many days. It is decorated with
beads and combs, but no hat is ever worn under ordinary circumstances. The weather may be bright or stormy, cold or hot, but none
of these conditions could induce the Chinese woman to patronize
the milliner. The parasol or umbrella takes the place of the American
hat, and the crowning ornament of women is in this way shown to
the best advantage.

Passing the windows one sees the cobbler at work on the paper-
soled shoes, using the most primitive implements for his work.
Next door will be the butcher of the town, who sells to all and
sundry from the animal which has been roasted whole in his great
oven. This saves the necessity of every cook in the town cooking a
small piece for each meal. Then one comes to the bric-a-brac dealer,
and is bewildered by the accumulation of thread, needles, matches,
punk-sticks, red paper, bird-kites, tumbling toys and fire-crackers;
but time and space would fail me to write down all that John the
merchant has in his little corner store for the curio hunter or for his
fellow countryman.

The vegetable store may be next, and one is puzzled at the variety
of strange foreign vegetables for sale. Some of them are imported, and
some are grown in our own soil — long roots like those of the golden
or white pond lily, turnip-like roots, peculiarly formed cabbages,
and a preparation of what is known as beancurd, which may or may
not be toothsome and nutritious to a Canadian system. Near by is
the dealer in fine silks, and here comes the temptation of the visitor,
for the texture, colors and designs are such as to attract a connoisseur
in such lines. The artistic quality of the Mongolian mind needs no
argument when one has witnessed the needle work and art designs
which are the product of China. One thinks of the long months and
even years it has taken to accomplish the task of such embroidery.

As we wander through Chinatown we come across the theatre, where the Chinaman finds much of his amusement. We have been told that no woman is allowed to take part in the drama, but where the *role* demands female characters men are provided to fill the place and play the part. This is the outcome of that pseudo sacredness with which the Orientals assume to regard the persons of their women. The plays which are most popular are those which have to do with the history of the nation and the events which have given rise to important epochs. To the ordinary listener it is one tumult of conflicting sounds, and even to those who understand the language it is generally one vast incoherency.

Passing an uncurtained window one sees a dozen men around a great dish of boiled rice, and with a dexterity which is positively bewildering these clumsy men are feeding themselves with chopsticks. It is as near to the proverbial 'supping gruel with a knitting needle' as it is possible to get. It is not true, as most of our vegetarian friends assert, that rice is the only food these people eat, for anyone who has had to do with the Chinese knows well that they consume large quantities of fish, fowl and pork. The latter is their staple meat diet, but no people we have ever met are more willing to pay outside prices for fowl for table and sacrificial use than are they. They are by no means vegetarians, as so many people believe, but they can live on rice exclusively when it is necessary so to do. Speaking of the food of these people we remember that they are the world's greatest tea drinkers. On the counters of the stores, over a little charcoal burner, the teapot is kept ready for the cup of tea either for personal friend or customer. Perhaps this is the explanation of the fact that while these people live in the most insanitary squalor, they escape many of the diseases with which those more scrupulous are smitten. They seldom drink raw water, and it is believed that this prevents the taking of those diseases which are communicated by the use of impure water.

One of the most interesting places to be visited in Chinatown is that of the confectioner. The making of confections is a fine art with the Chinese, for they are, above all others, lovers of the sweet and toothsome. The great days, such as Chinese New Year, are times when the people expend large sums on sweetmeats and sugar productions, with many kinds of dried fruit and nuts. Many of these are not as palatable to the Canadian as to the Chinese; but there is no way to account for human tastes, and we may be well satisfied if they are happy. What numbers of things one misses from these places without which we think we could scarcely live! The baker and milkman never call at the home of the Chinese housekeeper. The house furnishings are of the most meagre kind, and this seems to be the case among the well-to-do people as well as among the poorer classes.

Perhaps among all the memories which follow the visitor none will cling so long as that of the odors, which are so numerous that one becomes bewildered as to whether they are good, bad or indifferent. Someone has described a Chinese smell as 'a mixture and a puzzle, a marvel and a wonder, a mystery and a disgust, but nevertheless a palpable fact.'

The cause for all this, it appears, is found in the fact that the opium smoker is not far away, and the other smells, better and worse, filtering through this most abominable stench, produce effects not to be obtained otherwise. Another memory which one will carry from Chinatown is that of the sounds, which are ever to be heard day or night, from the outlandish fiddles and the booming of the worshippers' drum, together with the dulcet tones of the tongueless bells. The screech of a Chinese fiddle, or a number of them, is not just like any sound known to the ears of men, and the booming of the drum smites upon the ear with that dull monotony that breeds an unspeakable dread. But over against these we must place the sound of the bells which are touched by the soft hammer in the hands of the Confucian worshipper. Soft and liquid are these notes, like spirits lost among the discord of the drums and fiddles, and the memories of these tones heal the wounds of the harsh rasping of the other instruments. Heathenism as found in China, and transplanted to our own land, has neither sweet odors nor sweet music, with the one exception of the tongueless bells.

The dead walls are the places for the announcements of the various society meetings, and the notices are in the form of a red strip of paper upon which stand out the curious Chinese characters. Several societies have their headquarters in every Chinatown. Before these billboards there is to be found a crowd of people reading not only the notices of meetings of secret societies, but also many other items of interest which the writers keep posted for the information of the people. They have few, if any, books and no newspapers, and they read and discuss the notices by the hour.

It is evident that the social instincts of the Chinese are highly developed, for one cannot walk the streets of their towns without encountering groups of men everywhere engaged in conversation, and often in the excitement of good fellowship. One of the most pleasing sights to be witnessed is the attitude of the fathers to their sons, where the family has been established in this country. The affection of a husband for his wife is a quantity which is mostly wanting, but his whole affection seems to be placed on his little sons, and this may in some way account for the obedient reverence of the sons for the father, so that as long as he lives he remains true, and after the parent is dead the son becomes a worshipper at his shrine.

The Chinaman seems to think his love should be lavished upon his son that he may offer the proper devotion and sacrifices after he himself has departed this life. This is one of the few bright spots in the heathenized nature of the Chinaman. It is true that there are exceptions to this rule, but few husbands among the Chinese seem to think of the wife as higher than a chattel which it is convenient to have. The story is well authenticated by a medical missionary, who called to see a woman who was very sick in a miserable shed, with the rain dripping down upon the fever-stricken creature. The doctor appealed to the husband to provide a better place for the sufferer or there would be little hope of her recovery; but the husband declared that the only dry place was the other shed in which he sheltered his ox, and if it were to be turned out and get wet and die, he would have to buy another, but if his wife were to die it would cost him nothing for another. The missionary declared that there were many million women in China who were married to men who were not a whit better than this one. But, as we have said, the love of little children still burns in the breasts of the fathers, and this is a flame which the Christian religion feeds till it spreads to the whole nature of the darkened heathen.

One cannot leave Chinatown without seeing the Joss House. Victoria, B.C., has two or three, and they stand for heathen worship transplanted to this Christian land. It is worth while for those who affect to care nothing for the Christian church to spend a while in one of these dreary places, that they may feel how far above and beyond this kind of worship is the baldest kind of congregational service in a Christian church. An outer court, which has at its entrance a few smoking, ill-smelling punk-sticks; an aged caretaker who, with the utmost politeness, admits the visitors, many of whom are not over-considerate of the feelings of the 'heathen Chinee'; into a large square room, which is shrouded in semi-darkness and filled with the vile odor of the incense which is ever burning or smouldering on the altar, you are conducted. The place is decorated with the colors of the dynasty now on the throne, and the peacock feathers are in evidence. The people are well schooled in honoring the reigning monarch. Long strips of red and yellow paper hang from the walls, on which are written prayers or words which indicate that they are for the payment of a peace offering to the demons. On the side of the room, directly opposite the entrance, is a flue or open fireplace, and by the side of it a drum. The worshipper lights his prayer paper, and as it burns the draught of the flue carries it out of sight to the demons which await the offering. To attract their attention the drum is beaten, and its mournful notes awaken strange feelings in those who hear it for the first time in the gloomy precincts of this idolatrous temple. Turning away from the flue one faces the prayer mat upon which the devout Confucian falls, and to which he bows his forehead with many genuflections. In his hands he holds two half-round pieces of wood, in the form of split beans. If he is offering prayers for prosperity in the next cargo of rice or tea, he will, after offering his sacrifice in the form of a swine or a fowl, let fall these prayer sticks, and on the particular way they rest on the mat depends the answer to his supplication. If the answer be unpropitious he may repeat again and again till the sticks fall in the fortunate form; then he is satisfied.

A moment's observation touches one with the pathos of the whole performance, for the sincerity of the heathen none can doubt, but the childishness of the matter is saddening to those who have learned the better way. On an elaborately carved and gilded altar is the offering to the god of Joss. As intimated, it may be a swine roasted whole, or fowl; it may be tea or some other decoction as drink; but we have never seen the altar without a sacrifice on it in the many times we have been in these places. In a dark recess immediately behind the altar is the god, in the form of a most repulsive Chinese figure, with long black beard. Nothing can exceed the malignant expression of this idol as his dark features are illumined by the light which flickers from a crystal cup suspended in front by an invisible cord. The shrine is decorated, as are the other parts of the place, with much paper and feathers, which are covered with dust and cobwebs; and the odor of burning punk-sticks and smell of the half-roasted meat make the visitor feel that a charnel house is not far away. Depression of feeling to those who visit such places is an almost universal experience, and one there for the first time realizes the delights of worshipping in the Christian forms, where congregations gather as friends, and where to the power and sympathy of numbers are added the inspiring themes of sacred praise and sermonic instruction. The Joss House sees no congregation, hears no song of praise, and no inspiring discourse which lifts the thought and heart to better things for time and eternity, but gloom and uncertainty attend the solitary worshipper through all. Who that has 'tasted of the good gift of God, and the powers of the world to come,' can withhold pity for a brother redeemed who thus bows down to demons?

The funeral customs of the Chinese are peculiar. One of the most prized gifts that a child can bestow on a parent is a coffin. These may be received at any time in life, and many have stored the coffin in the home for years. On the other hand death has a terror of which we know nothing for the Chinese mind. The upper air being full of demons, who await the death hour, it is believed that the dying one should not be kept in the dwelling, but in some outhouse. This is a precaution against an invasion of these malignant spirits. On this account, instead of the patients passing away among the friends in the home, they are taken to some place where they may escape the notice of these denizens of the upper air. When a person of note and wealth is to be buried, the day is one of the greatest excitement, and large amounts of money have been spent in this country at such a time. At one funeral which took place in the city of Victoria, the street was laid with several platforms, on which was an abundance of many kinds of confectionery and other foods.

The secret orders to which the deceased belonged were out in full regalia, with banners and drums, and for hours the funeral services went on in the open street. The priests were dressed in robes of white, and went through numerous ceremonies and offerings of prayers. The funeral cortege was followed for a distance by hired mourners, men dressed to resemble women. Their pig-tails were combed out, and the long black hair, dishevelled and falling to the

ground as they bowed down in their assumed grief, made up a scene
which was pathetic in the extreme.

After the coffin came the attendant whose duty it was to scatter
the 'cash-paper,' which was to deceive the demons who were after
the soul of the departed. The red strips of paper, which were
scattered all the way from the house to the grave, were a sort of
bogus money which for the time being kept the demons back. When
the grave was covered the sacrificed swine was placed upon it as an
offering and safeguard. We have been told that in the early days in
British Columbia the offering at the grave was left there, but finding
that the Indians, without compunction, made a feast of the sacrifice,
the Chinese concluded that it was as well for them to bring it home
for the same purpose, and this rule is now followed. In all this we
behold the tremendous struggle of these dark-minded heathen to get
free from the terrors of evil in the world, and ever without finding
the way.

The Japanese question is a more recent one than the Chinese. It is
more serious, from the fact that Japan is an ally of Great Britain,
and a Japanese is not content to remain a hewer of wood or drawer
of water, but crowds into all lines of industries, and competes — and
successfully, too — with the white man. It is said that the British
Columbia fishing business is now almost entirely in the hands of the
little brown men. The latest development is the proposed establishment of a farm colony in Southern Alberta. The majority of the
recent arrivals have come from Hawaii, not direct from Japan. The
Mikado's Government has promised the Dominion authorities that
the clause in the treaty in regard to emigration to Canada will be
strictly enforced. By this clause only six hundred a year are allowed
to enter the Dominion; these must have passports, and no Japanese
are allowed to enter except direct from their native land. This, it is
hoped, will stop the influx from the Hawaiian Islands, and prevent
an inundation such as threatened British Columbia during the fall of
1907.

As for the Hindu problem, it is the most recent and in some ways
the most difficult of all, for the reason that the Hindu is a British
subject, and many of those who have arrived during the past year
have been veterans of the British army, proudly wearing medals of
honor. To bar them out, as British Columbia endeavored to do by

1 Japanese mining camp on Queen Charlotte Islands
2 Japanese mine owner (Christian) and miners, Queen Charlotte Islands
3 Chinese Methodist Mission, Vancouver
4 Japanese Methodist Mission, Vancouver

means of the Natal Act, which calls for an educational test, might, as can be readily seen, easily precipitate trouble in restless India. The uneasiness of the people of British Columbia, face to face with the possibility of the hordes of the Indian Empire swarming in upon them, can be readily imagined. The immigration of the Hindus rests a great deal upon the encouragement they get from the transportation companies. As these are now apparently endeavoring to discourage such immigration, it is expected that it will dwindle down without drastic measures.

Most of the Hindus who have come to Canada are Sikhs from the Punjab. As to the caste, they are said to be a mixture of Kshatrigas and Sudras. Physically they form a great contrast to the Chinese and Japanese; they are tall and gaunt, with dark skin and black hair, and their features are clear-cut. They appear intelligent, and their military bearing impresses one favorably.

The Hindu is a rather picturesque figure. When he arrives his dress consists of an undergarment, a pair of scanty pantaloons, and probably an old military coat; but he gradually adopts the Canadian costume, retaining his turban. The effect is often decidedly grotesque. So far the Hindus have been employed only in the lowest kinds of manual labor. They are very slow, and do not seem capable of hard, continuous exertion. Their diet is light, and physically, they are not adapted to the rigorous climate of Canada.

Owing to his peculiarities, the Hindu cannot work with men of other nations; indeed, only with Hindus of his own caste. He must prepare his own food, and that of a particular kind. Opinions differ as to the cleanliness of these Sikhs. They have certain religious ablutions, about which they are very punctilious, but since coming to this country they have lived herded together in the most wretched fashion. Poor people! This may have been their misfortune, rather than their fault. But their standards of living and manner of life and thought are far different from ours. However estimable they may be in India, they are sadly out of place in Canada.

Certain objections hold good with regard to all these Eastern peoples. It is true that they may be able to do much of the rough work, for which it is difficult to secure sufficient white labor; but where they enter, the whites are out, and out permanently. They constitute an entirely distinct class or caste. They have their own virtues and vices; their own moral standards and religious beliefs. The Orientals cannot be assimilated. Whether it is in the best interests of Canada to allow them to enter in large numbers is a most important question, not only for the people of British Columbia, but for all Canadians.

Chapter 16

The Negro and the Indian

NEITHER the negro nor the Indian are immigrants, and yet they are so entirely different from the ordinary white population that some mention of them is necessary if we would understand the complexity of our problems. We group them merely because both stand out entirely by themselves.

THE NEGRO

Contiguity to the United States is accountable largely for our negro population. The majority of the 20,000 negroes now in Canada are the descendants of those who escaped from slavery into British dominions. They are living chiefly in the towns of Western Ontario and the Maritime Provinces. In the cities they often crowd together and form a 'quarter,' where sanitary and moral conditions are most prejudicial to the public welfare. Blood, rather than language or religion, is the chief barrier that separates them from the rest of the community.

John R. Commons, writing in the *Chautauquan* (November, 1903), thus describes the negro: 'In Africa the people are unstable, indifferent to suffering, and "easily aroused to ferocity by the sight of blood or under great fear." They exhibit certain qualities which are associated with their descendants in this country, namely, aversion to silence and solitude, love of rhythm, excitability, and lack of reserve. All travellers speak of their impulsiveness, strong sexual passion, and lack of will power.' He points out what a momentous change it was to this people to be shifted from equatorial Africa to the temperate regions of America; from an environment of savagery to one of civilization. Then he speaks of their present relationship to the free institutions of America. 'The very qualities of intelligence and manliness which are essential for citizenship in a democracy were systematically expunged from the negro race through two hundred years of slavery. And then, by the cataclysm of a war of emancipation, in which it took no part, this race, after many thousand years of savagery and two centuries of slavery, was suddenly let loose into the liberty of citizenship and the electoral suffrage. The world never before had seen such a triumph of dogmatism and partisanship.' Whether we agree with the conclusion or not, we may be thankful that we have no 'negro problem' in Canada.

Many negroes are members of various Protestant churches, and are consistent Christians and highly respected citizens. The African

Methodist Episcopal Church, organized in 1816, has about 130 churches, with a membership of 3,000.

THE INDIANS

One of the most pathetic sights is that of an Indian stepping off a sidewalk to let a white man pass, or turning out of a prairie trail to give a white man the right of way. Once the Indians were proud autochthones; now they are despised natives; aborigines, yet outcasts; belated survivors of an earlier age, strangers in the land of their fathers.

Roughly speaking, the Indians may be divided into three classes — the Indians of Eastern Canada, those in the 'North-West,' and those in British Columbia. To these might be added the Eskimos of the far North, who, however, are yet outside our modern civilization. The last census gives 127,932 Indians and halfbreeds. The Indians of the East have already taken their place in the new life, and some are as prosperous as their white neighbors. Most of the Indians of the North-West have treaty rights. In general, each man, woman, and child receives annually $5.00, the councillors $15.00, and the chiefs $25.00, with a uniform every three years. In addition there is an annual allowance of ammunition, tools, etc. Reserves have been set apart allowing about 128 acres per head, and schools are maintained on the reserves. Many of the Indians are becoming successful farmers, but there are serious difficulties. The Rev. Thompson Ferrier writes:

On the reserve the white man's vices have taken a deeper root than his virtues. His fire-water has demoralized whole tribes, and the diseases he has introduced have annihilated many ... The Indian is growing up with the idea firmly fixed in his head that the Government owes him a living, and his happiness and prosperity depend in no degree upon his individual effort. Rations and treaty are all right for the aged, helpless, and infirm. Strong and able-bodied Indians hang around for rations and treaty, neglecting other duties and the cultivation of their land, in order to secure what in many cases could be earned several times over in the same length of time. The system destroys his energy, push, and independence ...

As fast as our Indian, whether of mixed or full blood, is capable of taking care of himself, it is our duty to set him on his feet, and sever forever the ties that bind him either to his tribe or the

Government. Both Church and State should have, as a final goal, the destruction and end of treaty and reservation life.

Mr. Ferrier thinks that the main hope lies in giving the young generation a good, practical training in specially organized industrial schools.*

The Indian population of British Columbia numbers 24,964. The income for 1907 was $1,541,922, or an average of $61.78 for every member of that population. Grouping them in families of four, the income becomes for the family $247.12. Of the British Columbia Indian, Dr. Whittington writes:

The sources of this income are catching, curing and canning fish; fur hunting; logging, boat-building, stevedoring, as sailors, farming, mining, etc. The women, of course, assist materially, and also the children, at inside work in the canneries, also in selling various kinds of handiwork. Apart from this the living of the Indians is easily obtained to a very considerable extent along the lines of fish, venison and small fruits, as well as farm produce. If it be a question of living, the Indian of to-day is very much nearer to the civilized white than to his pagan ancestor. Modern homes, modern clothing, modern education are, to a great extent, the order of the day, and are rapidly becoming more so. The Indian is in a transition stage from his old-time to his modern environment. I cannot but say that the journey is more than half done. The white man's vices are the most baneful of all the evil influences at work on the Indian. Another pernicious influence has been the mistaken kindness of the State in helping the Indian instead of simply helping him to help himself.**

Much missionary work, evangelistic, educational, industrial and medical, has been done among the Indians. Many are devout Christians living exemplary lives, but there are still 10,202 Indians in our Dominion, as grossly pagan as were their ancestors, or still more wretched, half civilized, only to be debauched. Surely the Indians have a great claim upon Canadian Christians!

  * See *Indian Education in the North-West*, by Rev. Thomson Ferrier.
 ** See *The British Columbian Indian and His Future*, by Rev. R. Whittington, DD.

Chapter 17

The problem of immigration

There are two classes who would pass upon the immigration question. One says, 'Close the doors and let in nobody'; the other says, 'Open wide the doors and let in everybody.' I am in sympathy with neither of these classes. There is a happy middle path — a path of discernment and judgment.
COMMISSIONER WATCHORN

To know anything about the actual character of recent and present immigration we must distinguish the many and diverse elements of which it is composed.
S. McLANAHAN

Emphatically too many people are now coming over here; too many of an undesirable sort. In 1902 over seven-tenths were from races who do not rapidly assimilate with the customs and institutions of this country.
PRESCOTT F. HALL

A circle ... including the sources of the present immigration to the United States would have its centre in Constantinople.
ASSISTANT COMMISSIONER McSWEENEY, quoted by HUNTER

Just as a body cannot with safety accept nourishment any faster than it is capable of assimilating it, so a state cannot accept an excessive influx of people without serious injury.
H. H. BAYESEN

IMMIGRATION and transportation are the two questions of greatest importance to Canada. From the situation, extent and character of the country, transportation must always be one of the leading factors in industrial and commercial development. But as men are greater than things, so immigration is greater than transportation. Canada has many problems, but they all dwindle into insignificance before the one great, commanding, overwhelming problem of immigration. Of vital importance to us are the character, the welfare and the development of the peoples who are to be the people of Canada.

Perhaps we can best approach our subject by studying the immigration movement in the United States. Great social and economic developments over-ride political divisions.

The following table shows the population and the foreign immigration during the last century:

Year	Population	Foreign immigration for decade
1790	3,929,214	
1800	5,308,483	50,000
1810	7,239,881	70,000
1820	9,633,822	114,000
1830	12,866,020	143,439
1840	17,069,473	559,125
1850	23,191,876	1,713,251
1860	31,443,321	2,598,214
1870	38,558,371	2,314,824
1880	50,155,783	2,812,191
1890	62,622,250	5,246,613
1900	75,559,258	3,687,564

Total immigration, 1820-1900, 19,229,224

Now, who were these immigrants, and why did they come, and what did their coming mean to the American Republic?

Going back to the old colonial days, the 'immigrants' to America were from England. In one sense they were immigrants. They 'came into' the country. But they ought rather to be distinguished as colonists. They set forth to unknown lands to found colonies in which they might enjoy those civil and religious liberties which were dearer to them than life itself. These colonists were some of England's noblest sons and daughters.

The Puritans in New England, the Quakers in Pennsylvania, the Cavaliers in Virginia — these laid the foundations. How different they and their coming from the immigration of to-day! They made great sacrifices. They had to undertake a long, expensive and perilous journey. They came to an unexplored wilderness inhabited only by savages. They had to create a civilization. To-day our immigrants, or their friends, pay a few pounds' passage money, and in a week or so are safely transported to a land with institutions similar to their own, and in which they hope at once to 'do better' than they did at home.

Besides the English of the early days there were the enterprising Dutch merchants who ventured forth across the seas and pushed their trade in regions unknown. Later two other elements were added, the Germans and the Scotch-Irish. The sturdy Germans came for political, military and economic reasons. They have had no small influence on the American national life.

The Scotch-Irish were a progressive class, well fitted to adapt themselves to new conditions and to help build up the new country. J. R. Commons, in the *Chautauquan,* says that 'they took the lead in developing the type now known as the American.'

A different and less desirable class of immigrants now began to arrive. Greatest in numbers and importance were the Irish. The potato rot in Ireland in 1846 drove thousands from their homes. Since then there has been a steady stream of those who sought to escape from poverty and from the hated rule of England. They have played no small part in the political life of the United States. Immigrants kept coming from England and Scotland and Germany. A large immigration of Scandinavians set in. Each decade drained a wider area of Europe; but the large majority were people fitted for the new civilization.

About 1882 a remarkable change took place in the character of immigration. Southeastern Europe had been tapped and the stream came with a rush.

J. R. Commons, in the article above quoted, says:

A line drawn across the Continent of Europe from northeast to
southwest, separating the Scandinavian Peninsula, the British Isles,
Germany and France from Russia, Austria-Hungary, Italy and
Turkey, separates countries not only of distinct races but also of
distinct civilizations. It separates Protestant Europe from Catholic
Europe; it separates countries of representative institutions and
popular government from absolute monarchies. It separates lands
where education is universal from lands where illiteracy predomi-
nates; it separates manufacturing countries, progressive agriculture
and skilled labor from primitive hand industries, backward agriculture and unskilled labor; it separates an educated, thrifty peasantry
from a peasantry scarcely a single generation removed from serfdom;
it separates Teutonic races from Latin, Slav, Semitic and Mongolian
races.

Prescott F. Hall writes in his valuable book on *Immigration and
Its Effect upon the United States:*

How marked the change in nationality has been is shown by the fact
that in 1869 not 1 per cent of the total immigration came from
Austria-Hungary, Italy, Poland and Russia; in 1902 the percentage
was over 70. On the other hand, in 1869 nearly three-quarters of the
total immigration came from the United Kingdom, France, Germany
and Scandinavia. In 1902 only one-fifth was from these countries.
Or, to put it another way, in 1869 the immigrants from Austria-
Hungary, Italy, Poland, and Russia were about one-hundredth of the
number from the United Kingdom, France, Germany and Scandinavia; in 1880 about one-tenth; in 1894 nearly equal to it, and in
1902 three and one-half times as great. In 1903 the largest element
in immigration was the Southern Italian with 196,117 souls, and the
next largest was the Polish, with 82,343. Considering the immigration of 1904 by the great racial divisions, we have the following
result, in striking contrast to the days when immigration was almost
entirely Teutonic and Celtic:

	Number	Per cent total immigration
Slavic	272,396	33.5
Teutonic	195,287	24.0
Iberic	186,607	22.9
Celtic	98,635	12.1
Mongolic	20,616	2.5
All others	39,329	4.8

Another way of looking at the subject is by comparing the total immigration of certain nationalities for the period, 1821 to 1902, with that for the year 1903:

	1821-1902		1903	
Country	Number	Per cent	Number	Per cent
Austria-Hungary	1,316,914	6.5	206,011	24.0
England and Wales	2,739,937	13.4	26,219	3.0
Germany	5,098,005	24.9	40,086	4.7
Ireland	3,944,269	19.3	35,300	4.1
Italy	1,358,597	6.7	230,622	26.9
Norway and Sweden	1,334,931	6.6	70,489	8.2
Russia and Poland	1,106,362	5.4	136,093	15.9
British North America	1,050,682	5.1		

The foregoing table shows not only the nations which have added chiefly to our population in the past, and which are adding to-day, but how the percentage of each has varied in the period before 1902 compared with 1903. If the same proportions had obtained in the earlier period as during the later, how different might our country and its institutions now be!

Just at this stage Canada becomes a field for immigration. Just when restriction leagues are being formed in the United States and rigid immigration laws are being enacted, Canada adopts a 'progressive immigration policy,' and puts forth every effort to secure immigrants. It is true that our relations with the Mother Land are such that we are receiving a large number of Britishers. But we are also receiving immigrants from all parts of Europe – that is, we are taking our place side by side with the United States as the Old World's dumping ground. As the sluices are closed there, the flood will be diverted to Canada, whatever the policy of the Government may happen to be. As the free lands are taken in the United States, and the pressure of population begins to be felt, the flood will flow in upon us as surely as water finds its level.

Compare the population of Canada with that of the United States a century ago:

1790	United States	3,929,214
1891	Canadian	4,833,239
1800	United States	5,308,483
1901	Canadian	5,371,315

It will be seen that the United States stood a century ago, with regard to numbers, where we stand to-day. But what a difference in immigration!

From 1800 to 1810 there was an immigration to the United States of 70,000, or 7,000 a year. During the corresponding decade it seems probable that the immigration to Canada will be between 2,000,000 and 3,000,000.

In Canada our immigration for 1901 was 49,149, a number not reached in The United States until 1831.

Last year our immigration was over a quarter of a million, a mark not reached in the United States until 1849.

When the United States contained our population they received one settler – and found it difficult enough to Americanize him. We receive thirty-six. What about our task?

In 1906 the immigration to the United States was about 1.4 per cent of the population. Until recently it has not exceeded 1 per cent. Our immigration last year was about 4 per cent of our population.

When it is considered how slow is the natural increase in a nation – that is, the excess of births over deaths – it becomes evident what an enormous strain is being put upon our institutions. We, as Canadians, must do in one year what under normal conditions would be spread over many years. Fancy a mother with her own baby to care for adopting half a dozen other babies — some of them, too, of very uncertain tempers!

Fancy a family increased suddenly by the presence of several strange children! What a problem to feed and clothe them — to train them and educate them — to instil into them the family traditions and impart to them the family spirit!

English and Russians, French and Germans, Austrians and Italians, Japanese and Hindus — a mixed multitude, they are being dumped into Canada by a kind of endless chain. They sort themselves out after a fashion, and each seeks to find a corner somewhere. But how shall we weld this heterogeneous mass into one people? That is our problem.

Chapter 18

The causes of immigration

History, from our standpoint, may be considered the story of race immigration and its effects. The Tartar invasion of Europe, the Roman invasion and conquest of a considerable part of three continents, the Germanic invasion of the Roman Empire, the invasion of America by the Spaniards and afterwards by the English, as well as the peaceful immigration of recent times on an enormous scale, are facts of the greatest magnitude.
HALL

MIGRATION is one of the most primitive instincts of the human race. The approach of winter drives the birds to a warmer climate. A drought drives the bison to new feeding grounds. Similar causes have driven wandering tribes of hunters to seek new hunting-grounds, or pastoral peoples to discover better grazing for their flocks. Then came the desire of conquest, as when the vast hordes of barbarians swept across Europe, pillaging the country as they went. In the process of civilization, higher motives influenced men; they could not live by bread alone; they must have freedom of thought and action. Unable to live out their highest lives at home they set sail for the New World in search of freedom. The hard realities of existence, or the desire for a better existence, are the primary causes of all migrations.

Emigration and immigration are the two sides of the shield. People *go out* of one country to *come into* another. The causes of emigration and immigration are the same – a dissatisfaction with the life at home – the hope of a better life elsewhere.

Why do people emigrate from Europe? Why seek a better country? Take those from Great Britain. Many of them are from the great cities where work is often difficult to obtain, wages are low, and all the effects of a relentless competitive system are most keenly felt. There is nothing to hope for. The workhouse probably lies at the end of the journey. Then there are young men and women who are keen to make their fortunes, but who feel the limitations of the old land. Again there are parents who desire for their children better things than they themselves have enjoyed.

In Scandinavian countries the hard struggle for existence has driven thousands of sturdy immigrants to search for more fertile lands.

If we pass to the countries of Southern Europe, we find that the conditions are almost intolerable. The poor peasants are taxed so heavily that there is little left to support life. In parts of Russia, for several months in the year, they are regularly on the verge of starvation. The course black bread fails. How they eke out an existence is a mystery!

In South Italy the pressure of the population is so great that people are driven out to seek food to maintain life.

Some, as the Poles, come to escape the tyranny of a government which they hate. Some, as the Jews, come to escape religious persecution. Christians from Turkish dominions flee for their lives.

1 Roumanians in national costume – the children attend All Peoples'
   Kindergarten, Winnipeg
2 A bit of Russia transplanted – a Greek Church ceremony, 'Blessing the
   Waters' – Bishop Seraphim blessing the waters of the Red River, Winnipeg

The trouble is often not merely the infertility of the soil; the whole social system is iniquitous. The new fortunate (?) live in luxury at the expense of the many. Privileged classes prey on the masses. The state exists not for the good of the people, but to gratify the ambition of a few leaders. Immense standing armies are maintained at an enormous expense, their existence perpetuating ancient jealousies and strifes. The church, organized to defend, joins in spoiling the people. Some one has bitterly said that the poor European peasant is working for two masters — for the church, for the salvation of his soul, and for the army, for the salvation of his body, so that he has no time to work for himself.

Asiatic immigration stands in a class by itself. China, Japan and India are the most densely populated countries in the world. The surplus population seeks an outlet.

Overcrowding, poverty, oppression, taxation, persecution, compulsory military service — these are the great causes of emigration.

Let us turn to the other side. Why do these people come to Canada? America, generally, has had a time of wonderful prosperity. It is a new land — almost an unoccupied land — of vast extent and wonderful resources. It is a land of freedom — of democratic government; a land where every man has a chance; a land without a past to darken the glowing colors of the ideal future. It appears to offer the immigrant just that which he has not had. So immigration has turned toward the New World — the United States, South America and now Canada.

Such are the great economic causes of emigration and immigration. Poverty there — prosperity here. In addition, there are important contributory causes that must be considered. First of all comes transportation. In the olden days travel was slow and costly. With the few small sailing vessels of a century ago any large movement of the peoples would have been impossible. Then, too, there was no means of conveying settlers inland from the ocean ports. Now all is changed. Our great ocean steamships and our railway systems make it possible to transport annually millions of people. It is only a few weeks now from Central Russia to Central Canada — only a few days from London to Montreal. With speed and capacity have come cheap rates. It is now comparatively easy for all except the poorest to cross the Atlantic. In fact, thousands of Italian laborers find it cheaper to return to Italy for the winter than to spend the cold months in New

York. Space has been almost annihilated; hence, the people are, as it were, at our doors.

How do the people know of our country of opportunity? Here come in the great advertising agencies. Of first importance are the settlers themselves; they come; they prosper; they write home to their friends. The successful immigrant is the best advertising agent. Dr. Allan McLaughlin states that 40 per cent to 55 per cent of the immigrants to the United States come on tickets prepaid by friends in the United States. The condition in Canada is much the same. One immigrant put it, 'We better our condition by selling our physical strength to the Canadian people. We make money and send it home to better the condition of those at home.' Immigrants send back for their relatives. Their letters are eagerly read by all the friends, often by the entire village. Next year scores or hundreds decide to come to such a good land.

Next comes the advertising done by the steamship companies. They and their agents are anxious to secure passengers and offer every inducement. We cannot state the position better than by quoting from the 1903 report of the American Commissioner-General of Immigration:

The deplorable political and financial conditions of the eastern and southern countries of Europe create a large natural emigration to our shores. The most convincing proof in thy eyes of the people in these countries of the exceptional prosperity of our country is the large sums of money, almost unprecedented to them, which annually arrive from friends and relatives residing in the United States. Besides this natural emigration, however, we are burdened with a dangerous and most injurious unnatural immigration which from year to year assumes larger proportions. This unnatural immigration consists of paupers and assisted emigrants, and is induced and brought about by the unscrupulous and greedy activity displayed by a large number of agencies and sub-agencies having well-established connections in the United States and abroad, apparently unknown to the steamship companies, which activity manifests itself in the peddling of steamship tickets and prepaids on the installment plan, both here and abroad; the constant agitation and offers of inducements by sub-agents in Europe, occupying semi-public positions, who in order to earn commissions play upon the grievance and susceptibility of the plain peasant, frequently inducing him to sell or mortgage all his belongings for the purpose of raising the necessary travelling expenses, which latter transaction is also turned to profit by such agent.

Then we have the advertising of those who desire to obtain cheap labor or to sell land. Again and again great contractors have sent to Europe for their men. Perhaps the most notable example in the United States was the securing of Slavs to operate the Pennsylvania coal mines. Here in Canada the presence of such large numbers of Hindus and Japanese is doubtless due to inducements offered by those seeking cheap labor.

We all know, too, the part that the real estate agent has had in encouraging immigration from the United States. Pamphlets issued by land companies have been sent broadcast throughout the Western States.

During the last few years charitable organizations have been responsible for the coming of many immigrants. In Great Britain, the Salvation Army, the Church Army, and several Children's Homes have assisted thousands of immigrants. So great has been the distress in the cities of the Old Land that the authorities themselves have spent large sums in sending the poor to Canada. This is much the easiest and cheapest way to get rid of them, and, from the Old Country standpoint, doubtless highly to be commended. The various Jewish societies, too, have been very active in assisting their co-religionists to emigrate. Many of our Jewish immigrants have been helped in this way.

In Canada the Government itself has become an advertising agency. Immigration offices have been opened in many countries, literature has been distributed and Canadian exhibits have been shown throughout the country. At every great exhibition Canada has had a splendid display. Lecturers go the round of the villages, and perhaps most effective of all, a bonus of $5.00 is paid on each immigrant from certain countries who is booked to Canada.

Whether such a 'progressive immigration policy' is the best for Canada is perhaps a matter of opinion — certainly a very vigorous and successful campaign has been carried on for some years. We append an extract from the last report of the Canadian Superintendent of Immigration; the character of the literature is indicative of the work of the department:

The volume of work at headquarters has not shown any diminution.
In the nine months ending March 31, 1906, 90,557 attachments
were made to our files; during the similar period covered by this
report the number of attachments was 102,956, and during this
same period 226,358 requests for information, direct and indirect,
were attended to, and 2,957,027 pamphlets, etc., were sent out.

The following is a statement showing immigration literature
ordered during the nine months referred to:

Gaelic pamphlet	10,000
The Canadian West	1,500
Symposium of Ideas and Prophecies	1,500
The Canadian West	100,000
Reliable Information	2,000
Western Canada, a Land of Unequalled Opportunities	2,000
Great Growth of Western Canada	2,000
Western Canada, a Land of Unprecedented Progress	2,000
Book of Lectures	200
The Story of Western Canada Crop	300,000
Farm and Ranch Review	5,000
Canadian Year Book	5,000
Prince Edward Island pamphlet	30,000
Immigration Act	40,000
Canada in a Nutshell	100,000
Home Building in Canada	115,000
Classes Wanted in Canada	50,000
Land Regulations	50,000
Canada Wants Domestic Servants	50,000
A Travers le Canada	20,000
Illustrated Pamphlet of Winnipeg	1,000
Everyman's Geology of Three Prairie Provinces of the Canadian West	5,000
Eastern Townships	30,000
Reduced Rates for Settlers	100,000
How to Succeed in Canada	200,000
Canada, Work, Wages and Land (English)	200,000
Canada, Work, Wages and Land (Danish)	20,000
Canada, Work, Wages and Land (Norwegian)	20,000
Canada, Work, Wages and Land (Finnish)	20,000

Canada, Work, Wages and Land (German)	20,000
Canada, Work, Wages and Land (Swedish)	20,000
Canada, Work, Wages and Land (French)	20,000
Canada, Work, Wages and Land (Belgian)	20,000
Canada, the Land of Opportunity (English)	200,000
Canada, the Land of Opportunity (Swedish)	50,000
Canada, the Land of Opportunity (Norwegian)	50,000
Canada, the Land of Opportunity (Finnish)	50,000
Canada, the Land of Opportunity (Danish)	50,000
Canada, the Land of Opportunity (Flemish)	50,000
Canada, the Land of Opportunity (French)	50,000
Western Canada	500
Climate of Canada	500
Western Canada Early Days	500
Western Canada Crop Prospects	500
What Canada Possesses	500
Letters from Successful Settlers (French)	20,000
Hangers	50,000
Facts for Settlers	100,000
Last Best West	375,000

MAPS

School Map of Canada (English)	30,000
School Map of Canada (French)	5,000
Battleford Map	10,500
Where and How (Folder Map)	100,000
Manitoba, Saskatchewan and Alberta Map	11,000
Small Dominion of Canada Map	5,000

NEWSPAPERS

Alberta German Herald	10,000
Morning Chronicle, Halifax	15,000
Le Courier de l'Ouest	10,000
Saskatoon Phoenix	10,000
Hungarian paper, Winnipeg	15,000
Polish paper, Winnipeg	10,000
German paper, Battleford	25,000
The Canada (Swedish weekly)	18,000
Der Nordwesten (German)	36,000

Logberg (Icelandic)	36,000
Outdoor Canada	450
Canadian Life and Resources	4,500
Danebrog (Danish)	9,000
Canada, London, England	18,750
Christmas Globe	200

There has been an extraordinary demand in recent years for farm help in the Province of Ontario, and in order to assist as far as possible in meeting this demand the plan will be tried this year of employing agents on commission. We have in view somewhere in the neighborhood of 200 men, residing in agricultural centres in this province, who will, I think, be found willing and able to render valuable assistance in the distribution of immigrants of the farm laborer class. A wide distribution of the help coming in will thus be insured, and the expense to the department will be very moderate, as we will only pay for work actually done.

The operations of the department for the fractional fiscal year in the United States are reported on by the Inspector of Agencies, Mr. White, and the medical service is dealt with in Dr. Bryce's report.

I have received a report from the Women's National Immigration Society, 87 Osborne Street, Montreal, showing that during the nine months ending the 31st March, 1908, 393 immigrants passed through the home maintained by this society at the above address, and the secretary states that the class of women arriving was most satisfactory, and that all are doing well.

The Ottawa Valley Immigration Aid Society, which received some financial assistance from the department, has continued to do good work during the year, the society's register showing an average of something over 200 visitors per month, and a large distribution of advertising matter. From the annual report I learn that the society arranged for ten lectures, and directed the placing of 661 settlers – 350 in New Ontario, 190 in New Quebec, and 121 in the Western Provinces.

The active and useful work carried on for a number of years by the Quebec and Lake St. John Repatriation and Colonization Society for the Province of Quebec has now been taken over by our department, and the secretary and some other members of the staff of the society have become employees of the department. Offices in connection with this special work are now maintained in Quebec and in Biddeford, Maine, and the arrangement is, I think, likely to be productive of good results.

Your obedient servant,

W. D. Scott,

Superintendent of Immigration.

Chapter 19

The effects of immigration

RACIAL, ECONOMIC, SOCIAL, POLITICAL

It is extremely undesirable that thousands of foreigners of questionable value from a mental, moral and physical point of view should be
allowed to freely invade well-governed and prosperous communities.
They underbid the labor market, raise important and vexatious
municipal questions, strain charitable resources to the utmost,
increase the cost of government, expose a healthy people to contagious diseases common to the poorer classes of Europe, corrupt
the body politic, and in every way complicate a situation none too
simple at best.
WHELPLEY

So far as mere commercial and material progress is concerned, a
heterogeneous people may be as successful as any. But where depth
and not breadth is concerned, that freedom from distraction and
multiplicity which results from the prevalence of a distinct type and
the universality of certain standards and ideals seems almost essential
to the development of extraordinary products in any line.
HALL

Foreign immigration into this country has from the time it first
assumed large proportions amounted not to a reinforcement of our
population but a replacement of native by foreign stock ... The
American shrank from the industrial competition thus thrust upon
him. He was unwilling himself to engage in the lowest kind of day
labor with these new elements of population; he was even more
unwilling to bring sons and daughters into the world to enter into
that competition. The more rapidly foreigners came into the United
States the smaller was the rate of increase, not merely among the
native population separately, but throughout the population of the
country as a whole.
F. A. WALKER

PRESCOTT F. HALL, in his splendid work on *Immigration and Its Effect upon the United States,* classifies the effects under four divisions – racial, economic, social, and political. We cannot do better than adopt his classification, at the same time urging our readers to study carefully this problem, which is essentially the same for the United States and Canada.

RACIAL EFFECTS

America is not American. Canada will not remain Canadian. During the first half of the past century there came to be a fairly well-defined American type – that is, the true American had certain distinctive physical, mental, and social characteristics. But so great has been the alien immigration that it is a question whether the older American type will predominate. New England was English. America is to-day, in many respects, more nearly German or Irish than it is English. If the Slavic or Latin elements predominate, what will it become?

We in Canada are at the beginning of the process, and can only speculate as to the result. It is conceivable that the various races coming to us might remain absolutely distinct. Canada would then simply be a congeries of races. But such a condition is not possible. Some peoples may not intermarry. The Mongolians, the Hindus, and the negroes will probably remain largely distinct. Even then the presence of these has a very decided influence on the other races. The Southern States would have had a vastly different history if the slaves had never been imported. The presence of incompatible elements changes the entire social and political life of a country; it is a fatal barrier to the highest national life. But in time most of these peoples will intermarry – Slavs and Celts, Latins and Germans, Hungarian and Semitic peoples, in varying combinations and proportions. From a physical standpoint, what will be the result? Mentally and morally, what type will prevail? Each has something to contribute. What form will each take in combination? All are poured into the crucible. Who can guess the resultant product?

It would be an interesting study to trace some of the modifications that are already taking place in the English people in Canada, some of them due to the presence of other peoples, some of them to environment. In a score of ways, Canadian English are not the Old Country type. But we must cross to the United States to see these modifications carried a little further. Physically and socially, what a difference! And these differences in type are bound to react on all our institutions. Grasserie compares the government possible in Latin and Germanic countries:

The ethnic character has a profound influence on the choice between the two modes of government. With some peoples individual autonomy — independence of character — is strongly traced; for example, among the Germanic nations. Each one engages only his extreme exterior in society. With nations of such temperament family life is strongly developed; the *home* is the sacred ark. With some other peoples — with the Latin nations in general — it is quite different. The autonomy is less refractory, they like to live in society, and prefer to discharge the functions of thinking and wishing upon others. The will not being carefully cultivated, it diminishes, and the State acts for the individual.

Very decidedly the social life and ideals of the people of the United States have been affected by alien races. Already government — especially the government in the cities where the proportion of foreigners is greatest — is being modified to a large extent.

We can already perceive changes in Canada. The Westerner differs from the Easterner, not merely because East is East and West is West, but because of the mixed character of the population of the West. The character of the Eastern cities, too, is changing. The people on the street differ in physique from those of a decade ago. Social distinctions, hitherto unknown, are being recognized. A hundred years from now who and what shall we be?

There is an unfounded optimism that confidently asserts that all this mingling of the races is in the highest interest of our country. We get the strength of the North, the beauty of the South, and the wisdom of the East; such is the line of thought often presented in after-dinner speeches.

We, too, must confess to a certain optimism, based not altogether on natural law, that ultimately a higher type may be developed. In the older and more permanent races and civilizations there is little variation from type; they are conservative, fixed, stationary. But with the mingling of the races there is a greater tendency to variation. The newer nations are in a state of unstable equilibrium. They are capable of being moved, of developing. There is the opportunity for change. Will the change be for better or worse?

Surely the whole conception of evolution is founded on the implicit faith that the world is moving toward higher things, and that spiritual forces are destined to prevail. Example, training, higher motives, religious impulses are more potent than race characteristics, and will determine the future of our people.

ECONOMIC EFFECTS

There has been much discussion as to the value of the immigrant. Immigrants from the United States to Canada have often brought thousands of dollars. This seems to be a straight gain to the country. But the amount of money brought from other countries is not great. Hall has prepared the following table, which shows the amount of money per capita owned by the immigrants at the port of entry in 1900; this will be approximately as true for the same nationalities in Canada as any table that could be compiled from Canadian statistics:

Scotch	$41 51	Irish	$14 50
Japanese	39 59	Syrian	14 31
English	38 90	Chinese	13 98
French	37 80	Finnish	13 06
Greek	28 70	Croatian and Slavonian	12 51
German	28 53	Slovak	11 69
Bohemian and		Ruthenian (Rusniak)	10 51
Moravian	23 12	Portuguese	10 47
Italian (Northern)	22 49	Magyar	10 39
Dutch and Flemish	21 00	Polish	9 94
Cuban	19 34	Italian (Southern)	8 84
Scandinavian	16 65	Hebrew	8 67
Russian	14 94	Lithuanian	7 96

In many cases the amount brought in will be more than offset by the money sent out of the country to prepay the immigrant's ticket. It will readily be seen that the immigrant's value lies not in what he has, but in what he is.

How much is he worth? Many have tried to estimate the money cost of 'raising' a man or woman, and have reckoned it at from $500 to $1,000. But such calculations are useless. A man's value to the country consists not in what he costs, but in what he can do – and does. Those who are physically strong can do much of the rough work of a new land. But if they are ignorant or immoral, it is decidedly a question as to whether they are, in the long run, worth much to the country. Some come in and crowd out native workers. In this case the net result is rather doubtful.

Hall, after an exhaustive study, declares: 'Foreign labor stands as a constant menace to the progress of the American laborer, and a check to his advancement. The moment foreign labor can do no harm to the native standard of living it ceases to come; while the moment conditions here improve, immigration comes to share in and limit the improvement.'

The general law seems to be that cheap labor tends to drive out higher-priced labor and lower the standards of living. The operation of this law is seen very clearly in the anthracite coal region. F. J. Warne, in his study of the Slav invasion, says:

Primarily and essentially this struggle was a conflict between two widely different standards of living. The English-speaking mine-worker wanted a home, wife, and children. A picture of that home represented, usually, a neat, two-story frame house, with a porch and yard attached. He wanted a carpet on the best room, pictures on the wall, and the house to be otherwise attractive. In that home he wanted none but his own immediate family, or very near relatives. His wife he liked to see comfortably and fairly well dressed. For his children he had ambitions which required their attendance at the little red schoolhouse on the hill. He was a type of man whose wants were always just beyond his wages, with the tendency for these wants to increase.

It cannot be said that all English-speaking mine-workers had exactly the same standard, but the tendency with all of them was toward one nearly uniform standard, and that a comparatively high one. This standard cannot be measured in money, because of the varying elements entering into its composition among different mine-workers, even of the same nationality. It is true that lower standards of living were continually coming into the region; but these were brought in, for the most part, by men of the same English-speaking races, the later arrivals being quickly absorbed and soon made to conform to the higher standard through family ties, intermarriage, and imitation.

But in marked contrast to all this was the mode of life of the Slav mine-worker. Escaping, as he was, from an agricultural environment which had barely supplied food, clothing, and shelter, the Slav came single-handed, alone. Wife and children he had none, nor wished for them. Placed in the anthracite region by the force of circumstances, without either the time or the means or the knowledge, even if he had the mental quality, to look elsewhere for work, the Slav could only supply his pressing physical demands by selling his labor. Under such conditions he was satisfied to live in almost any kind of a place, to wear almost anything that would clothe his nakedness, and to eat any kind of food that would keep body and soul together.

The Slav was content to live in a one-room hut, built by his own hands, on a hillside near the mine, of driftwood gathered at spare moments from along the highway, and roofed with tin from discarded powder-cans; or he crowded into the poorer and cheaper living sections of the large mining towns. He was not particular with whom or with how many he lived, except that he wanted them to be of his own nationality.

What was the effect on the English-speaking miner?

Not only did many voluntarily leave the industry; not only were workers being forced out of the mines, but many were compelled to lower their standard of living; others were prevented from raising their standard, while to many the struggle to exist became a most severe battle for the necessaries of life. The pressure on some miners was so great as to force their boys of tender years into the breaker and their girl children into the silk mill, in order that their pittance might add to the family income. This competition affected the lives of hundreds of thousands of people; it even determined the number of births in a community, as well as influenced powerfully the physical and mental qualities of those born into the world under such stress of conditions. Like all great fires, it had its beginning in small things — in the desire of the managers of capital to secure a lower cost of production; in the ability of one group of men to live on less than another group.

Small wonder if trades and labor unions cannot view with equa-
nimity the introduction of tens of thousands of Jewish and Italian
workers in the Eastern cities, or of Chinese and Japanese or Hindus
on the West coast. Hall sums up:

In conclusion it may be said that the chief economic effects of
immigration have been the settling of the new portions of the
country, the exploiting its industries more speedily than would
otherwise have been possible, the development of the factory system, and stimulating the invention and use of machinery requiring
no great skill for its operation. Immigration has also resulted in the
greater organization of industry and the stratification of society. All
these things doubtless would have come to pass sooner or later without immigration, but the influx of such large numbers of producers
has probably hastened their advent.

There is no doubt that our construction work could not have
been pushed forward so rapidly without the great numbers of
unskilled laborers who have come to us. There is no doubt that a
large immigration means general prosperity — at least for a time. The
immigrant must have food and clothing and houses and implements.
This makes trade good. Fortunately for us in Canada, we have had
vast areas of land to be settled, and so far a large percentage of the
immigrants have gone to the country. But as more and more remain
in the cities, we shall find competition keener. Now there is room
for all. Within a few years the people with lower standards of living
will drive out other competitiors. The economic question becomes a
social question. Our resources must be developed, but why such
haste? Can we afford, for the sake of immediate gain, to sacrifice
those standards and ideals which we have most carefully cherished?
True prosperity cannot be measured by the volume of trade or bank
clearings. It consists in the social and moral welfare of the people.

The competition of races is the competition of standards of living ...
As rapidly as a race rises in the scale of living and, through organization, begins to demand higher wages and resist the pressure of long
hours and over-exertion, the employers substitute another race, and
the process is repeated. Each race comes from a country lower in the
scale than that of the preceding, until finally the ends of the earth

have been ransacked in the search for low standards of living, combined with patient industriousness. Europe has been exhausted, Asia
has been drawn upon, and there remain but three regions of the
temperate zones from which a still lower standard can be expected.
These are China, Japan, and India. The Chinese have been excluded
by law, the Japanese are coming in increasing numbers, and the
Indian coolies remain to be experimented upon. *John R. Commons,*
in March (1904) *Chautauquan.*

SOCIAL EFFECTS

1 *Pauperism*
It is almost impossible to obtain statistics concerning the number of
immigrants who are dependent on our various charities. Our large
immigration, too, is so recent that such figures would be almost
valueless. To anyone, however, who knows the conditions it is
evident that immigration means a very heavy burden upon all our
charitable institutions.

The situation in the United States is clearly indicated in the
following excerpt from the *Report of the Associated Charities of
Boston,* 1894:

As we face the fact that nearly all those applying to us were of
foreign birth or parentage, that they included representatives of
some fifteen different nations, and that inefficiency and lack of
capacity were really the prevalent difficulties, we feel the importance of having changes made in our laws as to immigrants. This is a
primal necessity. The recent immigrants have been, generally speaking, much inferior to those who came in earlier times. They are
lowering the average standard of citizenship in our country, and such
immigration must be checked before we can adequately deal with
the problems of pauperism and crime in our cities.

Hall calls attention to another important aspect of the question:
'Much of the pauperism due to recent immigration is, therefore, not
to be found in the ranks of the immigrants themselves, but among
those who are displaced by their presence.'

The conditions in Montreal are set forth at length in the *Report of
the Secretary of the Charity Organization Society of Montreal,* 1905:

The question of immigration in Montreal has become much more acute during the past year, and we can see nothing ahead of us but that the difficulty will yearly increase with the national growth of the Dominion. You will remember last spring how we, as a city, were confronted with the serious problem of about one thousand Italians, without funds, without friends, unemployed, on our streets, and that a public subscription for bread had to be opened for them. A much more serious problem would have been upon us during the past winter in the arrival of not far from two thousand Hebrews from Russia, had it not been for the generosity of a gentleman of that faith, we understand, in London, who kindly sent a cheque for a large amount for the care of these unfortunate men ... During the last six months we have experienced great difficulty with immigrants from the British Isles, who came out in midwinter with only two or three pounds on their person upon arrival at the winter ports, either of Halifax or St. John, and, of necessity, a major part of this money had to be spent in transportation to Montreal, with the result of their coming to us penniless, or nearly so ...

They (the United States Bureau of Immigration in Canada) report that from the years 1901 to 1905 they rejected more than ten thousand applicants for certificates to enter the United States. If this is true, it would be interesting to know what became of these ten thousand people whom the Government across the line did not consider fit persons to become citizens of the United States ... Surely the Dominion of Canada, with all its needs for a large population to develop resources, cannot afford to be populated with outcasts from all the countries in Europe, thrown to be a burden on us by the United States officials in our midst.

In Toronto, during the past winter (1907-8) there was much distress. The greater number of those in need were recent arrivals from England.

A memorial presented by the Toronto and Montreal Boards of Trade states that of 243 patients treated in Muskoka Sanitarium 83 were foreign-born.

The following statements, made by the Hon. Mr. Hanna in the Ontario Legislature, show the conditions even in Ontario – one of the provinces least affected by foreign immigration:

During 1907 there were 1,163 admitted to asylums of the province, of whom 346 were foreign-born. During the past five years

Blessed with the gift of 'getting on'
1 Galician women picking potatoes on a western prairie
2 Milkwoman – the International Dairy, Winnipeg

the precentage of foreigners admitted to these institutions had increased from twenty to thirty per cent, while Canadian-born patients had decreased from eighty to seventy per cent. In the same period – from 1903 to 1907 – the cost of maintenance of foreign-born patients had increased from $24,613.20 to $51,744.30. While the foreign-born of the entire adult population were only twenty per cent, the total admissions to asylums from that class was thirty per cent. The figures showed the necessity of effective methods to prevent the dumping of undesirables by friends and others, aided by charitable associations, with no other object than to get rid of the responsibility of their maintenance. Taking into consideration the probable length of life of these patients, the cost of maintaining those admitted in 1907 alone would amount to $1,487,038.80, without including any proportion for capital expenditure.

Of the estimated total population of the province over sixteen years of age, 1,209,308 were Canadians and 291,675 foreigners, or twenty per cent of the whole. At the same time, of the commitments to jail thirty-eight per cent were of foreign birth, and the cost of providing for them amounted to $21,724.65.

Toronto Asylum gave a practial illustration of the position. Of 262 persons admitted, less than half were Canadians. Of course, many of the foreign-born had been resident in Canada for some years; but no less than seventy-seven were recent arrivals, who should have been deported if a satisfactory law had been in force. The majority of those people should not have been allowed to enter Canada. Owing to technicalities, only twenty-four came within the requirements of the Deportation Act, and therefore Ontario had to assume the cost of maintaining forty-three. That meant that the province would have to expend $224,000 for the support of people who had not the slightest claim for their consideration. No matter how it was regarded, the picture was one that could not be contemplated with equanimity. The figures, he claimed, showed that a proportion of insane among arrivals was twenty-six times greater than it should be, and there was a strong suspicion that many were deliberately sent out from Great Britain to be got rid of. An analysis showed that whole families of degenerates were included among arrivals, and weaklings of all objectionable types were represented, as well as many with criminal records. By deportation it was estimated that $450,000 had been saved to the province. The total deportations amounted to 108 since 1896.

In Winnipeg relief is given largely to those who have come to this country within the past few years. The most numerous class is that from Great Britain. There are many needy Jews, but the Jewish charitable organizations are largely responsible for their welfare.

The last report of the Winnipeg General Hospital shows the nationality of the patients as follows:

Canada	2,086	Ireland	151
England	960	Iceland	107
Scotland	281	Austria	107
United States	201	Russia	231
Galician	128	Wales	18
Sweden	118	France	5
Germany	113	Switzerland	2
Poland	49	Belgium	4
Denmark	21	Roumania	20
Norway	49	Others and unknown	76
Italy	14	Total	4,741

It will be seen that non-Canadians are out of all proportion to their number in the country, and it should be understood that a very much larger percentage of these are charity patients.

The following table shows the nationality of children cared for by the Children's Aid Society of Winnipeg:

Irish	24	Austrian	1
Canadian	147	French	7
French half-breed	17	German	21
English	97	Icelandic	5
Galician	36	Welsh	6
United States	9	Negro	1
Polish	9	Russian	3
Swedish	4	Scotch	12

We do not attempt to base any definite conclusions upon these figures. Many considerations enter into the problem. But we must not forget that, while it has its benefits, immigration also brings very heavy burdens. Many of our immigrants are below the average in their own countries.

2 *Physical condition*

Statistics in the United States show that the foreign-born 'furnished two and one-third times their normal proportion of insane. They have been the cause of epidemics and of the spread of much infection ... Favus and trachoma were practically unknown in the United States before the immigration from Southern and Eastern Europe ... Probably the worst effect of immigration upon the public health is not the introduction or spread of acute diseases, but of large numbers of persons of poor physique who tend to lower the general vigor of the community.' *Hall.*

How far this is true of Canada we cannot yet say. The same classes are coming to us as to the United States. The Canadian medical inspection is becoming more strict, and yet, as the chief medical officer says in his last report: 'Remembering that the immigrants are examined in groups often of 1,000 and over, and that as many as 7,000 have arrived in a single day, it will be understood that no attempt is made to make a clinical examination of persons who are not obviously in poor health.'

Tables I-IV from the departmental reports are of interest. They show the effort that is being made to admit only 'the fit.' But, with such a superficial examination, many diseased persons must pass unnoticed; and it may well be doubted if all who are released are permanently cured – e.g., out of 991 detained because of trachoma, 766 were released. But let each read these tables for himself, and draw his own conclusions.

This table [Table I], always interesting to the casual reader, is important, not only in indicating results compared with previous years, but also the degree to which the various peoples are impressed with the restrictions placed upon undesirable immigrants. As re-marked in previous years, of the total number, those destined to the United States show the proportionately largest number, there being 34 in a total of 198 at Atlantic ports, as compared with 164 destined for Canada, while the total immigrants destined to the United States were 17,887, as compared with 101,715 to Canada. The number of British debarred at Atlantic ports was 54, or 1 in 1,033, as compared with 1 in 1,669 in 1905-6. This increase, as compared with last year, of 3 to 2 in British rejections, is very worthy of note, since it has been the rule that the larger the total immigration of any class the

TABLE I
Statement by nationalities of number of immigrants debarred admission
to Canada during the fiscal year, 1906-7 (9 months)

Nationality	Total arrivals	Atlantic ports For Canada	For USA	Pacific ports For Canada	For USA	Totals For Canada	For USA	Totals
Austrian	562	1		1		2		2
Galician	1,652	6				6		6
Magyar	347	3				3		3
Ruthenian	303	2				2		2
Slovak	146	3				3		3
Chinese	92			1		1		1
French	1,314	4	1			4	1	5
German	1,889	2				2		2
English	41,156	42	2	2		44	2	46
Scotch	10,729	6				6		6
Irish	3,404	4		1		5		5
West Indian	64	1				1		1
Greek	545	1				1		1
Hebrew	544	1				1		1
Hebrew, Russian	5,802	24	3			24	3	27
Italian	5,114	29	1			29	1	30
Japanese	2,042			99	1	99	1	100
Poles	144	2	1			2	1	3
Poles, Austrian	375	1				1		1
Poles, Russian	492	6	4			6	4	10
Roumanian	431	1				1		1
Russian	1,927	15	15	1		16	15	31
Finns	1,049		3				3	3
Icelandic	46		4				4	4
Swedes	1,077	4				4		4
Turks	232	3				3		3
Armenians	208	2				2		2
Syrians	277	1				1		1
From U.S.A.	34,659			17		17		17
India	2,124			119		119		119
Totals	118,746	164	34	241	1	405	35	440

proportion detained is fewer, and British immigration has been
greater than for the same period of the previous year. The English
rejections were as 1 in 935; the Scotch as 1 in 1,788, and the Irish as
1 in 851.

TABLE II
Statement giving the diseases and other causes for which immigrants were
detained at the ports of entry – Quebec, Montreal, Halifax, St. John, Victoria,
Vancouver and New York, during the fiscal year, 1906-7 (9 months)

Class of disease	Cause of detention	Number detained	Number released	Number deported	Still in hospital
1 Contagious diseases	Chicken pox	1	1*		
	Typhoid fever	1	1		
	Mumps	1	1		
	Measles	4	4		
	Totals	7	7		
2 General diseases	Lupus	3		3	
	Tuberculosis	12	5	6	1
	Alcoholism	1	1		
	Delirium tremens	3		3	
	Rheumatism	2	1	1	
	Malarial fever	1			1
	Fever	3	3		
	Totals	25	10	13	2
3 The eye	Trachoma	991	766*	176	49
	Conjunctivitis	1,793	1,756	10	27
	Ulcer of eye	1	1		
	Cataract	1		1	
	Ophthalmia neonatorum	1	1		
	Blind	3	2	1	
	Partially blind	12		12	
	Totals	2,802	2,526	200	76
4 Nervous system	Spinal disease	1		1	
	Paralysis	7	5*	2	
	Convulsions	3	3		
	Apoplexy	1	1		
	Feeble-minded	8	4	4	
	Melancholia	1		1	
	Hysteria	1	1		
	Insane	15	13		2
	Epilepsy	3		3	
	Pott's disease	1		1	
	Paralysis of leg	1	1		
	Totals	42	15	25	2

TABLE II *continued*

Class of disease	Cause of detention	Number detained	Number released	Number deported	Still in hospital
5 Circulatory system	Heart disease	1		1	
6 Respiratory system	Bronchitis	4	4		
	Pneumonia	1	1		
	Empyema	1		1	
	Chronic pleurisy	1		1	
	Totals	7	5	2	
7 Digestive system	Hernia	5	1	4	
8 Genito-urinary	Syphilis	2		2	
9 The skin	Favus	9	7	2	
	Alopecia	2	2		
	Erysipelas	1	1		
	Scabies	1	1		
	Eczema	1			1
	Abscess on face	1	1		
	Tinea (Ringworm)	3	2		1
	Tubercular adenitis	2		1	1
	Totals	20	14	3	3
10 Locomotor system	Muscular atrophy	1		1	
11 Malformation –diseases of old age and infancy	Deaf	3	3		
	Cripple	1		1	
	Senility and debility	20	13	4	3
	Deaf and dumb	6	1	5	
	Hunchback	2	2		
	Lame	1	1		
	Rickets	1			1
	Old age	1	1		
	Totals	35	21	10	4
12 Accidents	Sprained muscle of groin	1	1		
	Lost fingers and toes	1		1	
	Totals	2	1	1	

TABLE II *continued*

Class of disease	Cause of detention	Number detained	Number released	Number deported	Still in hospital
13 Ill-defined causes	Poor physique	7	4	3	
	Nervous disease	2	1	1	
	Totals	9	5	4	
14 Other causes	Accompanying patients	213	190*	19	4
	Likely to become a public charge	159	69	90	
	Criminals	11	2	9	
	Traumatic lameness	1	1		
	For safe-keeping	4	4		
	Suspected immoral	4	4		
	Stowaway	18	11	7	
	Prostitute	8		8	
	Ran away from wife	1		1	
	Ran away from father	2		2	
	Eloped	2		2	
	Held for bond	1	1		
	For further observation	8	8		
	Waiting for tickets	3	3		
	Waiting for situation	94	94		
	To observe mental condition	1	1		
	Pediculosis	1	1		
	To observe eyes	16	16		
	Bad character	30	1	29	
	Artificial foot	1	1		
	Opium fiend	3		3	
	Procurer	1		1	
	Degenerate	3		3	
	Totals	585	407	174	4
Grand totals		3,543	3,012†	440	91

* 1 died   † 4 died

Table III shows the fate, so to speak, of the unfortunates in the great stream of favored people who have found their way to a new home in Canada. In all 201 have been sent out of Canada for some cause, of whom 157 were English, 8 Irish, 12 Scotch, and of the others, Galicians 4, French 2, Swedish 4, Italian 1, from the United States 5, Hebrew 3, Hungarian 1, Finnish 1, Danish 1, and Welsh 2.

While it is apparent that the number in some instances is too small to draw conclusions from, yet several nationalities show continued freedom from deported cases. For instance, only one Italian was deported this year as a criminal, and none in either previous year, although there were 16,546 Italian immigrants in the three years. Evidently they are remarkably free from insanity and tuberculosis, and in the latter cases this may be due to their outdoor life in sunny Italy. While the people of the United States stand first in the list as regards freedom from deportation, it will be understood that their being mostly agriculturists in the North-West and having resources will prevent their defectives from becoming, to a large extent, a burden upon the public. It is probable, too, that the remarkable interest and care taken by the Russian Hebrews for their own people is an explanation, in part, of the few deported; but it is probable that the fear of a forced return to Russia is an impelling force preventing their sick from becoming dependent inmates of public institutions.

3 *Illiteracy*
It is no light thing to introduce into our country tens of thousands of non-English-speaking immigrants. Ignorance of our language is a barrier that largely isolates these peoples from us and our institutions; and behind the language is the foreign mind and training which still further separates them from us. But more serious still is the fact that many of the immigrants are illiterates, uneducated even in their own language.

TABLE III
Statement showing the number, nationality and causes for which immigrants admitted to Canada were deported after admission to Canada during the fiscal year, 1906-7 (9 months)

Nationality	Whence sent for deportation	Male	Female	Class of disease	Cause of deportation
Deported at St. John					
English	Winnipeg	2		General diseases	Tuberculosis
English	Toronto	1		General diseases	Tuberculosis
Dane	Winnipeg	1		General diseases	Tuberculosis
English	Winnipeg	4		General diseases	Rheumatism
English	Toronto		1	General diseases	Rheumatism
Irish	Winnipeg	1		General diseases	Rheumatism
English	Winnipeg	2		Eye diseases	Failing eyesight
English	Winnipeg	3		Nervous diseases	Insanity
English	London	2		Nervous diseases	Insanity
English	Strathroy		1	Nervous diseases	Insanity
English	Toronto	2		Nervous diseases	Insanity
English	Hamilton	1		Nervous diseases	Insanity
English	Montreal	1		Nervous diseases	Insanity
English	Edmonton	1		Nervous diseases	Insanity
Welsh	Montreal	1		Nervous diseases	Insanity
Irish	Toronto	1		Nervous diseases	Insanity
Scotch	Toronto		1	Nervous diseases	Insanity
Scotch	Winnipeg		1	Nervous diseases	Insanity
Galician	Winnipeg		1	Nervous diseases	Insanity
English	Winnipeg	2		Nervous diseases	Physically and mentally weak
English	Winnipeg	1		Nervous diseases	Epilepsy
English	Winnipeg	2		Circulatory system	Heart disease

TABLE III *continued*

English	Winnipeg	Circulatory system	Empyema	1	
French	Winnipeg	Circulatory system	Varicose veins	1	
English	Cornwall	The skin	Ulcer on leg	1	
English	Winnipeg	Locomotor system	Locomotor ataxia	1	
English	Winnipeg	Malformation, etc.	Deaf and dumb	2	
English	Toronto	Malformation, etc.	Twisted neck and head	1	
English	St. John	Malformation, etc.	Cripple	1	
English	Winnipeg	Old age	Old age	1	
English	Winnipeg	Ill-defined causes	Physically unfit	1	
Scotch	Winnipeg	Ill-defined causes	Physically unfit	1	
English	Toronto	Accidents	Lost eye and thumb, feeble	1	
English	Winnipeg	Other causes	Accompanying patients	1	1
English	London	Other causes	Accompanying patients	1	5
English	Toronto	Other causes	Accompanying patients	3	2
Scotch	Toronto	Other causes	Accompanying patients	2	
English	Winnipeg	Other causes	Likely to become a public charge	3	3
English	United States	Other causes	Likely to become a public charge	3	
English	St. John	Other causes	Likely to become a public charge	1	
Swede	Winnipeg	Other causes	Likely to become a public charge	2	
English	Winnipeg	Other causes	Criminal	2	
English	Toronto	Other causes	Criminal	1	1
English	Montreal	Other causes	Criminal	1	
English	Quebec	Other causes	Criminal	1	
Italian	Quebec	Other causes	Criminal	1	
English	Quebec	Other causes	Pregnant	1	
English	Winnipeg	Other causes	Immoral	1	
Scotch	Winnipeg	Other causes	Vicious tendencies	1	
	Totals			62	20

TABLE III *continued*

Nationality	Whence sent for deportation	Male	Female	Class of disease	Cause of deportation
Deported at Montreal					
English	Winnipeg	4		General diseases	Tuberculosis
English	Montreal	2	1	General diseases	Tuberculosis
English	Ottawa	1		General diseases	Tuberculosis
Galician	Winnipeg	1		General diseases	Tuberculosis
Swede	Winnipeg	1		General diseases	Tuberculosis
U.S. Citizen	Montreal	1		General diseases	Tuberculosis
English	Winnipeg	5		General diseases	Rheumatism
Hebrew	Winnipeg	1		General diseases	Rheumatism
French	Winnipeg	1		General diseases	Rheumatism
Irish	Montreal	1		General diseases	Alcoholism
Irish	Ottawa	1		General diseases	Alcoholism
English	Port Arthur	1		Eye diseases	Failing eyesight
English	Winnipeg	8	1	Nervous diseases	Insanity
English	Kingston	1		Nervous diseases	Insanity
English	Montreal	6	3	Nervous diseases	Insanity
English	Toronto	4	1	Nervous diseases	Insanity
English	Hamilton	2		Nervous diseases	Insanity
English	Penetanguishene	1		Nervous diseases	Insanity
Scotch	Montreal	1		Nervous diseases	Insanity
Irish	Montreal	1	1	Nervous diseases	Insanity
Irish	Quebec	1		Nervous diseases	Insanity
Hebrew	Winnipeg	1		Nervous diseases	Insanity
Galician	Halifax		1	Nervous diseases	Insanity
U.S. Citizen	New Westminster	3		Nervous diseases	Insanity

TABLE III *continued*

U.S. Citizen	Montreal	1	Nervous diseases	Insanity
Swede	Toronto	1	Nervous diseases	Insanity
Galician	Bracebridge	1	Nervous diseases	Insanity
Scotch	Montreal	1	Nervous diseases	Insanity
English	Winnipeg	1	Nervous diseases	Insanity
English	Hamilton	1	Nervous diseases	Epilepsy
English	Winnipeg	1	Nervous diseases	Epilepsy
English	Cobourg	1	Nervous diseases	Physically and mentally weak
English	Winnipeg	1	Circulatory system	Varicose veins
English	Montreal	1	Digestive system	Chronic dysentery
English	Winnipeg	1	Genito-urinary system	Diabetes
English	Winnipeg	1	Genito-urinary system	Bright's disease
English	Winnipeg	1	The skin	Ulcer
English	Montreal	1	The skin	Abscess
English	Montreal	1	Malformation, etc.	Cripple
Welsh	Montreal	1	Malformation, etc.	Cripple
Russian Hebrew	Winnipeg	1	Old age	Old age
Hungarian	Winnipeg	1	Malformation, etc.	Cripple
English	Cornwall	1	Accidents	Frost bites
English	Ottawa	1	Accidents	Lead poison
English	Winnipeg	6	Other causes	Accompanying patients
English	Montreal	1	Other causes	Accompanying patients
English	Ottawa	3	Other causes	Accompanying patients
Scotch	Montreal	1	Other causes	Accompanying patients
English	Ottawa	1	Other causes	Likely to become a public charge
English	Winnipeg	2	Other causes	Likely to become a public charge
English	Toronto	2	Other causes	Likely to become a public charge
Scotch	Goderich	1	Other causes	Likely to become a public charge

TABLE III *continued*

Nationality	Whence sent for deportation	Male	Female	Class of disease	Cause of deportation
Deported at Montreal continued					
English	Lachute		1	Other causes	Pregnancy
English	Montreal	1	1	Other causes	Criminal
	Totals	82	29		
Deported at Quebec					
Irish	Quebec		1	Nervous system	Insane
English	Stanstead		1	Other causes	Pregnancy
	Totals		2		
Deported at Halifax					
English	Toronto	1		Nervous diseases	Insane
English	Penetanguishene	1		Nervous diseases	Insane
English	New Westminster		1	Nervous diseases	Insane
Scotch	Toronto	1		Nervous diseases	Insane
Scotch	Toronto		1	Other causes	Bad character
Finn	Halifax		1	Other causes	Pregnancy
	Totals	3	3		
Grand totals		147	54		

TABLE IV
Statement showing the number and nationality of immigrants deported
after admission to Canada during the three fiscal years,
1904-5, '05-6, '06-7

Nationality	Total number arriving	Deported	Ratio of deported to number arriving
Icelander	627	5	1 in 125
Danes	1,232	6	1 in 205
Welsh	2,069	6	1 in 345
English	155,138	313	1 in 496
Swedes	4,726	9	1 in 525
Norwegian	3,688	7	1 in 527
Poles	546	1	1 in 546
Hebrew	2,275	4	1 in 569
Finns	3,475	4	1 in 869
Irish	12,420	13	1 in 955
Dutch	1,064	1	1 in 1,064
Hungarian	2,219	2	1 in 1,109
French	4,705	4	1 in 1,176
Galician	14,234	10	1 in 1,423
Newfoundlander	1,559	1	1 in 1,559
Scotch	38,319	23	1 in 1,666
Russian	6,995	3	1 in 2,332
Belgian	2,552	1	1 in 2,552
Austrian	2,723	1	1 in 2,723
Russian Hebrew	18,064	3	1 in 6,021
German	6,338	1	1 in 6,338
Italian	16,546	1	1 in 16,546
From United States	136,319	5	1 in 27,263
Totals	437,833	424	1 in 1,033

According to the *Report of the United States Commissioner of Education*, the following is the general illiteracy for European nations:

Countries	Per cent	Category of population
German Empire	0.11	male
Sweden and Norway	0.11	male
Denmark	0.54	male
Finland	1.60	male and female over 10 years
Switzerland	0.30	male
Scotland	3.57	male and female
Netherlands	4.00	male
England	5.80	male and female
France	4.90	male
Belgium	12.80	not given
Austria	23.80	not given
Ireland	17.00	male and female
Hungary	28.10	male
Greece	30.00	male and female
Italy	38.30	male
Portugal	79.00	male and female
Spain	68.10	male
Russia	61.70	male
Servia	86.00	male
Roumania	89.00	male

The following table, showing the illiteracy of the different races contributing more than 2,000 immigrants each to the United States in 1904, will be largely true for Canada:

Northern and Western Europe
(chiefly Teutonic and Celtic)

Scotch	0.6	Irish	3.4
Scandinavian	0.7	Dutch and Flemish	4.1
English	1.3	German	4.8
Bohemian and Moravian	1.8	Italian (North)	12.6
Finnish	2.7		
French	3.2	Average of above	4.0

Southern and Eastern Europe
(chiefly Slavic and Iberic)

Spanish	9.8	Croatian and Slovenian	36.1
Magyar	14.1	Bulgarian, Servian and	
Greek	23.6	Montenegrin	45.4
Russian	26.0	Lithuanian	54.1
Slovak	27.9	Italian (South)	54.2
Roumanian	31.7	Ruthenian	58.8
Dalmatian, Bosnian and		Portuguese	67.5
Herzegovinian	35.6		
Polish	35.8	Average of above	42.6

Other races

Chinese	8.2	Hebrew	23.3
Cuban	8.7	African (black)	23.7
Japanese	21.6	Syrian	54.7

We add another rather curious table, which shows the general connection between illiteracy and poverty:

United States immigrants arriving at port of New York 1899

Race	Per cent illiterates	Money brought per capita
Southern Italians	46.56	$ 8.79
Ruthenians	45.83	9.53
Syrians	41.22	13.95
Poles	28.39	10.37
Germans	4.43	29.18
British	2.43	29.51

The more illiterate the less money. It should be remembered that the foreigners coming to us in the largest numbers are the Southern Italians and Ruthenians, or, as the latter are commonly called, Galicians.

The result of the incoming of immigrants will be that the average educational standing of the people will be lowered; and if school attendance is not made obligatory, it will be greatly and permanently lowered.

4 *Crime*

The situation in the United States may be presented in the following statements from Hall:

Roughly speaking, the foreigners furnish more than twice as many criminals, two and one-third times as many insane, and three times as many paupers as the native element.

In addition to the cost of supporting persons actually in institutions, there is a far larger cost for increased police and sanitary inspectors, for law courts and machinery of justice, for private charity, for public education, and for the effects of physical and moral contagion upon the rest of the population.

We might endure the criminality of the adult immigrants with more composure if we had any assurance that their children would be as orderly as the native-born. But we find just the opposite to be the fact. The children of immigrants are, therefore, twice as dangerous as the immigrants themselves.

The immigration to Canada has been so recent that here, again, we have no statistics on which to base conclusions of any value. The annual police returns for Winnipeg for 1907 show that immigrants are fairly prominent in the police court, more so than their numbers would warrant.

The following were the nationalities of the offenders:

Canadian	1,541	Welsh	17
English	992	Italians	15
Scotch	693	Assyrians	14
Irish	452	Austrians	19
Galician	379	Chinese	10
American	304	Indians	6
German	140	Bohemians	7
Swedes	128	Ruthenians	8
Icelanders	72	Australians	6
French	58	Roumanians	4
Hebrews	95	Bukowinians	5
Negroes	107	Finlanders	5
Poles	76	Hollanders	5
Halfbreeds	86	Mexicans	4

1 Galician children with some of our W.M.S. workers at Edmonton
2 A kitchengarden class of foreign children at All Peoples' Mission,
   Winnipeg

Russians	37	Swiss	2
Norwegians	31	Greeks	6
Hungarians	25	Belgians	13
Danes	21		

POLITICAL EFFECTS

Already our immigrants are making themselves felt in our political life. They soon obtain the franchise, and their votes are too numerous to be disregarded. Among nearly all the races there are political clubs. The political parties find it to their interest to maintain newspapers in the various leading languages. The non-English are frequently settled in 'colonies,' so that they have virtually the balance of power. Canada's future lies with her immigrants. Another word of warning from the United States: 'The heterogeneity of these races tends to promote passion, localism and despotism, and to make impossible free co-operation for the public welfare.' *Hall.*

Chapter 20

The city

SO IMPORTANT is the city, and so great its problems, that it demands a section to itself. One book dealing with this subject should be in the hands of all our readers, *The Challenge of the City,* by Josiah Strong.

We cannot do better in this necessarily brief treatment than quote certain passages which may at once state the situation and stimulate further study:

The social problem is the problem of man's relation to his fellows, which relations have been wonderfully multiplied and complicated by the industrial revolution. In the city, which is the most characteristic product of the new civilization, these relationships are more numerous and more intimate than elsewhere; and it is here that the evil effects of mal-adjustment are most pronounced.

If now it is true of modern civilization that materialism is its supreme peril, pre-eminently true is it of American civilization; and if material growth finds its comparative in the New World, the modern city furnishes its superlative. The modern city is at the same time the most characteristic product and the best exponent of modern civilization, and beyond a doubt it will determine the civilization of the future.

At the beginning of the nineteenth century the United States had only six cities of 8,000 or more; in 1880, 286; in 1890, 443; and in 1900, 545, among which are some of the greatest cities of the earth. In 1800 less than 4 per cent of our population was urban; in 1900, 33 per cent. In 1800 Montreal had a population of 7,000; in 1850, of 60,000 and in 1907, of 400,000. Toronto had 9,000 inhabitants in 1834, 25,000 in 1850, and 250,000 in 1907, an increase in less than sixty years of 1,000 per cent. Some have supposed that this remarkable movement of population from country to city was due to the exceptional conditions of a new civilization which would pass with time.

But this growth is not peculiar to new civilizations. London is probably two thousand years old, and yet four-fifths of its growth was added during the past century. From 1850 to 1890 Berlin grew more rapidly than New York. Paris is now five times as large as it was in 1800. Rome has increased 50 per cent since 1890. St. Petersburg has increased five-fold in a hundred years. Odessa is a thousand

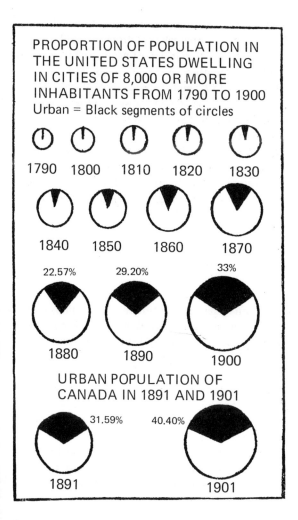

PROPORTION OF POPULATION IN
THE UNITED STATES DWELLING
IN CITIES OF 8,000 OR MORE
INHABITANTS FROM 1790 TO 1900
Urban = Black segments of circles

1790   1800   1810   1820   1830

1840   1850   1860   1870

22.57%   29.20%   33%

1880   1890   1900

URBAN POPULATION OF
CANADA IN 1891 AND 1901

31.59%   40.40%

1891   1901

Growth of urban population in the United States and Canada

years old, but nineteen-twentieths of its population were added
during the nineteenth century. Bombay grew from 150,000 to
821,000 from 1800 to 1890. Tokio increased nearly 800,000 during
the last twenty years of the century, while Osaka was nearly four
times as large in 1903 as in 1872, and Cairo has more than doubled
since 1850. Thus, in Europe, Asia and Africa we find that a redis-
tribution of population is taking place, a movement from country to
city. It is a world phenomenon.

Some have imagined that it would prove temporary; that this
flowing tide would soon ebb. But its causes are permanent, and
indicate that this movement will be permanent. The sudden expansion of the city marks a profound change in civilization, the results
of which will grow more and more obvious.

The accompanying chart shows the growth of urban population
in the United States and Canada:

Our population will continue to swell by this foreign flood, and
whatever strain it puts on American institutions, that strain is more
than three times as great in our large cities as in the whole country.
In 1890, of the male population in our eighteen largest cities,
1,028,122 were native-born of native parentage, 1,386,776 were
foreign-born, and 1,450,733 were native-born of foreign parentage;
that is, those who were foreign by birth or parentage numbered
2,837,509, or more than two and a half times as many as the native
American stock. This proportion has been largely increased by the
immigration of the last sixteen years.

These elements as the come to us are clay in the hands of the
political potter. If they remain uninstructed as to good citizenship
and incapable of forming individual judgments, the 'boss' will certainly rule the city when the city rules the nation.

When immigrants segregate themselves in various quarters of our
great cities, our language ceases to be a necessity to them. Ideas and
customs remain foreign. The most essential elements of their foreign
environment they have brought with them. Here are bits of
Bohemia, Russia, Italy, transferred to this side of the Atlantic and
set down in the city.

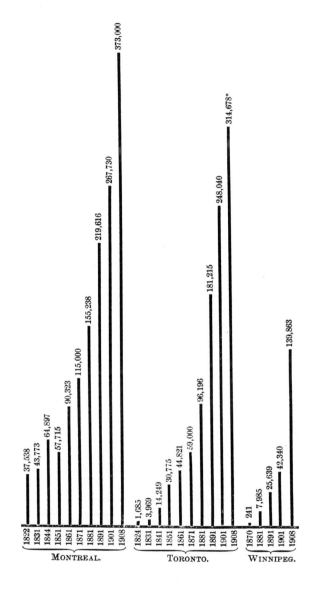

How our cities are growing   *Police census

Hall shows clearly the relation of the immigrant to the slum:

The proportion of those of foreign birth or parentage to the total population of the slums in Baltimore was (1900); 77 per cent; in Chicago, 90 per cent; in New York, 95 per cent, and in Philadelphia, 91 per cent ... Southeastern Europe furnishes three times as many inhabitants as Northwestern Europe to the slums of Baltimore, 19 times as many to the slums of New York, 20 times as many to the slums of Chicago, and 71 times as many to the slums of Philadelphia.

In Canada, the city and its problems are only beginning to require serious consideration. But already we hear much about municipal ownership of the great franchises, already city government is being remodelled. Within the last few years charity organization societies, city missions and institutional churches are being organized to meet hitherto unknown needs. Already we have our foreign-quarters, 'wards,' 'shacktowns,' 'China towns,' 'ghettos,' 'east-end,' and 'slum districts.' Silently, almost unnoticed, a change is taking place. Canada is leaving the country for the city. In 1891, 32 per cent of our population was urban; in 1901, 38 per cent – a relative gain of 6 per cent for the cities in ten years.

The population of Ontario more than doubled from 1851 to 1901, but the population of Toronto increased over six times during the same period.

The population of the Province of Quebec was almost twice as large in 1901 as in 1851, but that of Montreal was over four and one-half times as large.

Manitoba is an agricultural province, and yet one-quarter of the entire population is resident in the city of Winnipeg alone.

The following diagrams show the growth of our cities:

The present decade will bring us right into line with developments on the American side. Montreal, with a mixed English and French population, has now added very large Jewish and Italian elements.

In Toronto, St. John's Ward alone contains about 10,000 foreigners divided as follows: 5,000 Jews, 2,500 Italians, 2,500 of various nationalities. Rev. A. B. Winchester (December, 1907) estimated Toronto's foreign population as follows: Jews, 13,000;* Italians, 6,000; from the Balkan Peninsula, including Macedonians, Bulgarians,

---

* January, 1909, estimated number of Jews in Toronto, 15,000.

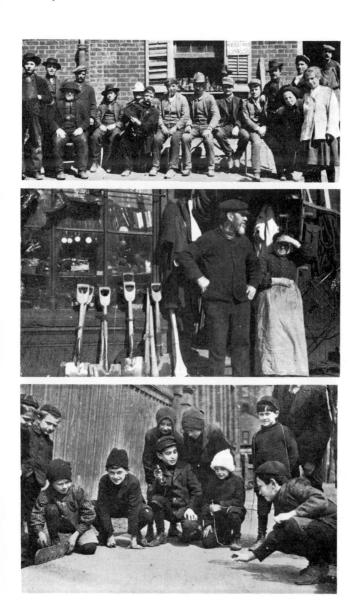

In 'The Ward' – Toronto's foreign quarter
1 Twelve nationalities represented
2 A prosperous merchant of 'The Ward'
3 Playtime

Roumelians, Servians, Albanians, Roumanians, Slovaks, Wallachians, Croatians, 2,000; Finns, 600; Syrians, 350; Greeks, 250;
Hungarians, 400; Russians, 200; Poles, 300; South American Re-
publics, 400; French, German, Swiss, Scandinavians, 2,000; Chinese,
1,000; total, 26,500. This is probably a very conservative estimate.
Then to the 'foreigners' we must add the very large number of
English immigrants who, on account of their poverty, made the
winter of 1907-8 one long to be remembered in Ontario.

In Winnipeg, it is estimated that from one-quarter to one-third of
the population are 'foreigners.' There are few Italians; proportionately as many Jews as in Eastern cities; large numbers of
Ruthenians, Poles, Germans and Scandinavians — after that representatives of all nationalities.

A careful estimate of the foreign population of Montreal gives us
the following: Jews, 25,000 to 30,000; Italians, 8,000 to 10,000;
Chinese, 1,000; Syrians, 800 to 1,000; with a considerable number
of Greeks and Roumanians, and a sprinkling of almost all other
nationalities.

We append the special census of 1906 for Winnipeg:

Canadian born	44,620	Norway and Sweden	1,689
British Islands	22,760	Roumania	613
British Possessions	254	Russia	4,594
		Spain and Portugal	24
Total British born	67,634	Switzerland	42
		Syria	80
Austria-Hungary	4,905	Turkey	51
Belgium	135	United States	3,875
China	362	West Indies	53
Denmark	155	Other countries	697
East Indies	26		
France	197	Total foreign born	22,432
Germany	2,547		
Greece	16	At sea	4
Holland	156	Not given	83
Iceland	1,882		
Italy	327	Grand total	90,153
Japan	6		

Ignorance of the language, high rents, low standards of living, incompetency, drunkenness and other evils are already producing conditions as bad as are to be found in the slums of the great cities. Unless certain tendencies are checked at once, it is appalling to think what will result with the growth of the city. We give an ordinary police court item from a Winnipeg daily paper:

M. Simok and M. Selenk endeavored to ascertain how many adults they could crowd into a given space. Selenk managed to accommodate forty-three occupants in five rooms where only fourteen could hope to find sufficient atmosphere for healthy respiration. Simok ran his neighbor close, having twenty-four in one room where only seven should have been. His rooms were too low, and lacked ventilation. In consideration of the immense profits made by such economic means, Magistrate Daly, at this morning's police court, charged Selenk $15 and costs, and Simok $10 and costs.

Fancy such conditions with 'illimitable prairies' stretching to the north and west!

A worker in a city mission gives the following typical cases of the poorer foreign homes:

Jacob Lalucki is employed in the Canadian Pacific Railway shops. He is a Ruthenian, his wife Polish. They are both Roman Catholics, but occasionally attend a Protestant mission. They have two young children. They live in one room, and have nine boarders, and the wife goes out washing.

Michael Yakoff and his wife are Russians. They have four children. He has only one leg, and acts as caretaker in a hall for which he receives $12.00 a month. They live in three rented rooms for which they pay $8.00 a month. They keep some roomers. Pieter, the oldest boy, eight years old, has to go out along the streets and lanes where he can find sticks of wood, empty barrels, etc., for which he gets a few cents to help to keep the family. Of course, he does not got to school. This family is Orthodox Greek.

Pieter Dagchook and wife are Ruthenians. He is a laborer — works 'steady' but drinks heavily. They have eight children. The eldest daughter is married and doing well. One boy ran away from home.

Another boy is in jail. A thirteen-year-old girl is at present in the hospital, and the four younger children are at home.

Stanislau Yablonovich is a teamster. He owns his own team, and his wife goes out cleaning. They own their house and several lots. They live in two rooms, and have five roomers. The furniture consists of three beds, a table, two chairs, a stove and some boxes. The attic is full of pigeons.

Ignace Lagkowski is a Little Russian. He is in the employ of the Street Railway Company. The family is very industrious. The mother goes out to work. Two of the boys sell papers. One boy works in a factory. They are Orthodox Greek, but the children attend the mission Sunday School, and their mother the Mothers' meetings.

John Doerchuchs' little boy, Lader, who attends the Kindergarten, had a sad accident last year. He was crossing the railroad track and an engine crushed his leg, so that it had to be amputated. The parents could get no compensation — they were only 'foreigners.'

Dunka and Nastaoma Ladowska are two of our Kindergarten girls. Their mother is a Ruthenian woman. She does not live with her husband, who was cruel to her. She has tried her best to get rid of him, as she can do better alone. She works by the day, and keeps two or three roomers. She needs help and advice to lead a clean life.

Mrs. Machterlincks is a widow; she has a rented house in which there are five rooms. She has two families as tenants, and between fifteen and twenty men boarders. She has several lots nearly paid for.

John Luelbachyl and his wife Mary came out from Galicia last spring. When he reached Winnipeg it was discovered that he had 'sore eyes,' and he was deported. His wife remained in the Immigration Hall for several months. Then she had a bad ankle, and had to be taken to the hospital. The three children were sent to the Children's Aid.

Pieter Yabroof is employed in a slaughterhouse. He and his wife and two children live in two rented rooms, and keep from fifteen to twenty men roomers. The place is nearly all beds. There are also a table, a stove and some boxes.

Michael Franchicinski is a laborer, but has at present no work. He and wife and five children live in two small rooms for which they

Double-decker tenements, Winnipeg
1 A tenement built on the rear of a lot so that several similar
   buildings may be built in front
2 In this building, owned by a Syrian, there are many homes,
   and generally in each home some boarders

pay $4.50 a month; this must come out of the summer earnings.
They have had great trouble and expense with one of the children.
Little Pieter took sick when they were coming out here, and was
sent back to Austria. The father hopes to save enough money to go
for his little boy.

John Klenbyel and wife and six children, and from fifteen to
twenty boarders live in four rented rooms. The place is 'beastly'
dirty. The boarders bring home kegs of beer nearly every day. Two
of the older girls are 'working out.' One of them told our visitor the
other day that she cannot stay at home; she is happier away.

Comment is hardly necessary. These are some of our immigrants
– our coming citizens. How about standards of living – decency –
morality? What about education and religion? Is it too high a flight
to ask, what about our Canadian ideals?

Chapter 21

Restriction of immigration

All countries are concerned with keeping their own useful citizens at home. All countries are concerned in preventing the ingress of foreign criminals, deficients or diseased.
WHELPLEY

The situation is grave and threatening, for, no matter how favorable may be the laws of Europe as applied to emigration, until each nation is compelled by sentiment from within or without to bear its own social burdens, they will be unloaded as freely as possible along the line of least resistance. Our immigration tide unless thoroughly policed carries with it the germs of anarchy, crime, disease and degeneracy.
WHELPLEY

While each of the colonies enforces more or less restrictive laws governing those who seek to enter, it is only necessary to note the experience of the United States to reach the conclusion that, should the popular tide of emigration turn toward these British Colonies, attracted by prosperous conditions or deftly directed that way by transportation interests, it would be equally impossible for South Africa, Australia or Canada to wholly exclude the undesirables.
WHELPLEY

The atmosphere of the Old World is permeated with the spirit of emigration. In all cases of hardship, of lack of employment, of misery and want, of misfortune and crime, the sufferer is urged to emigrate. If an industry is languishing, the workmen are told to emigrate. If the poorhouses are crowded, the authorities try to empty them on the colonies. If the country is deserted for the city, the city is to be depleted for the colonies; and the persons who have once deserted the soil are to be placed on it again. If population is constantly increasing by an excess of births over deaths, the remedy lies in cutting down at the other end by sending away the adults.
R. MAYO SMITH

WHEN it has become necessary in the United States to form an Immigration Restriction League, it is surely high time that we examined closely the character of our immigration, and shut out those whose presence will not make for the welfare of our national life.

President McKinley thus expressed the situation: 'A grave peril to the Republic would be a citizenship too ignorant to understand, or too vicious to appreciate the great value and beneficence of our institutions and laws, and against all who come here to make war upon them, our gates must be promptly and tightly closed.' In his message of 1903, President Roosevelt said: 'We cannot have too much immigration of the right kind, and we should have none at all of the wrong kind. The need is to devise some system by which undesirable immigrants shall be kept out entirely while desirable immigrants are properly distributed throughout the country.'

Canada, eager to secure immigrants, has adopted the system of giving bonuses. The United States, on the other hand, levies a head tax that more than defrays the cost of inspection. The following figures, quoted by Mr. Monk, a member of the Canadian Parliament, contrasts the American and Canadian systems:

United States

Year	Immigrants	Head tax	Money brought in
1904	812,870	$1,599,472	$20,894,383
1905	1,026,499	2,082,473	25,109,112
1906	1,100,735	2,290,901	25,109,413
1907	1,285,349	2,782,103	25,599,893
Total	4,225,453	$8,755,350	$96,712,801

So far, Canada has paid in bonuses, to attract immigrants, $781,613. The proportions are: British, $252,230; Continental, $446,811; United States, $82,571.

'Thus,' says Mr. Monk, 'we have paid over three-quarters of a million, besides meeting the expenses of inspection, etc., while the United States have paid no bonuses, have made their immigrants defray the whole expense of their inspection, and have obliged them to bring nearly a hundred millions of money into the country in the last four years. Our total outlay for immigration was $950,000 last year, and is to be $1,045,000 this year.'*

According to our Immigration Act in Canada, provision is made for the appointment of immigration officers, regulations are drawn up for the protection of immigrants, and restrictions are made *re* the immigration of certain classes.

The following clauses give the law which prohibits certain persons from landing, and provides for deportation:

26. No immigrant shall be permitted to land in Canada, who is feeble-minded, an idiot, or an epileptic, or who is insane, or who has had an attack of insanity within five years; nor shall any immigrant be so landed who is deaf and dumb, blind or infirm, unless he belongs to a family accompanying him or already in Canada, and which gives security, satisfactory to the Minister, and in conformity with the regulations in that behalf, if any, for his permanent support if admitted into Canada.

27. No immigrant shall be permitted to land in Canada who is afflicted with a loathsome disease, or with a disease which is contagious or infectious, and which may become dangerous to the public health or widely disseminated, whether such immigrant intends to settle in Canada or only to pass through Canada to settle in some other country; provided that if such disease is one which is curable within a reasonably short time, the immigrant suffering therefrom may, subject to the regulations in that behalf, if any, be permitted to remain on board where hospital facilities do not exist on shore, or to leave the vessel for medical treatment, under such regulations as may be made by the Minister.

28. No person shall be permitted to land in Canada who is a pauper, or destitute, a professional beggar, or vagrant, or who is likely to become a public charge; and any person landed in Canada who, within two years thereafter, has become a charge upon the public funds, whether municipal, provincial, or federal, or an inmate of or a charge upon, any charitable institution, may be deported and returned to the port of place whence he came or sailed for Canada.

29. No immigrant shall be permitted to land in Canada who has been convicted of a crime involving moral turpitude, or who is a

* See Appendix no 2.

prostitute, or who procures, or brings or attempts to bring into Canada prostitutes or women for purposes of prostitution.

30. The Governor-in-Council may, by proclamation or order, whenever he considers it necessary or expedient, prohibit the landing in Canada of any special class of immigrants, of which due notice shall be given to the transportation companies.

(2) The Governor-in-Council may make such regulations as are necessary to prohibit the entry into Canada of any greater number of persons from any foreign country than the laws of such country permit to emigrate to Canada.

31. Acting under the authority of the Minister, the immigration agent, the medical officer, and any other officer or officers named by the Minister for such purpose, may act as a board of inquiry at any port of entry to consider and decide upon the case of any immigrant seeking admission into Canada.

(2) The decision of such board touching the right of any such immigrant to land in Canada shall be subject to appeal to the Minister.

(3) The Governor-in-Council may make regulations governing the procedure in connection with inquiries by such boards of inquiry and appeals from their decisions.

32. All railway or transportation companies or other persons bringing immigrants from any country into Canada shall, on the demand of the Superintendent of Immigration, deport to the country whence he was brought any immigrant prohibited by this Act, or by any order in council or regulation made thereunder, from being landed in Canada who was brought by such railway, transportation company or other person into Canada within a period of two years prior to the date of such demand.

33. Whenever in Canada an immigrant has, within two years of his landing in Canada, become a public charge, or an inmate of a penitentiary, gaol, prison, or hospital or other charitable institution, it shall be the duty of the clerk or secretary of the municipality to forthwith notify the Minister, giving full particulars.

(2) On receipt of such information the Minister may, in his discretion, after investigating the facts, order the deportation of such immigrant at the cost and charges of such immigrant if he is able to pay, and if not, then at the cost of the municipality wherein he has last been regularly resident, if so ordered by the Minister, and if he is

a vagrant or tramp, or there is no such municipality, then at the cost of the Department of the Interior.

(3) When the immigrant is an inmate of a penitentiary, gaol, or prison, the Minister of Justice may, upon the request of the Minister of the Interior, issue an order to the warden or governor of such penitentiary, gaol or prison, commanding him to deliver the said immigrant to the person named in the warrant issued by the Superintendent of Immigration as hereinafter provided, with a view to the deportation of such immigrant; and the Superintendent of Immigration shall issue his warrant to such person as he may authorize to receive such immigrant from the warden or governor of the penitentiary, gaol or prison, as the case may be, and such order and warrant may be in the form given in Schedule 2 to this Act.

(4) Such order of the Minister of Justice shall be sufficient authority to the warden or governor of the penitentiary, gaol or prison, as the case may be, to deliver such immigrant to the person named in the warrant of the Superintendent of Immigration as aforesaid, and such warden or governor shall obey such order; and such warrant of the Superintendent of Immigration shall be sufficient authority to the person named therein to detain such immigrant in his custody in any part of Canada until such immigrant is delivered to the authorized agent of the transportation company or companies which brought him into Canada with a view to his deportation as herein provided.

(5) Every immigrant deported under this section shall be carried by the same transportation company or companies which brought him into Canada to the port from which he came to Canada without receiving the usual payment for such carriage.

(6) In case he was brought into Canada by a railway company, such company shall similarly convey him or secure his conveyance from the municipality or locality whence he is to be deported to the country whence he was brought.

(7) Any immigrant deported under this section as having become an inmate of a penitentiary, gaol or prison, who returns to Canada after such deportation may be brought before any justice of the peace in Canada; and such justice of the peace shall thereupon make out his warrant under his hand and seal for the recommittal of such immigrant to the penitentiary, gaol or prison from which he was deported, or to any other penitentiary, gaol or prison in Canada; and such immigrant shall be so re-committed accordingly and shall

Some conditions which produce 'a foreign problem'
1 Interior of a Polish home
2 A home in which six persons live

undergo a term of imprisonment equal to the residue of his sentence which remained unexpired at the time of his deportation.

No one will quarrel with the provisions of this Act, but it should go further, and provision should be made for more strict enforcement.

The following additional classes of persons are denied admission to the United States: polygamists; anarchists, or persons who believe in, or advocate, the overthrow by force or violence of the Government of the United States, or of all forms of law, or the assassination of public officials; those who have been within one year from the date of application of admission to the United States deported as being under offers, solicitations, promises or agreements to perform labor or service of some kind therein; persons whose ticket or passage is paid for with the money of another, or who is assisted by others to come unless it is affirmatively and satisfactorily shown that such person does not belong to one of the excluded classes. But any person in the United States may send for a relative or friend without thereby putting the burden of proof upon the immigrant.

The prohibition or careful selection of assisted immigrants is of the greatest importance. Tens of thousands have been assisted to emigrate from Great Britain. Many of them are not criminal, or paupers, or diseased, but utterly incapable and unfitted for the life here. A recent regulation seeks to mitigate this evil by insisting that assisted immigrants should, before sailing, pass an inspection of the Canadian officials. This certainly is a move in the right direction. If the inspection is at all thorough this arrangement will probably prove very satisfactory. The object is not to shut out all who are unable to pay their passage, but all who will be unable to earn a living in this country.

But while the law looks well on the statute book, what provision is made for enforcing it?

'No immigrant shall be permitted to land in Canada who is afflicted with a loathsome disease, or with a disease which is contagious or infectious,' etc. When 'immigrants are examined in groups often of 1,000 and over, and as many as 7,000 have arrived in a single day,' how can we have any guarantee that there are no loathsome or contagious or infectious diseases?

Broughton Brandenburg, President of the National Institute of Immigration for the United States, testifies to the weakness of our system:

'If there are members of the family who are physically unfit to be sent to Ellis Island, the sub-agents persuade the family to separate at the point of embarkation, and the diseased and deformed are sent across the channel into England, and dumped in the charitable institutions. *Sometimes they are sent from England, perhaps even from the port of embarkation, into Canada.*'

'No person shall be permitted to land in Canada who is a pauper, or destitute, or a vagrant.' But who is there to detect the pauper? It is true a man is asked to show how much money he has, but many an assisted immigrant has a little money, and many who have practically no money are allowed to pass.

What means are taken to detect criminals and prostitutes? What, indeed, can be taken?

Then, as to deportation – a few of the worst cases are deported; but thousands of incapables are filling our cities and being 'carried' by the community. The winter of 1907-8 has shown the real conditions and how difficult it is to enforce the Act.

The trouble is that we are *working at the wrong end.* The examination in every case should be not at the ports of entry, but at the ports from which the immigrants sail – or better still at the homes from which they come. Such a course would be at once kinder to the immigrants and much safer for our country. The present mode of deportation is necessarily cruel. Poor people are sent back and forward across the Atlantic, often suffering great hardship; children are torn from their parents and sent back among strangers. A scant living in the old land is sacrificed in the hopes of the fortune in the new land. After failure here comes deportation, but not always the old position at home.

Again, the examination where the people are known is the only effective method. Diseased, paupers, criminals, prostitutes and undesirables generally are known in their home neighborhood.

The Canadian Government should insist on the immigrant presenting a satisfactory certificate from the Government officials of his own country. If the foreign governments would not co-operate, if any are too despotic or corrupt to make such an arrangement practicable, then we should appoint our own agents in Europe who would make most thorough investigation.

We again quote Mr. Brandenburg, who says:

No matter what our standard of requirements may be, the immigrant will evade it if he is permitted to state his own qualifications uncontradicted. The only place to ascertain the truth is where he has lived. After he has reached New York, can he be held till his record is looked up in Europe? Can he be detained at Bremen or Naples while his career in Russia or Greece is investigated? Both are absurd. The important examination must take place in the locality where the evidence exists. Any other plan is folly and a waste of time, nothing more than a costly and dangerous makeshift.

There are several countries that would lend their aid to the establishment of an inspection service within their borders. There are others that would not. Place a head tax of $50.00 on every immigrant from any country that will not permit such inspection, and in three months there will be a reversal of that Government's policy. The foreign steamship companies will attend to that.

But if we had provision for thorough examination, what standard should we require? In addition to those already in the list of the prohibited, persons of poor physique, persons mentally deficient, the hopelessly incapable, the morally depraved – these surely should be excluded. In this matter our sympathies are divided. We pity the poor man or woman or child who cannot come up to the standard. There may be exceptional cases in which such people would 'do well' in Canada. But we cannot but think that we must protect the highest interests of our own land. Each country should be forced to care for its own criminals, paupers and diseased. To relieve any country of the burden is only to delay the application of measures that will abolish the conditions which produce these classes.

But there is here a larger question – the advisability or the justifiability of excluding not merely certain individuals, but certain classes. There is the live question of the Orientals on the Pacific coast. The Chinese, Japanese and Hindus are – or the majority of them are – physically and mentally 'fit.' They are in no sense paupers or incapables. Indeed, one of the most frequent and serious charges against them is that they are able to drive out other labor. Should they be excluded – if so, on what grounds? Much has been said on both sides. There is, no doubt, a national prejudice that should be overcome. On the other hand, the expression, 'This is a white man's country,' has deeper significance than we sometimes imagine.

The advocates for admission argue that we ought not to legislate against a particular class or nation, and that the Orientals are needed to develop the resources of the country. Their opponents believe that white laborers cannot compete with Orientals, that the standard of living will be lowered, and white men driven out, and they claim that a nation has the right to protect itself.

Needless to say, the economic aspects are those that really divide men on this subject, for, generally speaking, capitalists and employers are ranged against the labor party. Perhaps in the early stages of development, Chinese labor was necessary. Perhaps, for some time, the presence of a limited number of Orientals may be advantageous. But it does seem that the exclusionists are right in their contention that laborers working and living as the Orientals do, will displace European laborers. It is generally agreed that the two races are not likely to 'mix.' Ultimately, then, the question resolves itself into the desirability of a white caste and a yellow, or black caste, existing side by side, or above and below, in the same country. We confess that the idea of a homogeneous people seems in accord with our democratic institutions and conducive to the general welfare. This need not exclude small communities of black or red or yellow peoples. It is well to remember that we are not the only people on earth. The idealist may still dream of a final state of development, when white and black and red and yellow shall have ceased to exist, or have become merged into some neutral gray. We may love all men and yet prefer to maintain our own family life.

Phillips Brooks has stated the ethics of a policy of restriction:

No nation, as no man, has a right to take possession of a choice bit of God's earth, to exclude the foreigner from its territory, that it may live more comfortably and be a little more at peace. But if to this particular nation there has been given the development of a certain part of God's earth for universal purposes; if the world, in the great march of centuries, is going to be richer for the development of a certain national character, built up by a larger type of manhood here, then for the world's sake, for the sake of every nation that would pour in upon it that which would disturb that development, we have a right to stand guard over it. We are to develop here in America a type of national character, we believe, for which the world is to be richer always. It may be the last great experiment for God's wandering humanity upon earth. We have a right to stand guard over the conditions of that experiment, letting nothing interfere with it, drawing into it the richness that is to come by the entrance of many men from many nations, and they in sympathy with our constitution and laws.

We, in Canada, have certain more or less clearly defined ideals of national well-being. These ideals must never be lost sight of. Non-ideal elements there must be, but they should be capable of assimilation. Essentially non-assimilable elements are clearly detrimental to our highest national development, and hence should be vigorously excluded.

Chapter 22

Assimilation

We may well ask whether this insweeping immigration is to foreignize us, or we are to Americanize it. Our safety demands the assimilation of these strange populations, and the process of assimilation becomes slower and more difficult as the proportion of foreigners increases.
JOSIAH STRONG

Until very recent years the power of assimilation has apparently been sufficient to carry on this process without any serious breakdown of the political machinery. Of late, however, there are signs that the task is becoming more difficult, and that we are suffering under serious evils due to this constant addition to our voting population of persons not altogether fitted to exercise the right of suffrage.
MAYO SMITH

The suffrage means literally self-government. Self-government means intelligence, self-control and capacity for co-operation. If these are lacking, the ballot only makes way for the 'boss,' the corruptionist and oligarchy under the control of democracy. The suffrage must be earned and not merely conferred if it is to be an instrument of self-protection.
JOHN R. COMMONS

FOREIGNERS in large numbers are in our midst. More are coming. How are we to make them into good Canadian citizens?

First of all, they must in some way be unified. Language, nationality, race, temperament, training, are all dividing walls that must be broken down. Proper distribution may do much. There is a very natural tendency for people of the same nationality to settle in large colonies. We have Mennonite, Doukhobor, Galician and Mormon colonies. Some contain 10,000 people in almost a solid block. Isolated from Canadian people, they are much slower to enter upon Canadian life. Such colonies are really bits of Russia or Austria or Germany transplanted to Canada. Not only are they less open to Canadian ideas, but, closely united, they can control the entire community. The social, the educational, the religious, the political life is dominated by alien ideas. It would seem a wise policy to scatter the foreign communities among the Canadian, in this way facilitating the process of assimilation.

In the cities even worse conditions prevail. Already we have the Chinese quarter and the Jewish or Italian settlements. In the United States this tendency toward segregation is more manifest; within the foreign section everything is foreign. Hunter writes: 'To live in one of these foreign communities is actually to live on foreign soil. The thoughts, feelings and traditions which belong to the mental life of the colony are often entirely alien to an American. The newspapers, the literature, the ideals, the passions, the things which agitate the community, are unknown to us except in fragments.'

The social settlements in some of the larger cities have done something toward coming in sympathetic touch with the foreign communities, but their best work so far has been in bringing to light the actual and almost desperate conditions.

How are we to break down the walls which separate these foreigners from us? First of all comes the Public School. Too great emphasis cannot be placed upon the work that has been accomplished and may − yes, must − be accomplished by our National Schools. It is most unfortunate that in Canada we have Separate School systems, and, in some provinces, what is worse than a good Separate School system.

In the recent number of the *Labor Gazette* the provisions in the various provincial statute books dealing with the compulsory attendance of pupils at school are thus summarized:

An indispensable factor in solving the foreign problem
1 A Public School in western Canada
2 Public School children in Winnipeg's foreign section –
   many nationalities represented

Nova Scotia Children between the ages of 6 and 16 years, if physically and mentally capable, must attend school for at least 120 days
in the school year, but a child over 12 years of age who passes a
satisfactory examination in grade seven of common school work,
and any other child over 13 years of age, who has attended school
60 days during 14 consecutive weeks in the preceding year, if necessity requires him to work, may be exempted from the above
provision on permission of the local school board.

New Brunswick A comprehensive Act providing for the compulsory
attendance of children at school between the ages of 7 and 12 years
was passed in the year 1903. Provision was made in a special way
under the Act with reference to the employment of children below
the school age.

Quebec The payment of the fees of school children is compulsory,
but there is no provision under the law compelling the attendance of
children at school.

Ontario Under the terms of a special Act respecting truancy and
compulsory school attendance, every child between the ages of 8
and 14 years must attend school for the full term each year, unless
he has passed the entrance examination for high schools, or under
certain other specified conditions. The employment of school children during school hours is prohibited under a penalty of $20, unless
the child is required in husbandry or in urgent or necessary household duties, or for the necessary maintenance of himself or some
person dependent on him. The Act also provides for the appointment of truancy officers, and defines their duties. The onus of proof
as to the age of the child lies with the defendant in any action.

Manitoba Under the Manitoba Public School Act it is declared that
every person in rural municipalities between the ages of 5 and 16
years, and in any cities, towns and villages between the ages of 6 to
16 years, shall have the right to attend some school. Attendance,
however, is not compulsory.

Saskatchewan and Alberta The attendance at school of children
between the ages of 7 and 12 years, inclusive, is compulsory for a

period of at least 16 weeks each year, eight weeks of which time must be consecutive. Provision is made for the investigation of cases of non-attendance and the appointment and proceedings of truancy officers.

British Columbia Every child from the age of 7 to 14 inclusive, must attend some school, or be otherwise educated for six months in every year. Exemption is granted in case the child has reached a standard of education of the same or greater than that to be obtained in the public schools of British Columbia.

In Montreal, out of a total of 10,000 children under the Protestant School Commission, 3,500 are Jews, and this proportion is rapidly increasing.

In Toronto there are about 700 Jewish children in the schools. Many of the Italian children attend the Separate Schools. Compulsory attendance in Ontario is almost regretted by some, as many of the foreigners are forced to decide for the Separate School. But better a Separate School than none.

In Manitoba there is no compulsory education – a crying shame! Thousands of children are growing up without any education. In the city of Winnipeg itself hundreds of children run the streets, and there is no law to deal with them. True, there is a law by which an habitual truant may be handed over to the probation officer, but a child who never has gone to school is not a truant; he can do as he pleases. And he does. Nearly a hundred boys and girls are out on suspended sentence – convicted of crime, but released because the magistrate hesitates to send them to jail with hardened criminals. Hundreds of others are as guilty, but have never been 'caught.'

It is a disgrace that such conditions exist in our country – a worse state of affairs than obtains in most of the countries from which the immigrants come. We know that there are political difficulties and religious prejudices behind these conditions, but surely there are a sufficient number of men who love their country well enough to insist that every boy and girl in Canada have a chance to obtain at least an elementary education.

A move in the right direction has been made by the Manitoba Provincial Government in the appointment of agents to organize school districts in foreign communities. Under ordinary circumstances the initiative lies with the residents of any district; but if residents are ignorant or indifferent, they ought to be advised or compelled to organize.

In the other Western provinces the school system, though not ideal, seems to be working out fairly satisfactorily. Public Schools are rapidly multiplying, an additional Separate School being a rare exception. There are still, however, many communities where schools have not been established.

In addition to the work among the children, the school boards in several cities have been experimenting in work among adult foreigners. Last winter, in Winnipeg, about four hundred were instructed in English and other branches three nights in the week. The results were very gratifying, and the night school will be permanently established. We have often thought that our Public Schools, with their splendid equipment, might extend their operations by establishing industrial classes and literary clubs, thus becoming the centre of the life of the community.

It is not in the school, however, but on the street and in the shop that the foreigners acquire their knowledge of Canada. One of the most effective agencies for breaking down national differences is the labor union. Men of all languages and creeds band themselves together to maintain their 'rights' against employers. Every strike reveals the strength of trades and labor unions. Few think of the education that has been going on for months before united action is possible. Whatever its faults, the union is doing an immense amount in breaking down, at least, certain national prejudices and educating the foreigner to think.

Then the press wields a mighty power. The first English the foreigner reads is the headline in the evening paper. Even before he reads English the questions of the day are discussed in the papers published in his own language. Already in Canada there are newspapers in most of the European languages, and even in Chinese and Hindu.

Then we have the political clubs and organizations. The political parties are not slow to recognize the importance of the foreign vote; we have our Hungarian, Jewish, Syrian and Polish societies, and a dozen more. There are discussions and organization and canvassing; how intelligent the discussion, how disinterested the organization, and how clean the canvass is a matter of question.

What are the first lessons the foreigner receives in the government of our country? A thoroughly disreputable fellow, who is useful because he can speak several languages, is engaged to secure voters. He 'rounds up' as many as he can, and enters their names on the voters' lists. Here is a description of a common scene on registration day:

In a certain booth, when we entered, was a group of Galicians in tow of an interpreter of the same nationality. We listened to the methods of registration in one case where every question was asked in Ruthenian by the interpreter, and answered in the same tongue by the said Canadian citizen. When the declaration was read, the citizen-voter stood by with stolid face and unresponsive eyes. The clerk enquired, 'He understands this?' And the interpreter replied, 'Oh, yaas; I explaan to heem bee-fore.' 'Can he write?' asked the clerk. The interpreter repeated the question, and received a shake of the head in reply. Therefore, did this voter make his mark? Well — what of it? That is the same mark required on the ballot. Besides, he will probably be allowed an interpreter in the voting booth. *North-West Baptist*

This is the way voters are made. Their qualifications? They are supposed to have been resident in the country for three years.* And the vote of one of these foreigners 'kills' the vote of the most intelligent Canadian!

When the election comes, the services of the aforesaid disreputable fellow are again required. With his knowledge of English and the foreign tongues he commands the situation. The party must have him and must depend upon him. Big promises and a little money will go a long way. He 'fixes' a few of the leaders in the settlement. Then, on election day, the beer and whiskey flow freely. The election is won! This is no fancy picture and no isolated case. How can the foreigner have any high regard for our institutions? How can our free institutions be maintained?

Peoples emerging from serfdom, accustomed to despotism, untrained in the principles of representative government, without patriotism — such peoples are utterly unfit to be trusted with the ballot.

* See Appendix no 6.

Prof. Shaler says of the European peasant: 'Centuries of experience have bred in him the understanding that he is by nature a peasant, and that, save in rare instances, he can acquire no other station in the land of his birth. It is characteristic of peasants that they have accepted this inferior lot. For generations they have regarded themselves as separated from their fellow-citizens of higher caste. They have no large sense of citizenly motives; they feel no sense of responsibility for any part of the public life, save that which lies within their own narrow round of action.' *Atlantic Monthly.*

Our democratic institutions are the outcome of centuries of conflict by which to some extent we have been fitted for self-government. It is as absurd as it is dangerous to grant to every newly arrived immigrant the full privilege of citizenship. Just what qualifications should be required cannot be discussed here. The next reform should look to the restriction rather than the extension of the franchise.

In this making of Canadian citizens, the churches should take a greater part than they have hitherto done. The language is a difficulty, but business men and politicians readily overcome this difficulty, and why not the church? Then, the strangers bring their own religions with them, and religious prejudice is the most difficult to overcome. But overcome it must be. The churches to whom has been granted a vision of the Kingdom of God cannot ignore the presence of such large numbers of foreigners. 'Difficult to reach them?' Of course it is, but this is *the problem* of the church in Canada.

Several considerations are essential if we are to assist our immigrants to become Canadians. In the first place we must divest ourselves of a certain arrogant superiority and exclusiveness, perhaps characteristic of the English race. Our untravelled Canadian despises all foreigners alike. We must remember that many of the world's greatest and best men were from the very countries which our immigrants call home. We must learn that the world is wide, and that there are a great many other types than our own, and some just as good, though different. Other languages, customs and religions have their value. Again, we must not expect the foreigners at once to abandon the old in favor of the new. Such a course would show only weakness of character. Loyalty to the old is the best guarantee of loyalty to the new. As someone has put it, 'the light abandonment of ties, whether inherited or voluntary, because they had ceased to be pleasant, would be the uprooting of social and personal virtue.' J. C. Monaghan says (*Catholic World,* US): 'The people who come to us and have no love for the land left behind will be wanting in one of a strong man's best characteristics. I would not be understood as advocating a continuance of the separate schools, papers, churches, etc. If the assimilation is to go on rapidly, every school, paper and church in which a foreign tongue figures is in some measure a hindrance.'

We must in many ways meet these people half way — seek to sympathize with their difficulties, and to encourage them in every forward movement.

Only those who in time can take their place as worthy fellow citizens should be admitted to our Canadian heritage.

Chapter 23

A challenge to the church

The great problem raised by immigration is not embodied in the question, Will these diverse races blend? but in that which enquires, Of what quality will the product be? For as the rivers always set toward the sea, so do these streams of immigration all set toward the common centre of a new national life, and all must reach it soon or late. But as the waters of the ocean are flavored by the salts of alkali plains and the sulphur of mountain springs, by the leaves that drift down from the hillsides and the reeds and grasses of the fertile fields, so shall the life of this nation be seasoned by all the varied characteristics that differentiate the nationalities of the world. In this truth there are elements for our comfort and for our agitation. On the one hand, we may consider that every nationality is a storehouse of strong and enduring qualities which have been the guarantee of its survival; and considering this we well may dream of the nation yet to be, when into the generous texture of this New World life there have been woven the impulse of the Celt and the endurance of the German, the patience of the Slav and the daring of the Northman, the romance of Italy, the suavity of France, the buoyancy of Ireland, the shrewdness of Scotland, the enterprise of England. But on the other hand, there is cause for some alarm when we consider that as these peoples come to us we take them for better for worse, for richer for poorer, in sickness and in health. And, as we view their uncouth ways, their laxity of morals, their alien ideals, the ignorance and superstition of many of them, we sometimes have reason to fear that to us is coming a tremendous contribution of the worse — a contribution against which we will have cause to measure our highest ideals of manhood, our noblest conceptions of womanhood sanctified by faith in the God of the nations and a knowledge of the Gospel of His Son.

North-West Baptist, March 1st, 1907

'GO YE into all the world and preach the gospel to the whole crea-
tion.' Now, when all the world is coming to us, what an opportunity
is presented to the Christian church! The old distinction of home
and foreign missions is being broken down. We have now forced
upon us a new department — 'Foreign work at home.'

Until recent years there have been only two great religious bodies
in Canada, Protestants and Roman Catholics. The French population
was almost entirely Roman Catholic and the English largely Protestant. Both Roman Catholics and Protestants have established
missions among the native tribes. Among the Protestant churches the
Church of England and the Methodist Church have been most active
in this kind of work. Much has been done, and yet there are whole
tribes who are still living in the densest, grossest heathenism.

Several of the Protestant churches have established missions
among the French. The Presbyterian and Methodist churches have
been working along evangelistic and educational lines. Much difference of opinion exists as to the value of this work. One of our
correspondents gives the following spirited defence:

With us French missionaries the question is not, Can Roman
Catholics be saved in their own church? For we believe that souls are
saved in all religions, even among the heathen (Acts iv. 34). But the
question is, Is our church justified in maintaining missions among
the French Catholics of Quebec? It goes without saying that the
answer of every French Protestant is strongly in the affirmative, and
the following reasons are given:

(a) The Word of God is a closed book to the vast majority of the
inhabitants of the Province of Quebec. Here, as in other Roman
Catholic countries, the Church of Rome has confiscated the Sacred
Book. This is an incontrovertible fact. A short visit in the homes of
any village in Quebec will show, not only that the Bible is not in the
possession of the people, but that they are afraid of it, having been
told it was a dangerous book. I was called upon last fall to take the
oath before the Mayor in one of my appointments; the book presented to me to swear upon was the Roman Catholic Prayerbook or
Mass-book, as it is called. Hence, in harmony with the Great Commission, 'Go and preach the gospel to every creature,' we French
Protestants say that as long as there is a man in our country who is
deprived of the opportunity to read the Scriptures, it is the duty of
the church to give him that opportunity.

(b) Again, our work is justified on the ground that large numbers of the French-Canadians are falling into the abyss of free-thought. Even here in a small town I meet people, nominally Catholics, who have rejected all religious tenets. (Some of these can neither read nor write.) Unles the pure and undefiled religion of our Lord and Master, Jesus Christ, is presented to the people of Quebec, we shall see them follow the example of the people of France.

(c) Again, we claim that Rome is a national peril. The Church of Rome is the sworn enemy of our liberties and our principles. Her attitude is in perfect accord with the principles laid down by her theologians and the decrees of the Councils and Popes. Here is what St. Thomas said: 'Though heretics must not be tolerated because they deserve it, we must bear with them till, by second admonition, they may be brought back to the faith of the church; but those who, after a second admonition, remain obstinate in their errors, must not only be excommunicated, but must be delivered to the secular power to be exterminated.' This is a standard theological work of the Church of Rome. The Vatican Council of 1871 anathematized the idea that 'it is no longer expedient that the Catholic religion be held as the only religion of the State, to the exclusion of all other modes of worship.' Pope Pius VI, 1786, in the *Bull Super Solidate,* declared 'that the Pope can deprive kings of their authority to rule, and absolve subjects from their allegiance.' Pope Pius IX declared in 1851 that 'the Roman Catholic religion must be exclusively dominant, and every other worship must be banished and interdicted.' Such are her decrees, and if she does not enforce them to-day, it is due to her lack of power to the *'malheur des temps,'* as one French writer puts it. You know the position she takes in educational matters, and you know, also, for you are just now coming in contact with Galicians, etc., how ignorant and superstitious are her devotees.

In your letter you say that 'apparently our French missions have not been a great success.' It is only 'apparently' so, sir, for since this work has begun some 40,000 French Catholics in Quebec have accepted the Gospel and become Protestants, and our church has contributed its share in bringing about this result ... But why is our present membership so small? This can easily be explained. In the past, and to some extent in the present, most of our converts had to emigrate to the United States, on account of persecutions in our own country. It is a well-known fact that over a hundred French churches have been organized across the line, these being largely composed of our converts. But these are not lost to Protestantism. Again, there are results which cannot be tabulated. A great − a marked − change is slowly, but surely, taking place among my people. My people have become broader, more tolerant, and more independent. *They are beginning to think for themselves,* and our work to-day is largely one of education. The fruit is not yet ripe, but is ripening. It is not possible to change in a year, or even in fifty years, the *'mentalité'* of a people, especially when it is under the control of a church who does her best to prevent assimilation or any close union with other peoples. We must be patient, work and pray, and believe in the power of the truth and of holy lives to overthrow error and dispel darkness.

For some years the Methodists and Presbyterians have carried on small missions among the Chinese in British Columbia. The problem is thus stated in the Report of the Methodist Missionary Society for 1907-8:

The presence of large numbers of Asiatics in some of the provinces of the Dominion has become, from the political and economic points of view, a serious problem. The forces of organized labor see in these Oriental strangers what looks like a dangerous competing element, and if they are permitted to come in large numbers many workmen believe the result will be that wages for both skilled and unskilled labor will rule at much lower figures than if white men only were in control of the situation. This sentiment is very strong, especially in British Columbia, and during recent years steady pressure has been brought to bear − not without success − to induce the Dominion Government, if not to banish the Orientals now in the country, at least to prevent the entrance of any more. To those who can look at the question from an unprejudiced and non-partisan point of view, this seems to be a short-sighted policy. The trend of events points surely to the fact that in the not distant future, perhaps within a generation, Japan and China will be the great markets for our surplus products, especially foodstuffs, and anything which might induce these countries to adopt a retaliatory policy − which they are quite capable of doing − and boycott our products, would be most unfortunate.

But these are selfish considerations which ought not to weigh much one way or the other. The question is one to be settled on broad grounds of justice and international comity, and in the long run a dog-in-the-manger policy will not answer. It is a fundamental mistake to suppose that problems arising from great migrations of the world's populations can be solved by Acts of Parliament or labor combinations that take no account of God and His plans for the world. Still less can they be solved by angry outbursts and mob violence. Let us face the question fairly. The Orientals are here, and a time will come when they will be here in larger numbers. How shall we deal with them? Shall we regard and treat them as barbarians, a menace to society, to be mobbed, boycotted, driven out of the country? That were only to proclaim that we are barbarians ourselves, utterly unworthy of the freedom of which we boast so much. Surely there is 'a more excellent way.' These strangers from the Far East are human beings like ourselves, of the 'one blood,' and just as capable, under proper leadership, of rising in the scale of civilization and becoming a useful element in our cosmopolitan population as are the immigrants from other countries.

If, as stated in the Annual Report of the Methodist Missionary Society for 1906-7, the protection of our country from the 'yellow peril' depends upon 'saving it,' then the efforts of the churches appear rather insignificant. A few Chinese and Japanese evangelists, several 'Homes,' and a few churches and Sunday Schools are all that the church has contributed toward the solution of this problem which means so much to at least one of our provinces. We plead for foreign missions in China and Japan; we have here at home abundant opportunities of reaching these peoples. The work is here, minus the enchantment lent by distance.

But during the last few years the large influx of immigrants has brought the church face to face with new problems and responsibilities of tremendous magnitude. To supply the English-speaking communities which are so rapidly multiplying throughout the great West has taxed the resources of the churches. Hundreds of ministers have been imported from the Old Land, and yet it is difficult to keep pace with the development. This summer (1908) one hundred new prairie towns are being located on the Grand Trunk Pacific Railway and on a branch of the Canadian Pacific Railway.

Accustomed only to work among English-speaking peoples, and
intent on meeting their needs, we have hardly yet realized the claims
of 'our people of foreign speech.'

The Scandinavians and Germans have generally brought their
ministers and church organizations with them. In Winnipeg, in
addition to large Roman Catholic churches, there are fifteen Protes-
tant German churches and missions, including Lutherans, Reformed
Evangelicals, Adventists and Baptists. There are almost as many
Scandinavian, including the Lutheran mission church, Baptists and
Icelandic Unitarian. These various churches have missions throughout the country. The Evangelical Association, or German Methodist
Church, is extending its work in the West. The Moravian Church, or
Unitas Fratrum, has a strong cause in Alberta. Many Germans and
Scandinavians, especially those from the United States, unite with
the various English-speaking congregations. The Methodist and
Presbyterian churches have had one or two Scandinavian missionaries. Of the Canadian churches, the Baptists have been the most
aggressive in working among these peoples. In the prairie provinces
they report twenty-one German churches with a membership of
about 1,500, and sixteen Scandinavian churches with a total of over
360 members. Many of these were, of course, Baptists in the Old
Country.

On the whole, it may be said that these immigrants from Northern Europe are able to care for themselves. If our Canadian churches
desire to work among them, probably this could best be done by
co-operating with some existing organization. For instance, the
Methodist Church ought to be able to come to a working agreement
with the Evangelical Association. In the poorer districts in the cities,
all missionary organizations require German-speaking workers, as the
German language is used by a great variety of peoples.

When we come to the immigrants from Southeastern Europe, we
face an entirely different problem. Most of these are Roman or
Greek Catholic, or Jews. They, too, bring their religions, but often
these are not of a very high order.

The majority of the Jews come from Russia, Austria and Roumania, and constitute an entirely different class from those who
come from England or Germany. Up to the present the Christian
church has done little to reach the Jews in Canada. The London
Society for Promoting Christianity amongst the Jews has a small

mission in Montreal and another in Ottawa. The Presbyterian Church has a mission in Toronto, where there is also a non-denominational Jewish mission. In Winnipeg, for a short time, there was a mission under the auspices of the Anglican Church, but this has been discontinued. Has the Christian church no duty toward the Hebrew people, or do we despair of leading them into fuller light? Poor people, it is a strange kind of Christianity that they have known! The experience of one little Jewish girl may be regarded as typical. Sarah is only nine years old, but her young life has been crowded with experiences. The family lived in Russia. She remembers well one dreadful day when a mob began killing the Jews. Her father took her mother and her to a stable and hid them. She lay for hours under some hay in a manger while her 'Christian' persecutors searched everywhere for the hated Jews. She hardly dared to breathe. The terror of that day is branded deep into her very being. Then came the perilous flight across the border – months of hardship – the long sea voyage – and then the new land. Little Sarah says: 'In Russia I hated the Christians. I would spit when the name of Christ was spoken. But here my teachers are so good and kind. I know now that Christians are not all bad. I know Jesus must be good.'

Or let me quote from a letter written by a young Jew in our night school:

I was born in N____, eight miles from Berlin. When I was three years of age my father moved to a little village not far from the town of W____ in Russia. At the age of four, I was sent to a Hebrew school, which I attended for two years. After that my father engaged a private teacher who lived at our house; he taught me reading, writing and arithmetic, and religious knowledge. I was instructed in the five Books of Moses, and in the Prophets according to the Jewish beliefs. This teacher stayed with us for four years, and by the end of that time I was being taught in the Jewish tabernacle. I worked on the farm for one year, helping my father. When I was eleven years, I started again to school in the town of W____ to learn the Russian language. I attended school for one year and three months, after which I went home for the summer holidays. During my holidays an incident transpired in my life which I shall always remember. On Sunday I was at a Catholic church, and listened to the priest who, to my mind and way of thinking, did not preach the unvarnished truth to the poor uneducated people. At the close of the service he came through the pews carrying a gold cross in his hand, and requesting all the people to kiss it. This I refused to do. Then he began to preach directly to me, telling me if I refused to obey I would invoke the anger of God. He finished by telling how cruelly the Jews treated Christ, and urged his people to be cruel to the Jews when they had the chance. At this I got up on a chair, and began to talk to the people. I cannot remember now exactly what I said, but the tenor of my speech was that the people should think for themselves and not be led astray by those who preached for material gain. Space will not permit me to go into details, but suffice it to say that my act was a grave offence against the Russian law, and a few hours after I got home two police officials came to my father's to take me to the jail. My father took me out on bail, and as I was under age I did not receive any punishment, but was warned if a like occurrence happened I would pay for the whole business. When I was about thirteen years of age I went back to school and got mixed up with Socialists. I was greatly influenced, and a few months found me a Socialist organizer and preacher. While I was thus engaged I learned that the law officers were hunting for me. I had to leave home and flee into Germany with friends, where I remained for three years, when I left and came here to Canada. I was sixteen years of age, I could not speak a word of English, and did not know any people here. I do not go to any place of worship. I spend my time reading.

This young man is now nineteen. In two years after coming to Canada he had made $1,500, and now has a responsible position with a city firm.

Let these stories plead the cause of Jewish missions. The old faith is being lost. Have we a better to offer? Then, can we refuse to make the Jews sharers of our Gospel liberty? Surely we are debtors both to Jews and Gentiles.

We now approach the most difficult problem of all — the attitude of the Protestant churches toward the Catholic peoples of Southern and Eastern Europe. This is not the French Catholic question over again. So different are the two, that if we declined absolutely to establish missions among the French, we might still consider the advisability of missions among these peoples.

Let us consider first the needs of the Italians. The Roman Catholic Church attempted to graft Christianity on to a heathen civilization. The column of Marcus Aurelius was crowned with a statue of St. Paul. In the Pantheon the statue of Venus was replaced by an image of the Virgin. Jupiter was worshipped as St. Peter. Christianity became a baptized paganism. Now this hybrid religion is losing its hold upon the people. Most of the Italians who come to us are ignorant and superstitious; they have been poor and oppressed. Though nominally Roman Catholics, many are bitterly opposed to the church. The women attend church, at least at the times of the great festivals. The majority of the men are indifferent to religious affairs; the younger men are rapidly becoming sceptics. It is not a case of fighting the Catholics, it is the need to save the people! These Italians are pouring into our country. Have we nothing to offer them? The Methodist and Presbyterian churches have small missions in Toronto and Montreal, but these are, to use the words of one of the workers, 'entirely inadequate.' An American authority says: 'Among no class of foreigners has American mission work seemed to yield quicker, larger or more abiding returns.' If we are to be successful in this work we must do two things at the start. First, take it up in real earnest – put money and brains and heart into it. Second, we must among Romans be Romans. Sometimes we emphasize Canadian customs as Christian duties, and fancy that methods adapted to work among English Protestants should be effective among Italian Catholics.

An Italian missionary says that several agencies should work concurrently – (1) The Mission, (2) The Press, (3) Social Institutions. 'The people should be surrounded by genuine Christian sympathy and love – and they are lovable, if understood; they are to be won by treating them as Canadians, by discouraging the prejudices that often exist against them, and by helping them in every way possible.' This Italian work still lies ahead of the Canadian churches. Are there not some who will devote their lives to this people, who will become one with them and champion their cause?

In our cities we have numbers of Syrians, Armenians and Bulgarians. Little has as yet been done for them. In Toronto the Presbyterians have taken an interest in the Bulgarians from Macedonia, and a few are found in the various missions. The Macedonian cry ought to have a new significance for us in these days.

Last of all, we come to the immigrants from Austria and Russia – a score of peoples, each with peculiar needs. Take one example alone, the Doukhobors. They are Christians – of a kind. But surely Canadian Christians may help them in many ways. The Society of Friends established a school among them. This is all that has been done. Is there not here, too, a call to some of our young men? Ten thousand people, deeply religious and, according to their convictions, faithful unto death. Will our churches remain apathetic?

But the great majority of the people from Austria and Russia are Roman or Greek Catholics. They are peasants, the majority illiterate and superstitious; some of them bigoted fanatics, some of them poor, dumb, driven cattle, some intensely patriotic, some embittered by years of wrong and oppression, some anarchists – the sworn enemies alike of Church and State. The Slav is essentially religious, but his religious instincts have never yet found true expression. The move to the new land means a shaking of the very foundations of belief. The old associations are left behind, the mind is prepared for new impresions, the individual is thrown into an entirely different social life, and is enveloped by a different religious atmosphere. Sometimes he may cling tenaciously, desperately, to the old beliefs; often he renounces them entirely. Modifications must take place. The desire for light and liberty lies behind even the excesses into which some plunge. Light and liberty – these are what are needed.

The Greek Church of Russia has established strong churches in the United States, and these have established missions in Western Canada. But as yet the work is not well organized or supported, and schisms are of frequent occurrence.

The Roman Catholic Church has, so far, done comparatively little for these peoples. In Winnipeg there is a large Polish church with missions in outlying points, and a Ruthenian (Greek Catholic) church with several missions. There are also a number of scattered missions among Poles and Hungarians. But a study of the Catholic Directory reveals a surprisingly small number of distinctively foreign churches. The Redemptorist Fathers at Brandon and Yorkton, and the Benedictine Sisters at Winnipeg devote themselves largely to work among Poles. The Basilian Fathers of the Greek United Rite at Winnipeg and the Sisters, Little Servants of Mary, are working among the Ruthenians.

Of the Protestant churches, the Church of England and the Congregational Church have done nothing. The Baptists have done considerable colportage work, and report a Hungarian Mission and several small missions among the Galicians and Russians. In this field the Presbyterian Church has done by far the greatest work, and to them belongs the honor of initiating one of the most remarkable movements in church history. They have four medical men working among the Ruthenians and four missionaries among the Hungarians, many of whom belong to the Reformed Church. But their most important work has been in connection with the Independent Greek Church of Canada.

The Ruthenians had originally been Greek Catholic, but under Polish dominion, Roman Catholicism was forced upon them about three hundred years ago. The Jesuits were the instruments of this enforced conformity and accompanying persecution. Concessions were made, the Greek rite was maintained, and the priests allowed to marry. But only the higher clergy really accepted the papal suprem-acy, the lower clergy and the people remaining Greek Catholics. After the division of Poland, Russian Poland returned to the Greek Church. Austrian Poland (Galicia, etc.), remained under the control of the Roman Catholic Church. Of our Ruthenian immigrants about one-quarter are Orthodox Greek Catholics, the other three-quarters being Uniats (that is, those Greek Catholics upon whom Roman Catholicism was forced). Only step-children of Rome, they needed but the opportunity to break from Rome.

Owing to quarrels between the Russian Greek Church and the Patriarchate of Jerusalem, an Independent Greek Church was estab-lished in the United States. Free alike from Rome and St. Peters-burg, this church won many adherents among the Ruthenian Uniats. The Independent Bishop came to Winnipeg and established a church. But there was dissatisfaction and jealousy, and finally the young priests refused to recognize the authority of the Bishop.

Now we come to the part played by the Presbyterian Church. Some of the Greek priests approached the Home Mission Commit-tee, asking for their co-operation; some wished to come directly under the authority of the Presbyterian Church. What was the best way to help these people, Catholics, yet in some ways Protestant? This was the problem before the leaders of the Presbyterian Church.

They decided to allow the Greek Church to work out its own salvation as an independent institution. So there was formed the Independent Greek Church of Canada. The Presbyterians assisted in preparing a catechism. They established scholarships in Manitoba College and arranged courses of lectures for the priests. They assisted in building churches and maintaining the missions. The last Home Mission Report shows that twenty-four Independent Greek ministers are employed – thirteen in Manitoba, seven in Saskatchewan and four in Alberta.

During the last five years the Independent Greek Church has built over fity churches, and claims to have a following of about 60,000. What is this independent church like? Sometimes the priests call themselves Catholics, sometimes Protestants. In some ways the church may be said to be Catholic in form and Protestant in spirit. 'On the paper,' as one of their priests put it, 'we are under the Patriarch of Jerusalem. We pray for the Patriarch in church.' The Government is Presbyterian in form, and yet the priests lay great emphasis on the fact that they are regularly ordained, even though they despise the erratic bishop who ordained them. Their catechism is pretty much that of the Free Churches of England, though they retain the seven sacraments. They use the Greek rite, but they read and expound the Scriptures.

How far is there evangelical teaching and personal religious experience among them? Perhaps that depends on the particular priest. Sometimes within the robes is a man who really feels and knows; sometimes the robes are everything. But the spirit of enquiry is at work. The people feel their liberty, and are eagerly seeking for more light. Gradually many of the outward forms are being sloughed off; the people are studying their Bibles. They are mingling with Protestant people and catching the Protestant spirit. Can they be expected at once to become Protestants? If it were possible, would it be wise to attempt this change? Mediaevalism transplanted to the twentieth century – who can tell what the result will be?

The Methodist Church has a hospital at Pakan, and has done some work among the Slavs in connection with All Peoples' Mission, Winnipeg. Recently work has been commenced among the Polish people. The Poles are and have been for generations Roman Catholic, but they are great lovers of liberty, and bitterly resent the domination and, it is claimed, the oppression of the Irish Bishops in the United States and the French Bishops in Canada. This has led to the establishment of strong Independent Polish Catholic churches in the United States. This Independent movement is extending to

Canada, and is being greatly accelerated by the success of the Independent Greek Church.

It would seem as if the Methodist Church might work among the Poles in some such way as the Presbyterian Church has been working among the Ruthenians. During the past winter two young Independent priests have been attending Wesley College, and now has come the purchase of the Independent Polish Church in Winnipeg.*

If we are to help these Catholic peoples, two courses seem open. Either we must try to make Methodists of them, or we must help them to work out their own salvation. The first is easiest to attempt, but seems to us doomed to failure. The second is most difficult, but seems to be in accord with the laws of true spiritual development. Reformation must come from within. Independence means that the people are taught to think for themselves; it means that the Bible is placed in their hands; it means that their children attend the Public Schools instead of the parochial schools; it means that the people ally themselves with Protestants rather than with Catholics. *Independence affords the opportunity for reformation.*

What relation should the Methodist Church bear to such an Independent Church? That must be worked out. These experiments are unique in the history of the Protestant Church. There might be an independent Catholic Church subsidized by Protestant money, or there might be a Protestant organization granted special concessions. But who can forecast the form which any religious movement may take? Thousands of people are groping after the light. Can we not help to throw open the doors?

Special attention should be drawn to the necessity of mission work in our cities.** Here we have all sorts and conditions of men — the most needy isolated from those who might help them. The church must work out some new organization, and adopt special methods to accomplish this work. It would seem that institutional work is most effective. The effort must be not merely to preach to the people, but to educate them and to improve the entire social conditions.

In view of the great work before us the familiar words of Punshon come to us with new force:

---

   * See Appendix no 3.
 ** See Appendix no 4.

All Peoples' Mission, Winnipeg
1 Polish Church   2 Stella Avenue Church
3 Maple Street Church   4 The Institute

Listen! the Master beseecheth,
    Calling each one by his name;
His voice to each loving heart reacheth,
    Its cheerfullest service to claim.
Go where the vineyard demandeth
    Vinedressers' nurture and care;
Or go where the white harvest standeth,
    The joy of the reaper to share.

Then work, brothers, work, let us slumber no longer,
For God's call to labor grows stronger and stronger;
The light of this life shall be darkened full soon,
But the light of the better life resteth at noon.

Seek those of evil behavior,
    Bid them their lives to amend;
Go, point the lost world to the Saviour,
    And be to the friendless a friend.
Still be the lone heart of anguish
    Soothed by the pity of thine;
By waysides, if wounded ones languish,
    Go, pour in the oil and the wine.
            Then work, etc.

Work for the good that is nighest,
    Dream not of greatness afar;
That glory is ever the highest
    Which shines upon men as they are.
Work, though the world may defeat you,
    Heed not its slander and scorn;
Nor weary till angels shall greet you
    With smiles through the gates of the morn.
            Then work, etc.

Offer thy life on the altar,
   In the high purpose be strong;
And if the tired spirit should falter,
   Then sweeten thy labor with song.
What if the poor heart complaineth,
   Soon shall its wailing be o'er;
For there, in the rest that remaineth,
   It shall grieve and be weary no more.
            Then work, etc.

Appendices

APPENDIX 1

The following condensed table, issued by the Department of the
Interior, gives the latest immigration statistics:

Immigration to Canada

	Fiscal period nine months, 1906-7	Fiscal year, 1907-8	Five months of fiscal year, 1908-9
British	55,791	120,182	37,539
Galician	1,652	14,268	6,295
Belgian	650	1,214	499
French	1,314	2,671	1,182
German	1,903	2,377	796
Russian	2,976	7,493	2,204
Icelandic	46	97	22
Swedish	1,077	2,132	635
From United States	34,659	58,312	29,574
All other countries	24,599	53,723	11,643
Total	124,667	262,469	90,389

APPENDIX 2

On the 11th of September last, the following Order-in-Council was passed referring to the money qualification of immigrants arriving in Canada on and after the 1st of January 1909:

His Excellency the Governor-General-in-Council, in virtue of the provisions of Section 20 of the Immigration Act, Chapter 93, Revised Statues of Canada, 1906, is pleased in view of the labor conditions and of the probable supply and demand for laborers in Canada during the coming winter to Order, and it is hereby Ordered, that in the case of immigrants arriving at Canadian Ports between the 1st day of January and the 15th day of February, 1909, the Immigration Agent at any port shall require every immigrant, male or female, 18 years of age or over, to have in his or her possession money to the minimum amount of $50.00, in addition to a ticket to his or her destination in Canada, unless satisfactory evidence is furnished that the immigrant is going to some definite employment, or to relatives or friends already settled in Canada who would take care of such immigrant, and that on the last mentioned date the money qualification above prescribed be reduced to the minimum amount of $25.00 for each immigrant, and so remain until further ordered.

APPENDIX 3

At a missionary convention held in Winnipeg in the autumn of 1904 the author of this text-book presented a paper on 'The Stranger within Our Gates.' This was subsequently published in the *Methodist Magazine* (July, 1905). In this paper the following suggestions were offered:

Would it not be a mistake to interfere directly with this work? (The Independent Greek Church, which was just then being organized.) Should we not instead allow them to work out their own salvation? We must choose one of three courses. We can oppose these reformers on the ground that they are not evangelical; we can act independently, to a certain extent and for a short time; or we can co-operate with them, supplying their confessed deficiencies.

Assuming that our work should be of a supplementary character, we find that they need sympathy, advice and practical assistance. Several avenues are already open. We have one medical missionary. The Presbyterians have a hospital at Teulon. Extend this work, which the immigration officials say is much appreciated.

But it is along educational lines that at present they need our help the most. Encourage some of our Methodist young men and women to accept positions in Government schools in these foreign colonies. The Inspector informs me that it is difficult to secure Canadian teachers for these schools, that special permits would be granted to competent teachers, that there is splendid work to be done. One of the immigration officials informs me that the Galicians would welcome the establishment of the Sunday School. This work would involve no extra expense to the Missionary Society. It does involve some self-denial on the part of the teacher. Who will go for us?

Let the Missionary Society establish scholarships at Wesley College or at Alberta College, which would assist bright foreign boys to fit themselves as school teachers. With the help of a Canadian Christian environment, our professors could leave their stamp upon these teachers, and thus help to mould the entire community.

From among our probationers at Wesley College, ask for volunteers for foreign work at home. Allow these to substitute German or Russian or Polish for Greek (or the candidate for Indian work substitute Indian). During their course, let them do practical work in connection with All Peoples' Mission, if possible living in a foreign home. (The Roman Catholics have missionaries who know the language, and have even sent priests to Galicia to study the language and the conditions of the people.) Our workers thus trained would be able to do effective service in the way that would open out, or that experience might prove best. At present, with no accurate knowledge and no trained workers and no definite policy, we cannot but blunder.

This brings us to the necessity for the establishment of an Advisory Mission Council in the West. Let there be representation from the Methodist, Presbyterian and Congregational Churches, and, if possible, from the Church of England, the Baptist and Lutheran Churches. For some years the Foreign Mission Boards in the United States and Canada have held conferences concerning the work in the foreign field. An Advisory Council is not impracticable. It is a necessity if we are to have anything like a mutual understanding – if we are to adopt any far-reaching policy – if we are to make any effort at all commensurate with the greatness of the work.

APPENDIX 4

Winnipeg City Mission Board
Chairman — Rev. J. Woodsworth, D.D.
Secretary — Geo. N. Jackson, Esq.
Treasurer — Rev. A. Stewart, D.D.

Mission Centres
Maple Street — All Peoples' near C.P.R. station
Stella Avenue — Bethlehem, corner Powers and Stella
Burrows Avenue — Polish Church
Euclid Street — New building, corner Sutherland

Staff
J. S. Woodsworth, Superintendent
S. East, Pastor, Bethlehem
Miss Marion Adair,
Miss Agnes Allen,   } Deaconesses
Miss Grace Tonkin,
Miss L. S. Mason,
Miss C. V. Wigle,   } Kindergarten Directresses
Miss James,
Miss Blanchard,   } Kindergarten Assistants
Miss A. Kochallea, Bible Woman (resigned)
Chinese teacher (work suspended for lack of funds)
B. Baligrodzki,
A. Sosnowski,   } Polish students at Wesley College
E. Chambers,   } Probationers training for foreign work
Wm. Wyman,   } at home
Volunteer workers from Wesley College
Volunteer workers from city churches

During the past year the Superintendent has considered that his
first duty was the organization and supervision of the Mission.
Various changes have been made, which, it is believed, will make
possible the unification and extension of the work. The emphasis has
been placed upon the work among non-English-speaking peoples
from Europe. A beginning has been made in the training of workers

for this field. A Polish church has been purchased, and a new building is being erected to serve the needs of the foreign population in Point Douglas North. We have endeavored to use every means in our power to spread information and stimulate interest in this work. Outside of his own immediate duties, the Superintendent has taken an active interest in the Children's Aid and the Associated Charities of the city of Winnipeg.

We desire to testify to the earnestness and efficiency of our staff, and to thank the many friends who have assisted us in such a variety of ways.

We submit the following brief report of the various departments. Interesting details are given from time to time in *The Christian Guardian.*

Kindergarden Department

We maintain two Kindergarten Schools for at least ten months in the year. In each is employed a trained directress and a competent assistant. For the past eight months the average attendance in the two schools was eighty-five. The children come and go a good deal, but one month's enrolment gives a fair idea of the nationalities reached: 57 Polish, 22 English, 17 German, 14 Russian, 10 Ruthenians, 5 Hungarians, 5 Jews, 3 Bohemians, 2 Roumanians, 2 Swedes, 1 Norwegian. Total, 138.

This means that our teachers have a friendly entree to two hundred homes. They help the people in many ways. Most of the kindergarten children are in our Sunday Schools.

Work among girls

Two deaconesses devote all their time to work among the older girls. They conduct sewing classes, cooking classes, kitchen garden classes, and various kinds of clubs. In these there is a weekly average of about two hundred and thirty girls. The lives of over three hundred girls are being directly influenced by these workers, and their bands of helpers from the various city churches. In these classes and clubs, Hebrews, British and Germans are most numerous, but there are also representatives of the following other nationalities: Poles, Ruthenians, Hungarians, Bohemians, Russians, Roumanians, Icleanders, Norwegians, Swedes, Danes and Syrians. Many of the older girls are from shops and factories. The elevating influences of these girls' organizations can hardly be over-estimated.

During the summer our deaconesses assist in the work of the
Fresh Air Camp.

Work among boys
This is the weakest department of our work. We have several small
Boys' Brigades and Clubs, but they have not received sufficient
attention and support. We are hoping to do better work in our new
building.

Sunday Schools
Our Sunday Schools have been growing steadily till we have now an
attendance in the two schools of about three hundred and seventy-
five. Many of the children are "foreign," but the majority can
understand English. There are adult classes for Germans, Poles and
Ruthenians. A number of Russian-Jewish children are taking an
active interest in the Sunday School. Auxiliary to the Sunday School
are the Bands of Hope, at which there is a weekly attendance of
about one hundred and fifty.

Night schools
Night schools have been carried on throughout the winter. Before
the city schools were opened we had an attendance of nearly one
hundred three nights in the week. Afterwards the numbers decreased, and it was possible to do better work. Through these
schools we have come into sympathetic touch with large numbers of
young people, chiefly Russian Jews and Roman and Greek Catholics
from Southeastern Europe.

Mothers' meetings
Mothers' meetings have been held regularly throughout the year with
an average weekly attendance of about forty-five. The mothers sew
for an hour or two, then have devotional exercises in English,
German or Polish, and before separating have a social cup of tea
together. The deaconess in charge is able to come into very close
relations with the lives of the sixty or seventy women who attend
these meetings.

Friendly visiting
One deaconess and a Bible woman give most of their time to visiting
the homes of the people. They are often able to give advice and
assistance, and to do personal religious work. Needless to say, the
workers in all departments are constantly in and out of the homes of

the people. The poor, the sick, the stranger, these always claim our sympathy and help.

Hospital visitation
Every week, sometimes more frequently, our workers visit the hospitals, where they are often able to speak a word of cheer or comfort to the lonely and discouraged.

Welcome to immigrants
During the immigration season a student is placed at the Immigration Hall. He meets the incoming Old Country Methodists, helps to direct and advise them, and conducts religious services in Maple Street, which we regard as our Immigration Chapel. Throughout the year we have every week a Strangers' At-Home.

Relief
Through the winter we gave relief, generally in small amounts, to the extent of two hundred dollars, distributed about sixty bales of clothing and sent out Christmas baskets, groceries, etc. In many cases we were able to secure work, or direct those in need to the right source of help, hospitals or Children's Aid. Then friends often made it possible to give treats to those whose living at best is very scanty.

Religious services
Religious services are conducted regularly in English at both Maple Street and Stella Avenue. At Stella Avenue there has been built up quite a good little congregation, chiefly of Old Country people. At Maple Street every Sunday evening half the congregation is gathered in from the hotels and boarding-houses and Immigration Hall. The students of Wesley College rendered valuable assistance in this work during the winter. Services are also held in German, Polish and Bohemian. The Chinese work has been suspended on account of lack of funds.

The purchase of the Independent Catholic Church has opened up a most interesting field for work. Here and at Hirzel, Saskatchewan, ministers, formerly Catholic priests, are endeavoring to lead their people into Gospel light and liberty. This work is difficult, yet full of promise.

Finance
All Peoples' Mission is maintained by grants from the General Board of Missions and the Woman's Missionary Society; by contributions

from the Methodist churches in Winnipeg, and by collections taken
in the missions. In addition to these regular sources of income,
friends in the city and in both Western and Eastern Canada sent in
last year special subscriptions amounting to $666. Without these it
would have been impossible to do many things, much needed, but
for which there was no provision whatever. The Superintendent
would be glad at any time to receive financial help toward carrying
on the work of the various departments.

Workers are needed

Above all, we need workers. Are there not among the young people
in our churches men and women who will consecrate their lives to
social service?

SUPPLEMENTARY NOTE

Since the above report was written, our new Institute has been
completed and is already being worked almost to its full capacity.
Classes have been started in the Burrows Avenue school-house. At
Stella Avenue we are much cramped for room, and should, in the
near future, have a building at least as large as the Institute. If we are
to keep pace with the needs, additional centres ought to be opened.
The financial problem is a serious one. This year, besides grants from
all sources, the Winnipeg City Mission Board has become responsible
for over $15,000. This must be raised by Winnipeg Methodism, *in
addition* to the General Mission Fund, the Woman's Missionary
Society and the Forward Movement Fund. When it is considered
that from one-quarter to one-third of the entire population of
Manitoba is resident in Winnipeg, and that from one-quarter to one-
third of this city population is composed of 'foreigners,' it will be
seen that we are 'tackling' not a small local affair, but rather a great
national problem. As such, it demands the consideration and the
united energies of the whole Canadian Church. We must express our
appreciation of the way in which scores of young people from the
various city churches and the students of Wesley College have rallied
to our assistance.

We subjoin the programme for the present year. In addition to
our four 'mission centres,' with their various activities, we have other
'stations.' In the *Immigration Hall* we have been assigned a desk, and
during the immigration season a college student devotes his time to
this department. The *hospitals* are visited regularly every week. A

Bohemian service is conducted on Sunday evenings in the home of
one of our members. The *homes* of the workers and the *Deaconess
Home* are centres of activity, and perhaps the best work of all is
done by *friendly visiting* in the homes of the people. Further, we
endeavor *to co-operate* with the City Health Department, the hospitals and Free Dispensary and Nursing Mission, the Public Schools
and the Children's Aid, the Associated Charities, and other institutions that minister to the needs of the people. We work:

> For the right that needs assistance,
> For the wrong that needs resistance,
> For the glory in the distance,
> > And the good that we can do.

PROGRAMME, 1908-1909

Maple Street (the old All Peoples')

Sunday	11 a.m. Morning service and class meeting
	3 p.m. Sunday School
	6.30 p.m. Street meeting or Canvassing Immigration Hall, station, hotels and boarding houses
	7 p.m. Gospel service
Monday	8 p.m. Service for Ruthenians and Poles
Tuesday	8 p.m. German gospel meeting
Wednesday	2 p.m. Mothers' meeting, English and German
	8 p.m. Prayer meeting
Thursday	7.30 p.m. Band of Hope
	8.30 p.m. Boys' Brigade Band practice
Friday	8 p.m. Choir practice

Stella Avenue (Bethlehem)

Sunday	11 a.m. Children's service
	3 p.m. Sunday School and Organized Adult Bible Class in Mission House
	7 p.m. English service
Monday	9.30 to 12 a.m. Kindergarten
	Prayer meeting
Tuesday	9.30 to 12 a.m. Kindergarten
	7.30 p.m. Loyal Legion
	7.30 p.m. Girls' Club in Mission House

Wednesday   9.30 to 12 a.m. Kindergarten
               4 to 6 p.m. Sewing School
               8 p.m. Foreign Mothers' Meeting
Thursday   9.30 to 12 a.m. Kindergarten
               3 p.m. English Women's Club
Friday   9.30 to 12 a.m. Kindergarten
               4 to 6 p.m. Kitchen Garden A
               8 p.m. Choir practice
Saturday   10 to 12 a.m. Kitchen Garden B
               8 p.m. Junior choir practice

The Institute (new building)
Sunday   11 a.m. Girls' Catechumen Class
               11 a.m. Boys' Catechumen Class
               3 p.m. Sunday School
               7 p.m. English service
               7 p.m. Ruthenian service (in contemplation)
Monday   9.30 to 12 a.m. Kindergarten Class A
               1 to 3.30 p.m. Kindergarten Class B
               4 to 6 p.m. Kitchen Garden A
               7.45 to 9.45 p.m. Maple Street Boys' Brigade
Tuesday   9.30 to 12 a.m. Kindergarten Class A
               1 to 3.30 p.m. Kindergarten Class B
               4 to 6 p.m. Sewing School A
               4 to 6 p.m. Stella Avenue Kitchen Garden B
               4 to 6 p.m. Stella Avenue Small Boys' Club
Wednesday   9.30 to 12 a.m. Kindergarten Class A
               1 to 3.30 p.m. Kindergarten Class B
               4 to 6 p.m. Kitchen Garden B
               7.45 p.m. Stella Working Boys' Club
               7.45 p.m. Orchestra practice
Thursday   9.30 to 12 a.m. Kindergarten A
               1 to 3.30 p.m. Kindergarten B
               4 to 6 p.m. Cooking class
               7.30 p.m. Girls' Club
               8 p.m. Monthly Concert
Friday   9.30 to 12 a.m. Kindergarten A
               1 to 3.30 p.m. Kindergarten B
               2 p.m. Foreign Mothers' Meeting
               7.45 p.m. Boys' Club, King Arthur's Knights
               7.45 p.m. New Boys' Club

Saturday   10 a.m. Small Boys' Gymnasium Class
                2.30 p.m. Stella Girls' Club, No. 2
                2 to 4 p.m. Sewing School B

Burrows Avenue (property recently purchased)
Use of church granted to former owners — the congregation of the
Polish Independent Catholic Church. In the school house we
conduct the following:

Sunday   3 p.m. Sunday School
                8 p.m. Evening meeting in English
Monday   4 to 6 p.m. Sewing School
                8 p.m. Occasional meetings of Polish Committee
Tuesday   2 p.m. Mothers' Meeting
                7.45 Night School
Thursday   7.45 Night School
Friday   Stella Boys' Brigade
Saturday   7.45 Night School and social evening

APPENDIX 5

The following services are announced weekly in the Winnipeg city papers:

Anglican
St. John's Cathedral
St. Martin's Mission
Holy Trinity
Christ Church
St. Mark's Mission
All Saints'
St. Luke's
St. Alban's
St. George's
St. Peter's
St. Matthew's
St. Margaret's
St. Barnabas' Mission
St. Michael and All Angels'
St. Cuthbert's
St. Philip's
St. Jude's
St. Thomas'

Roman Catholic
St. Boniface Cathedral
St. Mary's
Immaculate Conception
Holy Ghost (Polish)
St. Nicholas (Greek Catholic)
St. Joseph's (German)
Sacred Heart (French)
St. Ignatius
St. Edward's

Presbyterian
Knox
St. Andrew's
Westminster
St. Giles'

St. Stephen's
Augustine
Point Douglas
St. Paul's
Dufferin Avenue
St. John's
Home Street
Riverview
Elmwood
Norwood
Sherman Street
Clifton Street
Hungarian Mission
Free Presbyterian Church of
    Scotland

Baptist
First Baptist
Logan Avenue
Broadway
Tabernacle
Emmanuel
Nassau Street
Calvary
Olivet
Beulah
East Elmwood Mission
Swedish Baptist
German Baptist
North Side German

Methodist
Grace
Zion
Wesley
McDougall

Young

Fort Rouge

Maryland Street

Broadway

Norwood

Sparling

St. John's

Gordon

Epworth

All Peoples', Maple Street

Bethel

All Peoples', Bethlehem

St. James's

King Edward Street

Congregational

Central

St. James' Park

Evangelical Lutheran

First English Lutheran

Evangelical Lutheran (German)

Norwegian Lutheran, Mission
    Church

Christ Church (German)

Emmanuel (German)

First Icelandic

Trinity (German)

Zion (Swedish)

Tabernacle (Icelandic)

Reformed Church

Zion (German)

Christian Reformed (Dutch)

Salem

**German Evangelic Synod
    of North America**

St. John's

First Evangelical

Church of Christ (Disciples)

Sherbrooke Street

Church of Christ (Scientist)

Evangelical Association

Ebenezer

English Mission

Christians

Salvation Army

Citadel

Nena Street

Holiness Movement

Scandinavian

First Scandinavian

Elmwood Scandinavian

Unitarian

First Icelandic

All Souls'

Christadelphians

Jewish

Shaarey Zadek

Shaarey Shomayin (Orthodox)

House of Jacob

Apostolic Faith

Latter Day Saints

**Reorganized Church of Latter
    Day Saints**

Welsh United Church

Society of Friends

Spiritualistic Church

Gospel Meeting

Men's Own

Home and Foreign Mission

Young Men's Christian
    Association

Bijou Theatre Christian
    Endeavor Services

APPENDIX 6

AN ACT RESPECTING NATURALIZATION AND ALIENS

13. Any alien, who, within such limited time before taking the oaths or affirmations of residence and allegiance and procuring the same to be filed of record as hereafter prescribed, as may be allowed by order or regulation of the Governor-in-Council, has resided in Canada for a term of not less than three years, or has been in the service of the Government of Canada, or of any of the provinces of Canada, or of two or more of such governments, for a term of not less than three years, and intends when naturalized either to reside in Canada or to serve under the Government of Canada or the Government of one of the provinces of Canada, or two or more of such governments, may take and subscribe the oaths of residence and allegiance or of service and allegiance in form A and apply for a certificate in form B. R. S., c. 113, s. 8.

24. An alien to whom a certificate of naturalization is granted shall, within Canada, be entitled to all political and other rights, powers and privileges, and be subject to all obligations, to which a natural-born British subject is entitled or subject within Canada, with this qualification, that he shall not, when within the limits of the foreign state of which he was a subject previously to obtaining his certificate of naturalization, be deemed to be a British subject, unless he has ceased to be a subject of that state in pursuance of the laws thereof, or in pursuance of a treaty or convention to that effect. R. S., c. 113, s. 15.

OATH OF RESIDENCE

I, A. B., do swear (or, being a person allowed by law to affirm in judicial cases, do affirm) that in the period of   years preceding this date I have resided three (or five, as the case may be) years in the Dominion of Canada, with intent to settle therein, without having been, during such three years (or five years, as the case may be) a stated resident in any foreign country. So help me God.

Sworn before me at
           on the   A. B.
day of
R. S., c. 113, sch.

OATH OF ALLEGIANCE

I, A. B., formerly of (former place of residence to be stated here), in (country of origin to be stated here), and known there by the name of (name and surname of alien in his country of origin to be stated here), and now residing at (place of residence in Canada and occupation to be stated here), do sincerely promise and swear (or being a person allowed by law to affirm in judicial cases, do affirm) that I will be faithful and bear true allegiance to His Majesty King Edward VII (or reigning sovereign for the time being) as lawful Sovereign of the United Kingdom of Great Britain and Ireland, and of the Dominion of Canada, dependent on and belonging to said Kingdom, and that I will defend Him to the utmost of my power against all traitorous conspiracies or attempts whatsoever which shall be made against His Person, Crown and Dignity, and that I will do my utmost endeavor to disclose and make known to His Majesty, His heirs or successors, all treasons or traitorous conspiracies and attempts which I shall know to be against Him or any of them; and all this I do swear (or affirm) without any equivocation, mental evasion or secret reservation. So help me God.

Sworn before me at
                        this   A. B.
day of
4-5 E. VII., c. 25. s. 2.

CERTIFICATE OF NATURALIZATION

Dominion of Canada,
    Province of
    In the (name of court) Court of

    Whereas   formerly of (name of
country) now of   in the province of
                        (occupation), has complied with the several
requirements of the Naturalization Act, and has duly resided in
Canada for the period of   years;.
    And whereas the particulars of the certificate granted to the
said   under the fifteenth section of the said Act
have been duly announced in court, and thereupon by order of
the said court, the said certificate has been filed of record in the
same pursuant to the said Act:

This is therefore to certify to all whom it may concern, that under and by virtue of the said Act
has become naturalized as a British subject, and is, within Canada, entitled to all political and other rights, powers and privileges, and subject to all obligations to which a natural-born British subject is entitled or subject within Canada, with this qualification, that he shall not, when within the limits of the foreign state of which he was a subject (or citizen) previous to the date hereof, be deemed to be a British subject unless he has ceased to be a subject (or citizen) of that state, in pursuance of the laws thereof, or in pursuance of a treaty or convention to that effect.

Given under the seal of the said court this
day of   one thousand nine hundred and

A. B.
Judge, Clerk (or other proper officer
of the court).

This form may be altered so as to apply to the provinces of Saskatchewan and Alberta, and the Yukon Territory.

R. S., c. 113, sch.; O. C.'s, 21st Dec., 1903, and 3rd Nov., 1905.